Intranets:
The Surf Within

Intranets:
The Surf Within

J A M E S   C I M I N O

CHARLES RIVER MEDIA, INC.
Rockland, Massachusetts

Publisher: Dave Pallai
Interior Design/Composition: Reuben Kantor
Cover Design: Marshall Henrichs
Printer: InterCity Press, Rockland, MA.

CHARLES RIVER MEDIA, INC.
P.O. Box 417
403 VFW Drive
Rockland, Massachusetts 02370
617-871-4184
617-871-4376 (FAX)
chrivmedia@aol.com
http://www.charlesriver.com

This book is printed on acid-free paper.

James Cimino. *Intranets: The Surf Within*
ISBN: 1-886801-40-1

Printed in the United States of America
97 98 99 00 01 7 6 5 4 3 2 First Edition

CHARLES RIVER MEDIA titles are available for site license or bulk purchase by institutions, user groups, corporations, etc. For additional information, please contact the Special Sales Department at 617-871-4184.

Contents

Foreword

The growth of World Wide Web (WWW) technology instigated a surge of new software packages and applications to improve business practices and information resourcing. This technology enabled businesses to be more competitive on a global scale and effectively changed the way people conducted business. Soon after corporations made their presence on the WWW, many began to ask, Why not implement the WWW paradigm for internal use? From this began the inception of the "intranet" or "corporate Internet." Once again, technology is beginning to change the way people conduct business.

Easy to use intranet-centric tools and capabilities that empower employees and enhance the capability of corporations to effectively compete have become increasingly important. Functions such as online search; electronic commerce and workflow functions such as automated routing and notification of tasks and activities; and distribution of collaborative documents are in high demand. These applications will greatly increase a company's information-sharing and time effectiveness and enable employees to become more productive.

Information-sharing from a variety of sources in an open protocol environment is becoming the standard among businesses. Problems with traditional means of circulating information through employee manuals and paper memos have increased the importance of easily obtaining updated documents. Browser interfaces provide a common vehicle for ubiquitous and immediate distribution of corporate information. Equally important to providing information-sharing are tools that will also allow easy creation of and access to legacy information sources. As businesses continue to rely more and more on evolving technology, expectations for more interactive information exchange and time-critical applications will be dramatically heightened.

The future demands fully integrated, easy-to-use, and open systems products that will make businesses more competitive in a global market. Intranets, with their unparalleled capability to navigate and interact in today's electronic communication environment, will take us into the next century.

Dr. Prakash Ambegaonkar
CEO
Frontier Technologies Corp.
November 1996

Acknowledgments

I wish to acknowledge the following individuals for their help, support, and understanding throughout this project:

My wife, Victoria, for her support, love, and friendship.

My dog, Nikita, for laying at my feet and keeping me company those long nights I stayed up typing.

My mentor, Deni Connor, for acting as a sounding board, and helping keep me focused.

My publisher, Charles River Media, and especially Dave Pallai, for giving me this opportunity.

Kathy Mills for copyediting and Dena Bockleman and Debbie Reeves for their editorial contributions.

My father, Dennis J. Cimino, to whose loving memory I dedicate this work.

Introduction

With commercial acceptance of any technology comes the inevitable adaptation of that technology to better suit respective business models. That adaptation of Internet technology has become the "intranet." The intranet is one of today's hottest topics. Virtually every computer hardware and software manufacturer is making major announcements about their comprehensive intranet strategies. Even more significant is that businesses large and small have taken to the intranet concept, and are the very driving force behind the explosive growth of the intranet.

Intranets: The Surf Within targets the IS professional and assumes basic knowledge about networks and wide-area connectivity. This book also assumes that you also have some working knowledge of the Internet technology and methodologies. If you are trying to decide whether to establish a presence on the Internet, to configure an Intranet for your company, or both, this book is for you.

OBJECTIVES

The objectives of this book are simple. This book is intended to:

1. Define an intranet and the services it can provide.
2. Help you decide which intranet services to deploy within your organization.

3. Get you started developing intranet services for your organization

4. Provide practical intranet examples and ideas.

How This Book is Organized

Intranets: The Surf Within, is divided into three sections. The first section covers Internet and intranet terminology and differentiates between the two paradigms. In writing this book, I felt that it was important to establish the definition of what an intranet is, as well as to explain the roots of this technology. You cannot understand what a technology is until you know where it comes from. This book begins with a brief overview and history of the Internet. From there, I define the intranet, and the services that can be provided within an Intranet.

Once the basic definitions are covered, the book delves into the logistical and managerial requirements for running a successful intranet. After all, once you decide to build an Intranet, you need to get upper management to buy into the project. This book then gets into the nuts and bolts of what is required to set up and maintain the physical intranet severs and services. I cover server hardware and software, from the selection of the server hardware platform and operating system, to the installation of the Web server software.

The second section of the book covers some of the programming techniques you will require for your Intranet project. The HyperText Markup Language (HTML) has become the *de facto* standard for Internet and intranet design. I devote a two chapters to basic HTML and advanced HTML coding techniques, as well as include a CGI primer. I also have provided a basic overview of some cool third party tools you can use to "jazz up" you intranet, and to enhance to services your intranet can provide. All the techniques explained are used in the sample Intranet examples.

The sample intranet is the final section of this book. Rather than providing case studies, I have created a fictitious company and walk you through the creative process as the intranet is born and starts to develop. From a practical viewpoint, I start off with some rudimentary, but useful Intranet applications that **any** organization can modify to suit their purpose. The goal is to provide the reader with a template they can mold to fit their corporate intranet needs, quickly and easily. I even provide a section for creating your own intranet menuing system.

Intranets: The Surf Within contains appendices that cover topics ranging from Web hosting and outsourcing, a comprehensive listing of intranet products and providers, and a glossary of intranet terms. I have also included a CD-ROM containing sample programs, demonstrations, live product trial copies, and all the source code included within the book.

I hope you find this book useful and informative. If you are considering an intranet project, this book should provide you with the impetuous to forge ahead with the project. If you are currently implementing an intranet, this book may provide you with an idea or two to add to your project. Finally, if you are just in the intranet planning stages, this book should provide you with some useful guidelines on how to proceed, how to select a Webmaster, how to get your organization involved, keep the content fresh, and how to maintain the project momentum.

If you are currently working on an intranet project, or if you find the information in this book helpful, I'd want to hear from you. Drop me a line at ciminoj@bright-ideas.com.

The Internet:
An Expanding Universe

CONTENTS

Wait — I thought this was a book about "intranets." It is! However, it is important to understand the weaknesses of the Internet and the inherent security concerns to understand intranets and know what to avoid. In many ways, these concerns have accelerated the growth of intranets, private Internets within companies.

The Internet has gained a lot of attention lately. Once the exclusive domain for exchanging project information among the military agencies, subcontractors, and institutions of higher learning, the Internet is now the playground of "Web surfers," business entrepreneurs, techies, and computer Newbies. The Internet has become considerably more than just a vast electronic bulletin board service. It has become a virtually indispensable atlas where you can find information on just about anything.

Still in its infancy, the Internet has more than three million servers and more than 35 million users. Nobody really knows exactly how many computers and networks make up this network, or how many visitors a day the Internet has. Some estimates say there are as few as 5,000 networks connecting nearly two million computers and more than 15 million people around the world. Others say the figures are lower. Whatever the actual numbers, it is clear that Internet visitors and those who decide to take up permanent domicile on the 'Net are only increasing.

The beauty of the Internet is that it consists of a complex web of smaller regional networks connecting with multiple machines. To understand it, picture a modern road network of superhighways connecting large cities. Imagine dusty backroads connecting with two-lane black top roads, which connect with multilane divided interstate highways. (See Figure 1-1.)

These highways link large cities to smaller freeways and parkways linking smaller towns, whose residents travel on slower, more narrow residential byways.

The high-speed Internet is the data superhighway, representing the hub of electronic commerce. Connected to hubs are computers that use a particular system of transferring data at high speeds to smaller links. In the United States, the major Internet backbone can theoretically move data at rates of 45 million bits per second (Mbps). Compare this to the average home modem, which has a top speed of 9,600 to 28,800 bits per

FIGURE 1-1 *A Large Internet Service Provider's Private Backbone Network*

second. The internetworking "protocol," or manner of communicating data, lets network users in Battle Creek, Michigan, connect to computers in New York City or halfway around the world in rural Bangladesh. (See Figure 1-2.)

Connected to the backbone computers are smaller networks serving particular geographic regions, generally moving data at speeds of around 1.5 million bits per second (Mbps). (See Figure 1-3 on page 4.)

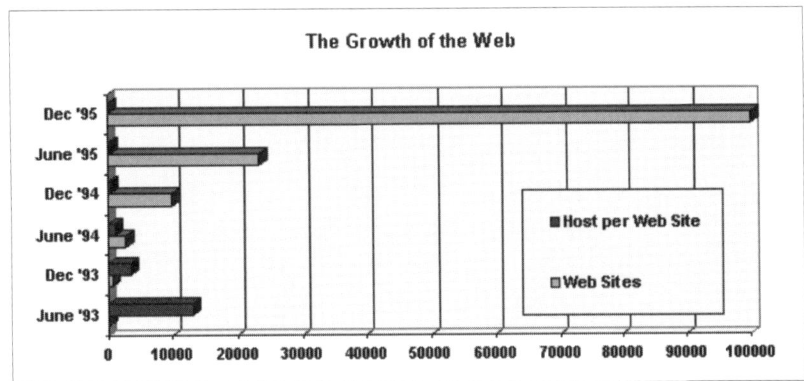

FIGURE 1-2 *The Growth of the Web*

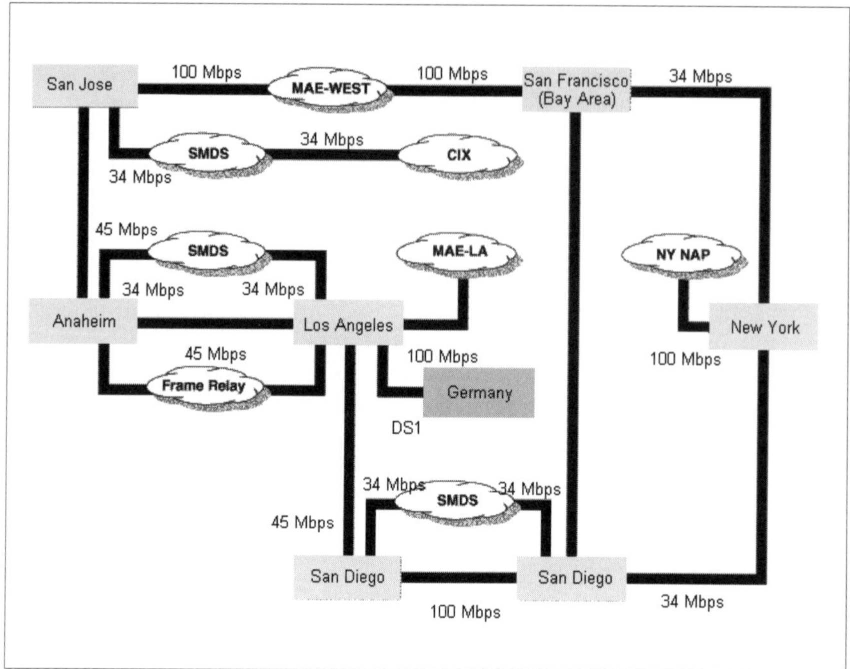

FIGURE 1-3   *Intersite Link Speeds for a Major Internet Service Provider*

Feeding these geographic turnpikes are, in turn, even smaller networks or individual computers. (See Figure 1-4.)

Add to the Internet links to commercial networks such as CompuServe and Prodigy, and you will see how global communication grows ever closer. Users of these commercial on-line services can now exchange electronic mail with their Internet friends. Some commercial providers, such as Delphi and America Online, are bringing their subscribers direct access to Internet services. And as the Internet becomes easier to use, more and more people will join. This ease of use is fueling the exponential growth of the Internet. In fact, according to SIMBA Information, Inc., of Wilton, CT, the online services market is projected to leap from 6.8 million subscribers in 1995 to more than 20 million subscribers by the year 2000. (See Figure 1-5.)

Unlike commercial networks such as CompuServe, America Online, and Prodigy, the Internet is not run by one central computer or comput-

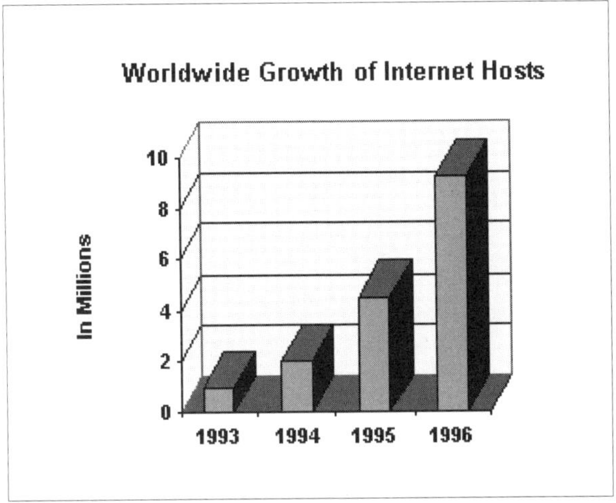

FIGURE
1-4
Worldwide Growth of Internet Hosts

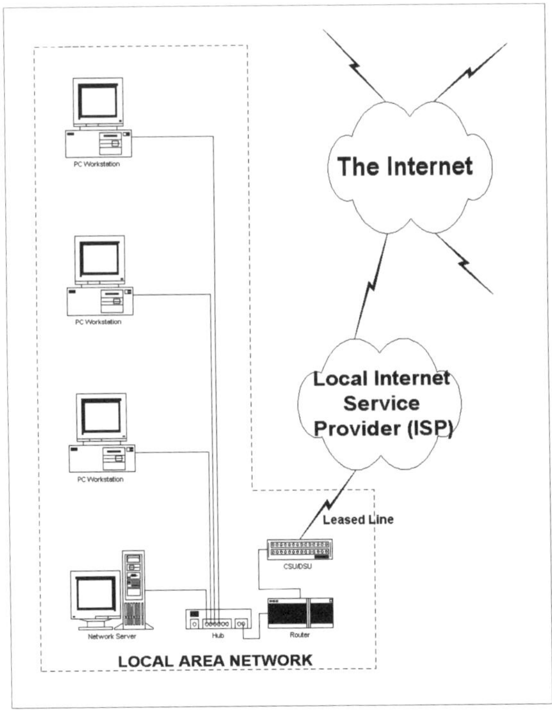

FIGURE
1-5
A Geographic Distribution of the Internet

ers, nor is it a paid service. This difference is both its greatest strength and its greatest weakness. It means that it is virtually impossible for the entire Internet to crash at once. Even if one computer shuts down, the rest of the network stays up. The design of the Internet also reduces the costs for an individual or organization to get on the network by parceling out those costs to individual organizations called "Internet Service Providers" (ISPs).

But, with these strengths of a universal navigation tool that an online service provides and an implied guarantee of computer uptime, the Internet is often difficult to navigate. It is frequently an arduous task to find what you want because different computers may have different commands for searching their resources. Only recently have Internet users begun to develop navigational tools and "maps" that let novices navigate the Internet without getting lost or waylaid. The Internet has been the domain, in many ways, of the technically elite who can get software to work on their own without needing technical assistance from the software vendor.

Major network providers continue to work on ways to make it easier for users of one network to communicate with those of another. Work is under way on a system that provides universal "white pages" in which users can look up someone's electronic mail address or find businesses that provide services users are looking for. This trend toward universal connectivity will accelerate in coming years as users begin to demand seamless network access, much as telephone users can now dial almost anywhere in the world without thinking about how many phone companies connect their calls.

THE BIRTH OF THE INTERNET

How, you may wonder, did the Internet evolve, or how did this connected revolution come to be? The Internet started as a method of communication between the U.S. Department of Defense and scientists as a means of improving military communication, allowing them to transfer data between project sites. In the 1960s, researchers began experimenting with linking a hodgepodge of different computer types to each other through telephone hook-ups using funds from the U.S. Defense Department's Advanced Research Projects Agency (ARPA). The intent of this network, called ARPANET (Advanced Research Projects Agency Network), was to facilitate the exchange of information between the military and its subcontractors on various government projects. Many of the top computer scientists in industry and academia gained access to this network through CSNET (the Computer Science Network), a project created by the National Science Foundation (NSF), another U.S. government agency. All U.S. military sites were soon connected to the ARPANET, marking its transition to a practical, rather than an experimental, network.

ARPA wanted to see if computers in different locations could be linked using what was then a new technology called "packet-switching." Packet-switching would let several users share a single communication link in which packets of data would be transmitted over the network to the recipient where they would be recombined. Earlier networking efforts had required a line between each computer on the network. The NSF helped fund building of a high-speed wide area network, opening its doors to all educational facilities, academic researchers, government employees, and international research organizations. This network allowed for creation of a data highway in which large numbers of computers could essentially share the same data link. Data was broken into packets to be transferred to another site. Each packet was given the computer equivalent of a map (an address) and a time stamp, so it could reach its desired destination. Once the packets had arrived, perhaps by different routes, they would then be reassembled by the receiving machine into a coherent message.

This newly formed network, which made transporting data interdependent on the end points, allowed computers to share data and researchers to exchange electronic mail among themselves. E-mail itself was something of a revolution. Before the advent of e-mail, transmitting documents had to be accomplished via fax, postal courier, or U.S. mail. E-mail sent via the Internet offered the capability to send detailed letters at the speed and cost of a phone call.

As ARPANET grew, enterprising students developed a way to use it to conduct online conferences. These conferences started as science-oriented discussions, but they soon branched out into virtually every other field as people recognized the power of being able to "talk" to hundreds, or even thousands, of people around the country who where introduced over this electronic wire.

In the 1970s, ARPA helped support the development of rules, or protocols, for transferring data between different types of computer networks. These "internet" (which was coined from the term "internetworking") protocols made it possible to develop the worldwide Internet. The "'Net," as we know it today, links all sorts of computers across national and international boundaries using a common protocol called the Transmission Control Protocol / Internet Protocol (TCP/IP). By the close of the 1970s, links developed between ARPANET and counterparts in other countries. The world was now tied together in a computer "mesh," or web.

In the 1980s, this network of networks, which became known collectively as the "Internet," expanded at a phenomenal rate. Thousands of colleges and universities, research companies, and government agencies began connecting their computers to this worldwide 'Net. Enterprising hobbyists and companies unwilling to pay the high costs of full-time Internet access (or unable to meet the stringent government regulations for such access) learned how to link their own systems to the Internet, even if only for e-mail and conferences.

The Web Is Spun

In 1989, the World Wide Web was born. The Web originated at the European Center for Particle Physics (CERN), located near Geneva, Switzerland. CERN, notorious for developing networking technologies and the collaborative needs of the physics community, gave birth to a method of distributing hypertext documents and hypermedia (pictures, sound, movies, and animation). The collection of these documents and hypermedia became known as the World Wide Web, or "Web" for short. It is important to note that the Web did not gain widespread use until

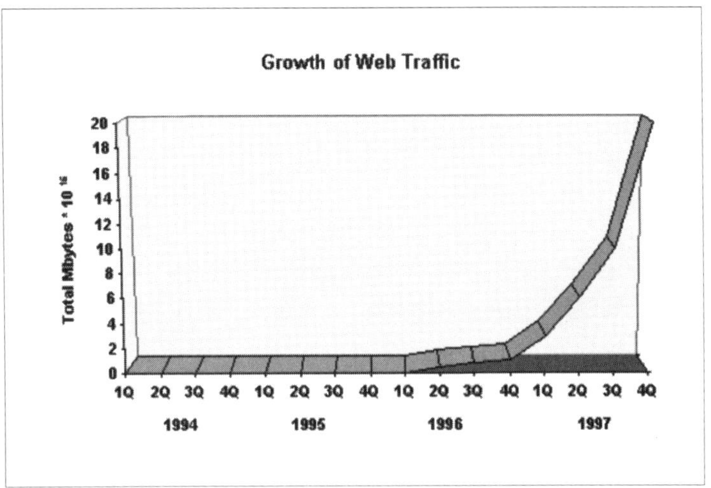

FIGURE 1-6   *The Growth of Web Traffic. (Source: The Internet Society, 1996)*

the National Computer Security Association (NCSA) Mosaic became available in early 1993. (See Figure 1-6.)

As we have witnessed in the 1990s, the 'Net is growing at exponential rates. Some estimates show the volume of messages transferred through the 'Net grows 20 percent each month. In response, government and other users have tried in recent years to expand the Internet itself. It wasn't long ago that the main 'Net "backbone" in the United States moved data at 1.5 million bits per second. That proved too slow for the ever-increasing amounts of data being sent over it, and in recent years the maximum speed increased to 1.5 million and then 45 (Mbps). Even before the 'Net was able to reach that higher speed, however, 'Net experts were already figuring out ways to pump data at speeds of up to two billion bits per second or "gigabits" (Gbps) — fast enough to send the entire *Encyclopedia Britannica* across the country in just one or two seconds.

Another major change has been the development of commercial organizations that provide internetworking services at speeds comparable to those of the government's system. By mid-1994, the U.S. government had removed itself from day-to-day control over the workings of the 'Net as regional and national providers continued to expand.

The Internet and Business

Almost every major publication has touted the wonders of the World Wide Web and the marvels of the Internet. Developers, manufacturers, and resellers see the Internet as a potential moneymaking opportunity. However, no one is sure exactly what that moneymaking formula is.

According to a recent report published by Forrester Research of Cambridge, MA, Internet-related software, hardware, and services will constitute a multibillion dollar industry by the year 2000. Forrester predicts revenues from the Internet access business will exceed $4 billion annually by the end of the decade. (See Figures 1-7 and 1-8.)

Jay Batson, senior analyst at Forrester, says the growth spurt will center around new tools for World Wide Web (WWW) viewing and

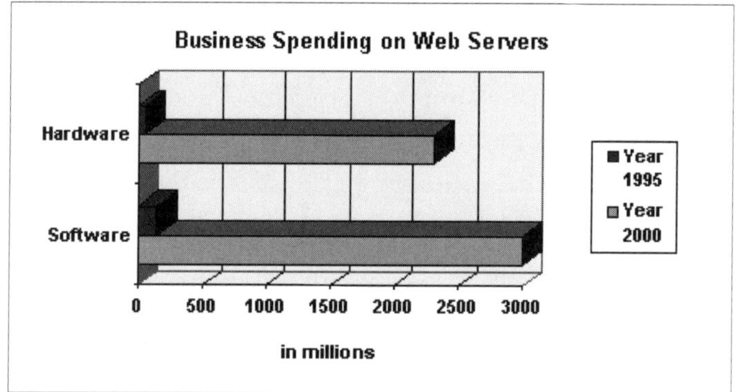

FIGURE 1-7   *Business Spending on Web Servers. (Source: Forrester Research, 1996)*

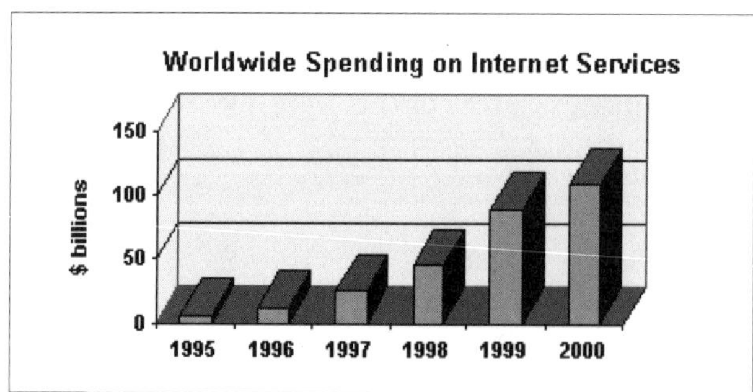

FIGURE 1-8   *Worldwide Spending on Internet Services. (Source: Information Week, March, 1996)*

authoring, combined with consulting fees and Internet services. The Forrester report says Internet growth will be due largely to a quick ramp-up for Internet adoption, with the Web as the catalyst.

According to a recent poll published in *Network Computing* magazine, more than 86 percent of the 1,000 companies surveyed already have some type of connection to the Internet, with 79.4 percent of the activity centered around browsing Web sites. In a related *Information Week* article, 70 percent of the organizations surveyed stated that access to the Internet improved overall productivity. Even resellers are getting on the "Internet-as-a-business-tool" bandwagon. A recent poll in *Computer Reseller News* showed 54 percent of the 200 resellers surveyed currently use the Internet for business, with more than 45 percent of the respondents using Internet services more than 30 percent of the time.

The Hermes Project, an Internet demographics study run by the University of Michigan, found that 59 percent of Internet users are professionals or managers making more than $66,000 annually and who spend 82 percent of their time on the Internet browsing Web sites. (See Figure 1-9.)

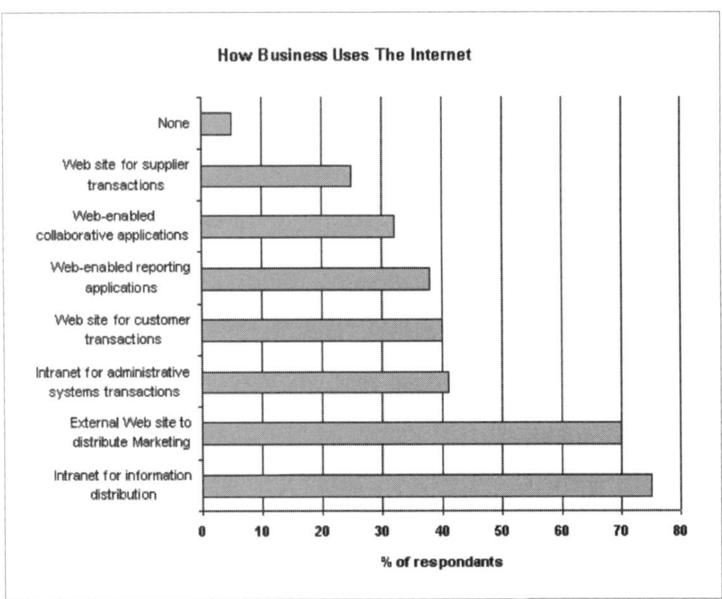

FIGURE 1-9 *How Businesses Use the Internet. (Source: Information Week survey of 225 IS managers, April, 1996)*

The Internet has evolved from an exclusive communications medium for the military and institutions of higher learning, into a viable business tool. Everyday, hundreds of new businesses and thousands of new users are exploring the possibilities and opportunities that can be obtained on the 'Net. While the technology exists for establishing a presence for your business on the 'Net, the skill sets and tools required to implement this technology are not as easy to obtain as they should be. The question often remains. "How can I get my business on the 'Net?".

What's Required to Get on the Internet	There are two ways to connect to the Internet. The first, and simplest, method is to obtain a dial-up account to an Internet Service Provider (ISP). An ISP can give you a shell account consisting of a Serial Line Internet Protocol (SLIP) or a point-to-point protocol (PPP) connection.

There are two ways to connect to the Internet. The first, and simplest, method is to obtain a dial-up account to an Internet Service Provider (ISP). An ISP can give you a shell account consisting of a Serial Line Internet Protocol (SLIP) or a point-to-point protocol (PPP) connection.

The other method of connecting to the Internet is by a leased line. This is more effective for large corporate accounts. The type of leased line you get and the speed of the connection depends on your organization's use of the Internet and the amount of sustained bandwidth it requires. Leased lines are available in various types and speeds, ranging from 56 kilobit per second (Kbps) lines to Integrated Services Digital Network (ISDN) or frame relay, all the way to fractional or full T1 or T3 lines.

No matter how you access the Internet, you will require an Internet Protocol (IP) address for your Internet access account. This IP address can be assigned to you by your ISP dynamically (meaning the IP address may change each time you access the Internet) or statically (you have the same IP address all the time). We will cover various methods for assigning IP addresses to network clients later in this book.

When you access Internet hosts, you typically don't know the IP address for that host; instead, you know its Uniform Resource Locator (URL). URLs are the common means we use to refer to and locate Internet hosts and devices. For example, www.bright-ideas.com will link you to the Bright Ideas Software World Wide Web home page. This URL is physically associated with the IP address of the Bright Ideas Web server. The mechanism that makes the association between the URL and IP address is the Domain Name Service (DNS).

A DNS server is a dedicated machine or server process that handles address and name resolution for the client and host devices on your network. The DNS server can be maintained by your ISP, or your organization can maintain its own. Just as we have telephone books, the DNS facilitates your ability to locate individuals by name instead of number.

DNS uses the same technique as directory information to determine where a person or device is located. If the individual is not part of the local listing, one DNS "operator" will contact the closest DNS "operator." View DNS as a distributed web of telephone and address listings, with each site's DNS host maintaining a list of the local names. When a search needs to be made outside of locally maintained names, the DNS server has pointers to other DNS hosts and queries the DNS servers as needed.

DNS management, like IP address management, is time- and bandwidth-intensive. For a host name to be published on a DNS host, it must be added to the domain name server. Any time your address changes, the DNS needs to be updated with the proper information.

What the Internet Really Costs	Many products are available that make it easy to connect your company to the Internet, and even connect your business on the Web. The fact of the matter is, these products only paint a rosy picture of an often difficult and cumbersome venture for the inexperienced user.

To connect your company to the Internet, you need five items: a communications protocol; an Internet Service Provider (ISP) (the company that supplies the connections to the Internet); a leased line (the physical link between your site and the ISP); a router (the device that connects your network to the CSU/DSU); and a CSU/DSU (a high-speed line driver that talks over the leased line). Numerous options are available for each of these items.

COMMUNICATIONS PROTOCOL

You can use various methods to communicate over the Internet or to other hosts from your TCP/IP workstation. SLIP is a simple protocol used to transmit a packet of data and delivery information across a serial line. Compressed SLIP (CSLIP) is also available. The Point-to-Point Protocol (PPP), another serial line transmission protocol, allows multiple protocols to be multiplexed across the communications link. The Challenge Handshake Authentication Protocol (CHAP) is used with PPP. The server or host you are logging in to must be configured to use CHAP, which provides an additional level of login and password authentication and is typically the third level of login authentication on systems that support CHAP. Figure 1-10 shows a typical SLIP or PPP connection.

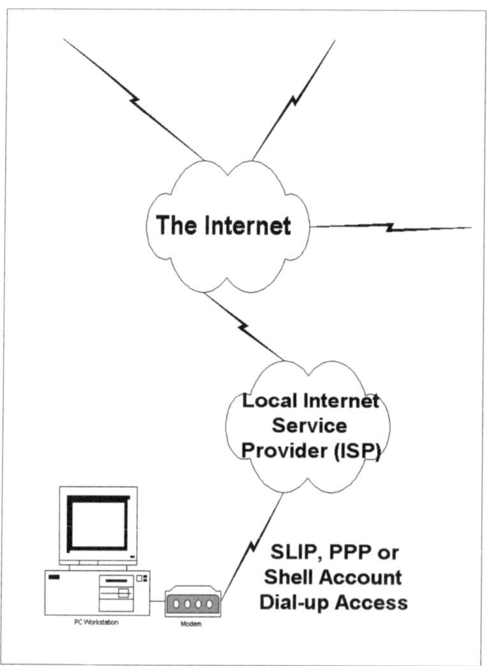

FIGURE *Examples of SLIP and PPP Connections*
1-10

INTERNET SERVICE PROVIDERS (ISPs)

An ISP provides front-end service and acts as your entry to the Internet. Although most Internet users have a dial-up account to an ISP, your company will require a connection that provides greater speed and bandwidth to accommodate multiple simultaneous connections from multiple users. Because of this, you must select an ISP who provides leased-line access. Figure 1-11 shows some ISPs and their leased line access charges.

Company	Startup Fee	56	128	256	384	512	T1
Global Access Incorporated	$ 1,000	$ 195	$ 250	$ 375	$ 500	$ 625	$ 750
Intellicom	$ 300	$ 1,000	$ 1,500	$ 1,700	$ 1,800	$ 2,000	$ 2,300
EMI	$ 1,000	$ 316	$ 494	$ 677	$ 874	$ 1,076	$ 1,523
DeltaNet	$ 1,500	$ 375	$ 500	$ 800	$ 1,200	$ 1,500	$ 2,700
PSI	$ 2,000	$ 300	$ 800	$ 1,000	$ 1,200	$ 1,500	$ 2,500

FIGURE *Monthly Service Charge (by line speed)*
1-11

Note: These leased line charges may vary due to geographic area and promotions the ISP may be running. These values should be used for reference purposes only.

Selecting an ISP is analogous to leasing a car: When you lease a car, you have a specific make and model in mind, and you shop around to find the dealer closest to you who will give you the best rate. In selecting an ISP, you want the fastest line speed for the lowest monthly charge. You also want to know how far removed your ISP is from the Internet backbone. The closer an ISP is to the backbone, the better its Internet response and access time will be.

Service is another important factor. Although you won't be bringing in your server every 3,000 miles like you would a car, you will want an ISP who is responsive and will help you when you have questions and problems.

You also want to know if your ISP has more than one connection to the Internet. On more than one occasion, a construction backhoe or some disaster has ruptured a fiber-optic cable, bringing a portion of the 'Net to its knees. In one experience, an ISP was out of commission for days due to a broken fiber-optic cable.

LEASED LINE

For access to the Internet, a standard phone line will not do. To facilitate multiple users simultaneously, you need a dedicated, leased line. The costs for your leased line depend on the type of circuit and the speed of the line. Circuit types range from ISDN, Switched 56, or frame relay, to T1. Of these circuit types, only frame relay and T1 circuits can be ordered in various line speeds, typically in increments of 56Kbps. The line speed determines the number of concurrent users who can be supported at any given time. The slower the line speed, the fewer concurrent users who can be supported.

In addition, there are several one-time and recurring charges associated with leased lines. These charges can be divided into two categories: ISP charges and phone company charges. (See Figures 1-12 and 1-13.)

	COST	Year 1	Year 2
ISP Setup Cost (one time): (Includes Router and CSU)	$ 6,000.00	$ 6,000.00	$ 0
ISP Monthly Charge:	$ 900.00	$ 10,800.00	$ 10,800.00
Telco Setup Charge (one time):	$ 408.00	$ 408.00	$ 0
Telco Monthly Charge:	$ 632.00	$ 7,584.00	$ 7,584.00

FIGURE 1-12 *Costs Breakdown Example: T1 Line*

	COST	Year 1	Year 2
ISP Setup Cost (one time): (Includes Router and CSU)	$ 1,995.00	$ 1,995.00	$ 0
ISP Monthly Charge:	$ 400.00	$ 4,800.00	$ 4,800.00
Telco Setup Charge (one time):	$ 509.00	$ 509.00	$ 0
Telco Monthly Charge:	$ 170.00	$ 2,040.00	$ 2,040.00

FIGURE 1-13 *Costs Breakdown Example: 56Kbps Frame Relay*

Note: Rates will vary depending on your local telephone company and your ISP. In addition, some ISPs do not provide a router and CSU/DSU in their monthly rate. In this case, you would be responsible for obtaining and configuring this equipment.

ROUTER

The first piece of hardware required is a router. The router is a sophisticated piece of hardware used to connect your network to the ISP. Think of the router as acting much like a bouncer at an exclusive club. At the club, if you don't know the "password," you don't get in. Here, if you are an Internet user trying to access an internal network and you don't know the TCP/IP address or domain name you are trying to access, the router will keep you out. Routers can also discriminate based on IP address.

Routers include software that determines the protocols (the language the router uses to communicate) and the levels of security the router offers. Also included are associated memory and interface modules that may be required, depending on the router manufacturer and model selected.

The router handles all Internet traffic coming to and from your network. This means the router you select must be robust, scaleable, and capable of growing as your network access needs grow.

When selecting a router, you may want to look for one that offers a dial-back option. In dial-back mode, the router switches to a lower-speed link if the primary link ceases to pass data. Typically, a slower leased line speed, or even an ISDN line, will be used for the dial-back circuit. Dial-back capability comes in very handy if your primary link fails. Some of the more advanced CSU/DSUs can now even be configured for this option. Keep in mind that dial-back capability requires a second leased line, which means an additional cost. This cost may be easily justified depending on your need for reliable Internet access.

CSU/DSU

The router requires a CSU/DSU to communicate over the leased line to the ISP. The CSU/DSU is similar to a modem in that it converts the network data from the router's serial port into information that can be sent over the leased line. The CSU/DSU is purchased based on the speed of the leased line purchased. Because the goal is to preserve your investment, you should also select a CSU/DSU that is scaleable and will allow you to upgrade your leased line service, without having to replace your CSU/DSU. To accomplish this, you might want to consider purchasing a CSU/DSU that supports fractional T1. This will allow you to increase your leased line bandwidth in increments of 56Kbps.

Beyond "Basic" Access

After obtaining these four items, your network users will be able to access services provided on the Internet. For the time being, we will assume your client workstations have the necessary TCP/IP protocol stack and Web browser software installed. We promise to cover these topics later.

Once connected to your ISP, your network clients will be able to access the various services of the Internet. These services include:

- mail services;
- search engines;
- file services; and
- Web services.

These Internet services make up the super set our universal client will need to access. The universal client can participate in any or all of these services, independent of client machine type and operating system. This means a Macintosh should be able to access file services, mail services, and Web services just as easily as a Windows or a UNIX workstation could.

MAIL SERVICES

Electronic mail has become a virtually indispensable business tool. But with all the various operating systems and mail packages available, sending mail between systems is still complicated and troublesome. That's where support for e-mail standards is important. The emerging e-mail standards are SMTP, POP, uuencode/uudecode, MAPI, and MIME.

The Simple Mail Transport Protocol (SMTP) is the foundation of all TCP/IP mail systems. SMTP provides direct, end-to-end mail delivery, which removes the host dependency from e-mail delivery paradigm. In the event of a delivery failure, the local system knows immediately. Both sender and recipient must be capable of handling mail, or mail must be routed to a mail server.

There are two widespread versions of the Post Office Protocol (POP): POP2, which is defined by Request For Comment (RFC) 937, and POP3, which is defined by RFC 1725. These are incompatible protocols, but perform the same basic functions. They verify the user's login name and password, then move the mail messages from the mail server to the user's workstation.

Message Application Program Interface (MAPI) is a set of functions that developers can use to create mail-enabled applications. MAPI-aware applications have an extra command on their FILE menu, the SEND command. This permits the application to send the current document in a mail message.

The Multipurpose Internet Mail Exchange (MIME) standard is an extension of existing TCP/IP mail systems. MIME focuses on the contents of your electronic mail, not how it is delivered. MIME addresses weaknesses in existing TCP/IP mail systems by defining encoding techniques for various forms of data and a structure for the message body that permits several objects to be carried by a single mail message.

There are other options than MIME for encoding binary data within an SMTP mail message. Uuencode and uudecode, although not standards and borrowed from UUCP, are still more widely used for encoding and decoding SMTP mail than MIME.

SEARCH ENGINES

These are Internet service tools that are desirable for file transfer, searching, and retrieval. The ability to provide a News reader search engine, Telnet, and Archie and Gopher services are desirable. A News reader allows you to find and read news articles, raise queries, issue announcements, and conduct discussions on the Internet. It accomplishes this through Usenet, the global news network. Usenet is similar to a forum for exchanging ideas and information, much in the manner of an electronic discussion group.

The Internet gives you methods of logging in to other computers. The Telnet command is typically used to let you connect to a host on which you do not have an account. Telnet allows you to emulate different terminals, with the two most common being TN3270 and TN5250 terminals.

Gopher, a popular Internet search and retrieval engine, gives you access to information, including text and graphics, through a network of gopher servers. Gopher servers are centers (many of them at universities) that provide information and make it available to anyone in the world. Gopher originated at the University of Minnesota as a general-purpose information retrieval tool.

The program Archie, whose name was derived from *archive,* performs its searches on the Internet in File Transfer Protocol (FTP) repositories. Like gopher, you can run Archie from your Internet site or from a Telnet session by logging in to an Archie server.

FILE SERVICES

The File Transfer Protocol (FTP) is the way computers on the Internet exchange files. FTP is a high-level protocol, which requires client and server components. A subset of FTP is the Trivial File Transfer Protocol (TFTP). TFTP, like FTP, is used to upload and download files, but requires minimal overhead. TFTP has no directory or password capability.

WEB SERVICES

If you want to publish information on the Internet, you'll need a Web server. We will delve into the hardware, software, and administrative requirements for a Web server in subsequent chapters of this book. The costs for providing these services within an organization and outside an organization are equal. Keep in mind that the moment you install a Web server at your site, you've opened a window into your local network that any user on the Internet can peer through. Most visitors are content to window shop, but a few will try to peek at things you don't intend for public consumption. Others, not content to look without touching, will attempt to force the window open and crawl in.

Security Issues   As the growth of the Internet has exploded, so have instances of Internet security breaches. With big business gravitating toward the variety of services that can be provided over the Internet, concerns about the security and reliability of the Internet have been raised. Justifiably so! Before the explosion of the home computer, in the heyday of the mainframe, security was largely a function of expense and unavailability of equipment. In those days, a terminal and a modem were expensive, and use was limited to large government and educational institutions. Today, there is roughly one computer per every two households and some homes have multiple computers. Hackers are getting younger and business is more vulnerable to attacks.

The software that powers the Internet has come under fire for many publicly disclosed shortcomings. The following section details the more recent security flaws that users have found in the more popular Internet browsers and Web servers. These security holes have been fixed or patched in the currently shipping versions of these products, but this does not mean that new holes haven't been created. they just haven't been publicized or exploited yet.

As far as security on the Internet is concerned, there's a lot to worry about. A false sense of security is not the same as security. Many in the industry feel that the International Trade and Regulation (ITAR) restrictions on cryptography should be repealed.

One of the more popular Internet browsers, Netscape Navigator, had several problems with its security and cryptographic code. In fact, several "hacks" published books that detailed the holes in Netscape's security. Netscape was forced to use a crippled cryptographic algorithm because of ITAR export restrictions. Some of the hacks are indicative of sloppy programming at Netscape, while some are indicative of the flaws inherent in releasing cryptographic code without a publicly available source.

There is a maxim in system security circles that says buggy software opens up security holes. Conversely, there is a maxim in software development circles that says large, complex programs contain bugs. Unfortunately for us, Web servers are large, complex programs that can, and often do, contain security holes.

Even worse, the open architecture of Web servers allows arbitrary Common Gateway Interface (CGI) scripts to be executed on the server's side of the connection in response to remote requests. Any CGI script installed at your site may contain bugs, and every bug is a potential security hole.

There are four overlapping types of risk:

1. Private or confidential documents stored in the Web site's document tree may fall into the hands of unauthorized individuals.
2. Private or confidential information sent by the remote user to the server, such as credit card information, may be intercepted.
3. Information about the Web server's host machine may leak, giving outsiders access to data that can potentially allow them to break into the host.
4. Bugs that allow outsiders to execute commands on the server's host machine to modify and damage the system are not uncommon risks. These risks include "denial of service" attacks in which the attackers pummel the machine with so many requests that it is rendered effectively useless.

SERVER AND OPERATING SYSTEM CONSIDERATIONS

Some operating systems offer more secure platforms for Web servers than others. As a rule of thumb, though, the more powerful and flexible the operating system, the more open it is for attack.

With the large number of built-in servers, services, scripting languages, and interpreters available, UNIX systems are particularly vulnerable to attack. This is because there are so many points of entry for hackers to exploit. Macintoshes and Microsoft Windows machines are less likely to be exploited. However, a tradeoff exists between convenience and security on these machines.

A UNIX system managed by a seasoned UNIX administrator will probably be more secure than a Microsoft Windows system set up by a novice. You always have to factor in the experience of the people running the server host and software.

Remember: The more features a server offers, the more likely it is to contain security holes. Simple servers that make static files available for requests and do little more are probably safer than complex servers that offer such features as on-the-fly directory listings, CGI script execution, server-side include processing, and scripted error handling.

Different server platforms and operating systems vary in their capability to restrict browser access to individual documents or portions of the document tree. Certain servers provide no restriction at all, while other servers allow you to restrict access to directories based on the IP address of the browser or users who can provide the correct password. A few commercial servers provide data encryption as well.

SOFTWARE AND PROGRAMMING CONSIDERATIONS

CGI scripts can be a major source of security holes. Although CGI is not inherently insecure, CGI scripts must be written with just as much care as the server itself. Unfortunately, some scripts fall short of this standard, and trusting Web administrators install them at their sites without realizing the problems.

Server-side includes, snippets of server directives embedded in Hypertext Markup Language (HTML) documents, are another potential hole. A subset of the directives available in server-side includes instruct the server to execute arbitrary system commands and CGI scripts. Unless the author is aware of potential problems, it's easy to introduce unintentional side effects. Unfortunately, HTML files containing dangerous server-side includes are seductively easy to write.

ROUTER AND DNS SECURITY ISSUES

Restriction by IP address is secure against casual nosiness, but not against a determined hacker. There are several ways around IP address restrictions. With the proper equipment and software, a hacker can "spoof" his or her IP address, making it seem as if he or she is connecting from a location different from the real one. Nor is there any guarantee that the person contacting your server from an authorized host is, in fact, the person you think he or she is. The remote host may have been broken into and is being used as a front. To be safe, IP address restriction must be combined with a mechanism that checks the identity of the user, such as a check for username and password.

IP address restriction can be made much safer by running your server behind a firewall machine that is capable of detecting and rejecting attempts at spoofing IP addresses. Such detection works best for intercepting packets from the outside world that claim to be from trusted machines on your network.

One thing to be aware of is that if a browser is set to use a proxy server to fetch documents, your server will know about only the IP address of the proxy, not the real user's address. This means if the proxy is in a trusted domain, anyone can use that proxy to access your site. Unless you know you can trust a particular proxy to do its own restriction, don't add the IP address of a proxy (or a domain containing a proxy server) to the list of authorized addresses.

Restriction by host or domain name has the same risks as restriction by IP address, but also suffers from the risk of DNS spoofing, an attack in which your server is temporarily fooled into thinking that an alien IP address belongs to a trusted host name. To lessen the risk of DNS spoofing, some servers can be configured to perform an extra DNS lookup for each client. After translating the IP address of the incoming request to a host name, the server uses the DNS to translate from the host name back to the IP address. If the two addresses don't match, access is forbidden.

Restriction by user name and password has its problems as well. A password is good only if it's chosen carefully. Too often, users choose obvious passwords such as middle names, their birthday, their office phone number, or the name of a favorite pet goldfish. These passwords can be guessed at, and WWW servers, unlike UNIX login programs, don't complain after repeated unsuccessful guesses. A determined hacker can employ a password-guessing program to break in by brute force. You should also be alert to the possibility of remote users sharing their usernames and passwords with other users. It is more secure to use a combination of IP address restriction and password than to use either of them alone.

Another problem is that the password is vulnerable to interception as it is transmitted from browser to server. It is not encrypted in any meaningful way, so a hacker with the right hardware and software can pull the password off the Internet as it passes through. Furthermore, unlike a login session in which the password is passed over the Internet just once, a browser sends the password every time it fetches a protected document.

This makes it easier for a hacker to intercept the transmitted data as it flows across the Internet. To avoid this, you have to encrypt the data.

If you need to protect documents against local users on the server's host system, you'll need to run the server as something other than "nobody" and set the permissions of the restricted documents and server scripts so they're not readable by any user in the world.

Firewalls

You can use a firewall to enhance your site's security in a number of ways. The most straightforward use of a firewall is to create an "internal site" that is accessible only to computers within your own local area network. If this is what you want to do, all you need to do is to place the server inside the firewall. (See Figure 1-14.)

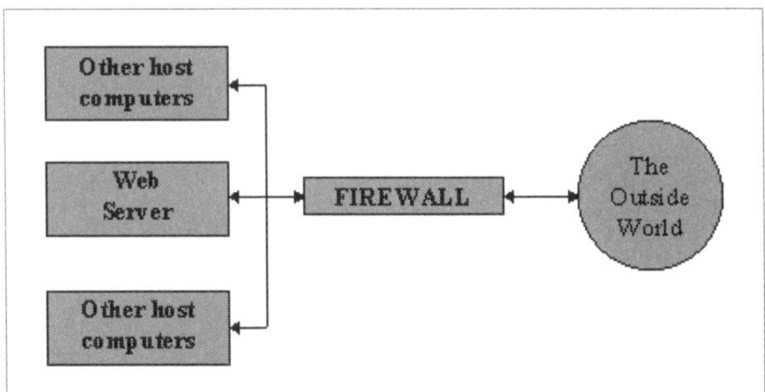

FIGURE 1-14 *A LAN Protected by a Firewall*

However, if you want to make the server available to the rest of the world, you'll need to place it somewhere outside the firewall. From the standpoint of security of your organization as a whole, the safest place to put it is completely outside the local area network. (See Figure 1-15 on page 26.)

This is called a "sacrificial lamb" configuration. The server is at risk of being broken into, but the firewall protects the security of the inner network.

It's not advisable to run the Web server on the firewall machine. If you do this, any bug in the server would compromise the security of the

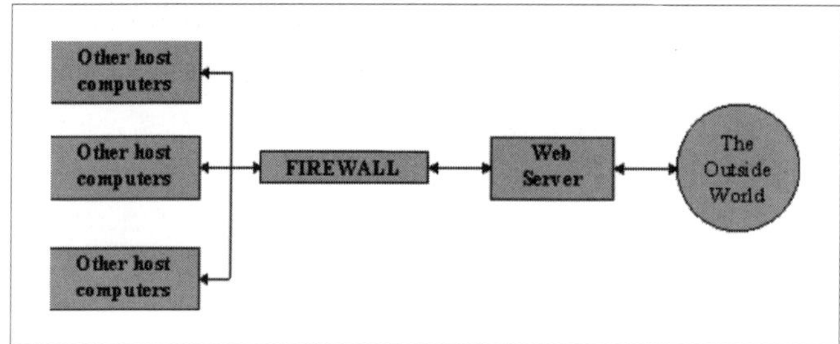

FIGURE *A Firewall Separating a Network from Its Web Server,*
1-15 *Thus Protecting the LAN*

entire organization. There are a number of variations on this basic setup, including architectures that use paired "inner" and "outer" servers to give the world access to public information while giving the internal network access to private documents.

Some firewall architectures, however, don't give you the option of placing the host outside the firewall. In this case, you have no choice but to open up a hole in the firewall. There are two options:

1. If you are using a "screened host" firewall, you can selectively allow the firewall to pass requests for port 80 that are bound to or returning from the WWW server machine. This has the effect of poking a small hole in the dike through which the rest of the world can send and receive requests to the WWW server machine.

2. If you are using a "dual homed gateway" firewall, you'll need to install a proxy on the firewall machine. A proxy is a small program that can see both sides of the firewall. Requests for information from the Web server are intercepted by the proxy and forwarded to the server machine, and the response is forwarded back to the requester.

A small and reliable Hypertext Transfer Protocol (HTTP) proxy is available from Trusted Information Systems at ftp://ftp.tis.com/pub/firewalls/toolkit/.

An excellent source of information about firewalls is available in the books *Firewalls and Internet Security* by William Cheswick and Steven Bellovin, and *Building Internet Firewalls* by D. Brent Chapman and Elizabeth D. Zwicky of O'Reilly & Associates, Inc.

Encryption

Encryption works by encoding the text of a message with a key. In traditional encryption systems, the same key was used for both encoding and decoding. In the new public key or asymmetric encryption systems, keys come in pairs: one key is used for encoding and another for decoding. In this system, everyone owns a unique pair of keys. One of the keys, called the public key, is widely distributed and used for encoding messages. The other key, called the private key, is a closely held secret used to decode incoming messages. Under this system, a person who needs to send a message to a second person can encrypt the message with that person's public key. The message can be decrypted only by the owner of the secret private key, making it safe from interception. This system can also be used to create unforgeable digital signatures.

Most practical implementations of secure Internet encryption actually combine the traditional symmetric and the new asymmetric schemes. Public key encryption is used to negotiate a secret symmetric key that is then used to encrypt the actual data.

Because commercial ventures have a critical need for secure transmission on the Web, there is very active interest in developing schemes for encrypting the data that passes between browser and server.

More information on public key cryptography can be found in the book *Applied Cryptography* by Bruce Schneier, published by John Wiley & Sons.

There are several proposed encryption and user authentication standards for the Web. Each requires the right combination of compatible browser and server to operate, so none is yet the universal solution to the secure data transmission problem.

Secure Socket Layer (SSL) is the scheme proposed by Netscape Communications Corp. It is a low-level encryption scheme used to encrypt transactions in higher-level protocols such as HTTP, NNTP, and FTP. The SSL protocol includes provisions for server authentication (verifying the server's identity to the client), encryption of data in transit, and optional client authentication (verifying the client's identity to the server). SSL is currently implemented commercially only for Netscape browsers and some Netscape servers. (Although both the data encryption and server authentication parts of the SSL protocol have been implemented, client authentication is not yet available.)

Using SSL-enabled servers and clients, you will be able to send encrypted messages without fear of interception. However, to use public key encryption for the purposes of user verification, other issues are involved, including the need to obtain a verification certificate from an officially recognized Certifying Authority such as Verisign, of Verisign, Inc., Mountain View, California.

Secure HTTP (SHTTP) is the scheme proposed by CommerceNet, a coalition of businesses interested in developing the Internet for commercial use. SHTTP is a higher-level protocol that works only with the HTTP protocol, but is potentially more extensible than SSL.

Shen is the scheme proposed by Phillip Hallam-Baker of CERN. Like SHTTP, it is a high-level replacement for the existing HTTP protocol. It hasn't yet been implemented in production-quality software.

Server Security Problems

The following are examples of past security issues that have been found in both commercial and public domain Internet server products.

NETSCAPE COMMUNICATIONS SERVER FOR WINDOWS NT

There are a security bug on the Windows NT version of Netscape server that allow users to read secured documents without entering their username and password. According to Netscape, this bug has been fixed by version 1.12 and above of the Windows NT Server.

The Windows NT versions of the Netscape servers (both the Netscape Communications Server version 1.12 and the Netscape Commerce Server) had two problems involving the handling of CGI scripts. One of these problems is also shared by the O'Reilly WebSite Server.

The Netscape server did not use the Windows NT File Manager's associations between file extensions and applications. Thus, even though you may have associated the extension .pl with the Perl interpreter, Perl scripts weren't recognized as such when placed in the cgi-bin directory. Until very recently, a Netscape technical note recommended placing the perl.exe file into cgi-bin and referring to your scripts as /cgi-bin/perl.exe?&my_script.pl.

Unfortunately, this technique allowed anyone on the Internet to execute an arbitrary set of Perl commands on your server. This is not a good idea. A Netscape technical note suggested encapsulating your Perl scripts in a .BAT file. However, because of a related problem with batch scripts, this method was no safer.

Because EMWACS NT Server, Purveyor and WebSite NT servers all use the File Manager extension associations, you can execute Perl scripts on these servers without placing the perl.exe file into the cgi-bin directory. They are safe from this bug.

O'REILLY WEBSITE SERVER FOR WINDOWS NT AND WINDOWS 95

WebSite versions 1.1b and earlier had the same problem with DOS .BAT files that Netscape does. However because WebSite supports three different types of CGI scripting interfaces (native Windows, standard CGI for Perl scripts, and the rarely used DOS .BAT file interface), the recommended action was to turn off the server's support for DOS CGI scripts. This will not affect the server's ability to run Visual BASIC, Perl, or C scripts.

This bug has been fixed in version 1.1c and above. You should upgrade to the latest version with the patch provided at the WebSite home page. You can obtain detailed information on the actions necessary to close the WebSite .bat file security hole at the WebSite's developer page.

PURVEYOR SERVER FOR WINDOWS NT

The EMWACS NT server, from which Purveyor is derived, appears to be safe from this problem. According to the developers of Purveyor, they anticipated the .bat file security hole during the software's development. Purveyor is immune to the .bat file security hole.

MICROSOFT IIS WEB SERVER

Versions of the Microsoft IIS server downloaded prior to March 15, 1996, contain the same .bat file bug that appears in other NT-based servers. In fact, the problem is worse than on other servers because .BAT CGI scripts don't even have to be installed on the server for a malicious remote user to invoke any arbitrary set of DOS commands on your server.

NCSA HTTPD FOR UNIX

Version 1.3 of NCSA's UNIX server contains a serious security hole. Discovered in March of 1995, this hole allows outsiders to execute arbitrary commands on the server host. If you have a version 1.3 httpd binary whose creation date is earlier than March 1995, don't use it.

WHAT'S NEXT?

In this chapter, we have learned the basic requirements for providing network access to the Internet. This was in no way intended to be a comprehensive guide, but rather an overview of what is required to get started. However, what if you don't really need to provide Internet access? Here is one of the driving forces behind the intranet. Companies want to provide services within the organization without the expense of providing external access to the 'Net. Besides, once you "open the floodgates" so to speak, you will need to provide an additional layer of network administration. Internet administration has become a full-time job in many organizations. Unfortunately, Internet administration is often being dumped in the laps of overextended LAN administrators.

We have also learned that there are glaring holes in Internet security. The holes can be patched, prevented, or worked around. However, some solutions in providing additional layers of security may be cost-prohibitive. These costs can arise from additional required hardware, software, and administrative overhead. This is another reason that intranets are growing in popularity. Just as with any other LAN-based service, you have the same control and constraints over your intranet services. What control do we have over the Internet? None. The only real control over the Internet is provided by the InterNic, which governs only domain name usage. Everything else is really a free-for-all. You can't even guarantee bandwidth and service availability.

And so, with all the problems inherent in providing external Web services, perhaps we should investigate providing these services internally. And thus is born the intranet!

2

The Intranet:
Surfing Within

CONTENTS

In its simplest form, an intranet is defined as "Internet services provided within an organization." If we expand this concept, we need to add the client software that will be used to access these services. The client software used is the true differentiator between Internet and intranet services.

As we learned in Chapter 1, Internet services consist of mail services, file services, news services, and Web-based services. All these services can be accessed through your browser software. If you analyze today's LANs, you will find that most already offer file and mail services, but are lacking the news and Web-based services common to the Internet. You might assume that by adding these missing services, you will have the makings of an intranet.

That's not exactly true. The Internet is based on industry-adopted, codified standards, while most network operating systems and electronic mail systems are based on interpretations or adaptations of standards with proprietary features mixed in. For example, Novell's Internetwork Packet Exchange/Sequenced Packet Exchange (IPX/SPX) Protocol suite is not a standards-based networking protocol. Yet today, it is one of the most widely deployed network transport protocols. Lotus Development's cc:Mail is not a true standards-based electronic mail package, yet it, too, is very widely used.

Getting non-standards-based or *de facto* network technologies and standards-based Internet technologies to work together is a task that takes specialized software — in this case, the intranet client.

The Intranet Client

We need to take a closer look at the client software that will be used on your intranet. Here's a simple example: Take a workstation running Novell's IPX/SPX protocol. It cannot access file services on a UNIX, Digital, Macintosh, or Windows NT server unless one of these conditions is met:

- those "host" systems are running an IPX protocol stack interpreter, or
- the client workstation is running a multiprotocol stack LAN driver.

Take a look at Figure 2-1. This figure shows a multiprotocol network and the tasks that would be involved in accessing file services from one workstation to all the operating systems depicted. This configuration

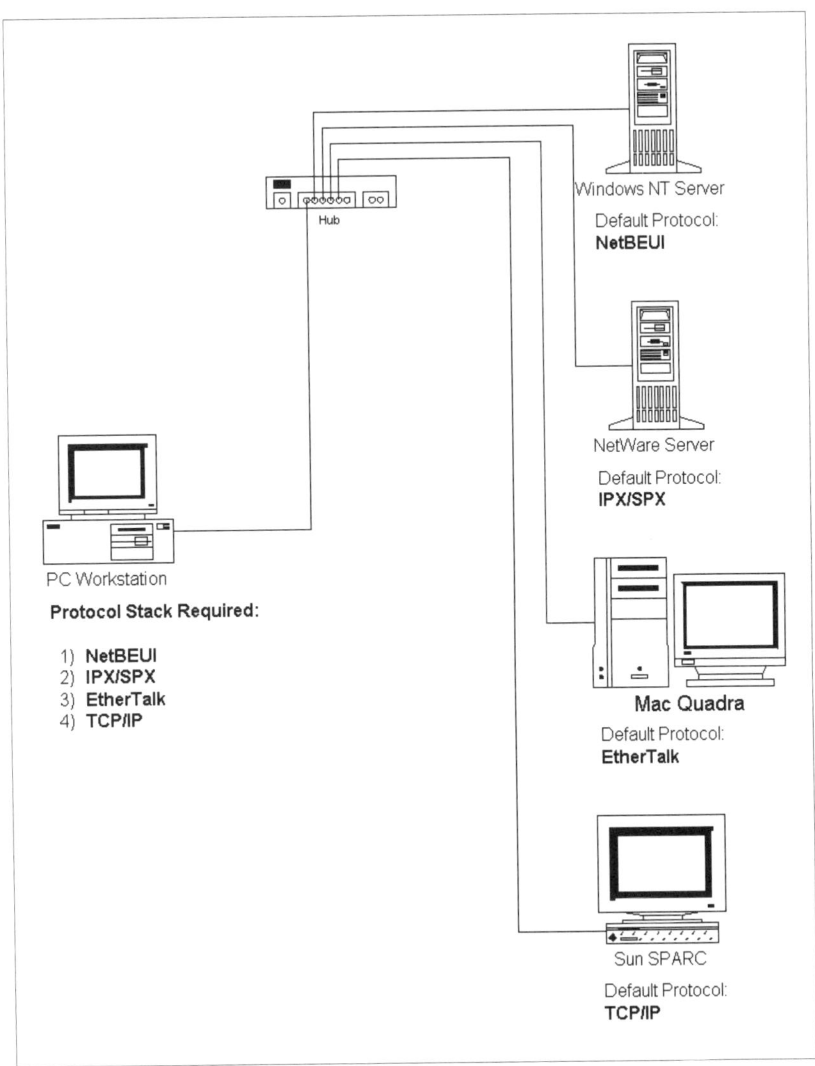

FIGURE *A Multiprotocol Network*

2-1

would use a good chunk of memory on the client workstation. It would use so much memory that memory-intensive applications might not run at all, and attempting to open multiple applications on the client PC might cause it to freeze, hang-up, or crash.

If we expand on this example beyond basic file services, we'll see the same is true for a workstation running an electronic mail package such as

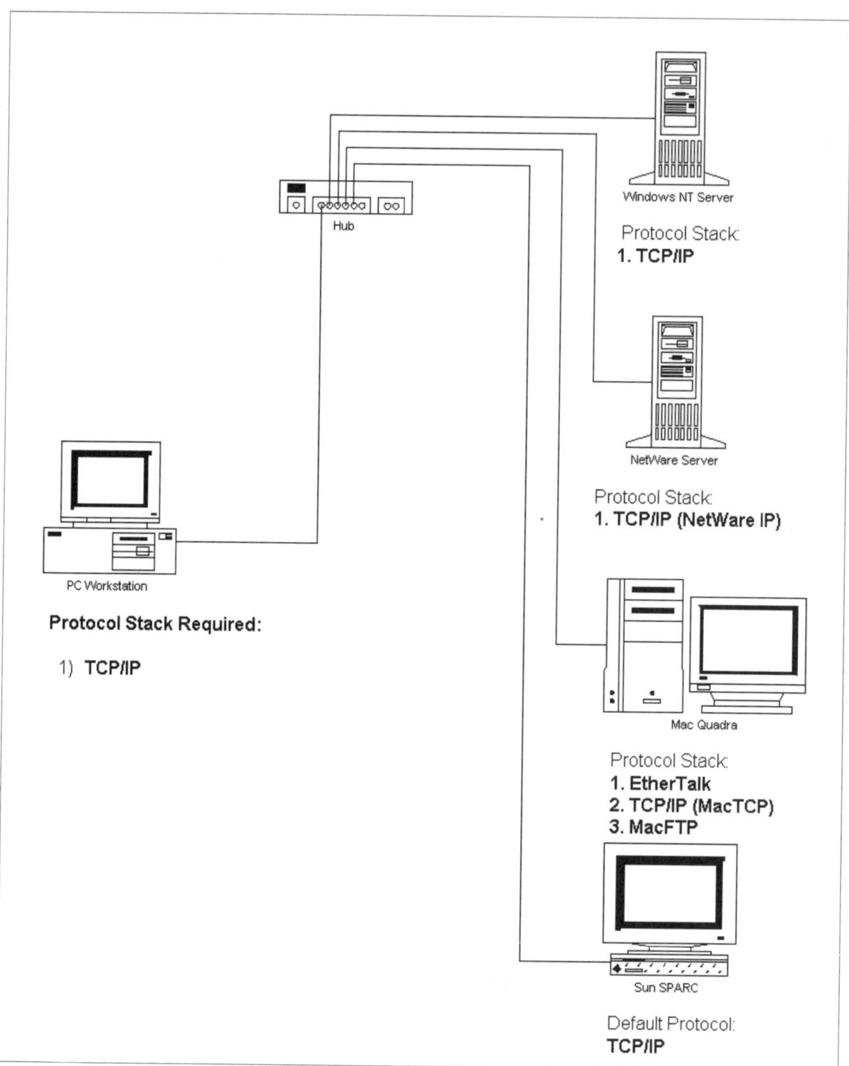

Figure A Single Protocol Network
2-2

cc:Mail. That client cannot exchange mail messages with other systems or networks unless one of the following conditions is met:

- those other mail systems are running cc:Mail and are recognized by the cc:Mail domain, or
- a mail gateway exists that can translate between different mail systems.

In a standards-based environment, our client could exchange messages with any other standards-based messaging system, and could access files on any standards-enabled network operating system. Ideally, this would be accomplished through a single protocol stack and a single application (or a tightly integrated suite of applications), as shown in Figure 2-2.

In Figure 2-2, we show the same multiprotocol environment used in Figure 2-1. The only difference is that we have replaced the multiprotocol stack at the client workstation with a single TCP/IP protocol stack. We've added additional software at the server to support protocols that may not be native to the various operating systems. And, in some cases (the NetWare and Macintosh OS), we will need to add additional software to support the file transfer protocol (FTP). Because file servers are more robust and have a different memory model than the client workstations, they are better equipped to handle multiple protocol stacks. More importantly, the client PC, with a single protocol stack, has more memory available to run applications.

The Universal Client	We touched on the concept of the universal client in Chapter 1. We said the universal client could access the various services we were to provide, independent of operating system and client machine type. For this to be true, our services must support the same standards and protocols used by our universal client. In addition, other services we might want to introduce into our intranet beyond the core Internet services must also support the same standards and protocols used by our universal client.

Within the context of this book, the universal client will be defined by our browser software and our protocol stack. We will get into the protocol portion of our universal client a bit later in this chapter. As for browser software, you will want to select a client such as Netscape Navigator, the Microsoft Internet Explorer or NCSA Mosaic. There are other commercial and freeware browsers available, most of which are based on NCSA's Mosaic. You may also want to consider the Internet services supported by each client because not all clients support every possible Internet service. Another consideration, especially for intranets, is the support for third-party add-ins and modules (sometimes referred to as plug-ins). See Table 2-1 for a partial list of browsers.

Table 2-1. Internet Client Software Packages

Browser	Windows	Windows 95	Windows NT	Macintosh	UNIX	FTP	Mail	Telnet
Netscape Navigator	√	√	√	√	√	√	√	√
NCSA Mosaic	√	√	√	√	√	√		
Microsoft Internet Explorer	√	√	√	√		√	√	
AttachMate	√	√	√			√	√	√
QuarterDec InterSuite	√	√	√			√	√	√

If you examine Figure 2-3, you will see a sample of a simple intranet. By simple, I mean this intranet is using the Netscape Navigator browser as the universal client on the three different workstation types (Windows, Macintosh, and UNIX).

Although software exists on the NetWare file server that will allow these three different clients to share file and print services (NetWare, NetWare for Macintosh, and NetWare NFS), this does not make it an intranet. It is when you add the Netscape Navigator client software that all three clients can access both NetWare and Microsoft Windows NT servers and their respective Web, FTP, mail, and video services.

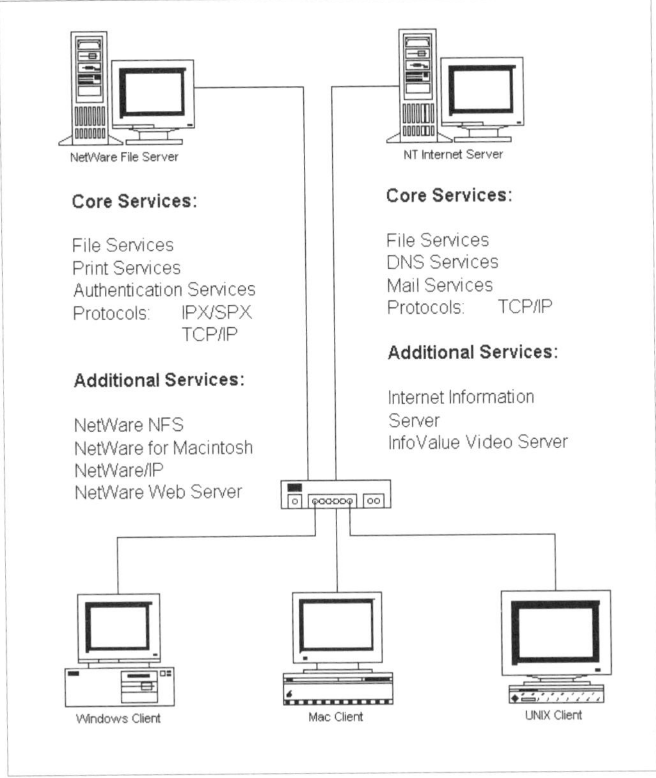

FIGURE *A Multiclient Intranet*
2-3

We could even add clients to this intranet that support only the universal client. This would allow secure services to be run on the NetWare or Windows NT server, and shared services to be run over the intranet.

CONSIDERATIONS FOR STARTING AN INTRANET

Make the decision for your intranet based on the services or suite of services you will offer your users, not on the operating system or Web server software you just happened to "download for free." These services will help dictate the required server hardware and software, and even the client software, you will need.

Take a look at Table 2-2 and use this as your starting point for narrowing down your client and server platforms. Keep in mind that you may select a combination of server and clients on your intranet (just like on the Internet). However, the best possible solution would be to try to have only one client type and one server type to support and maintain.

Table 2-2. Intranet Service Matrix

Service	To Be Provided? (Yes / No)	Existing on LAN Today? (Yes / No)	Platforms to Support (Windows, MAC, UNIX)
World Wide Web			
Mail			
FTP			
Telnet			
News			
Audio			
Video			

Web services are the most common selection and the most obvious services you can provide over your intranet. However, the types of Web services, and the nature of any server-side scripting or programming, will dictate which software you use. If, for example, you can write Perl scripts, you can select virtually any Web server software. However, if you can write only in Visual Basic, your selection of available Web servers that work with Visual Basic may change.

The operating system the Web server software runs on can also be a limiting factor. You would probably not want to use a Windows NT-based server if you run a Macintosh shop and you never have worked on a Windows NT platform. Instead, you might want to look for a Macintosh-based Web server package to simplify system administration and management duties. After all, bringing an alien operating system into your network adds one more layer of complexity to your day-to-day administrative responsibilities.

Your current network operating system already provides some level of file services to your LAN clients. However, you may want to add FTP capabilities to existing servers. By doing this, you can provide file services from within the universal client. Adding FTP services will vary depending on the operating system you are using.

There are other service-based considerations. Some really cool Web-based services, such as audio servers and video servers, run on specific operating system platforms and microprocessor hardware. To provide these services to your users, you will have to deal with these system requirements and limitations.

You must also take into account the client mix you will be providing these services to. We've already discussed the intranet client to some degree, but your network may use a mix of protocols, or you may not have the time, money, or resources to re-deploy a single protocol stack on all your workstations.

This is probably a good time to take a full inventory of your network environment. After all, this may be something you have been meaning to do for some time, anyway, so planning the implementation of an intranet gives you a good excuse. You need to determine the mix of client operating systems, protocols, and even the Internet client software your workstations are running. For a small departmental intranet, it may be a simple task to manually collect this information. However, once your intranet client base crosses the "over 50" mark, the collection and organization of this client configuration database becomes a daunting task. This makes an excellent case for obtaining a solid network hardware and software inventory program.

Your inventory should detail the types of client workstations, the operating system and version those clients are running, and the protocols and frame types running on those workstations. You might want to use the form on the following page as a template for your network inventory sheet. This form is in no way all-inclusive. (See page 40.) This form has been included in Microsoft Word 6.0 format on the companion CD-ROM in the back of this book.

Network Client Inventory

Inventory Collected By: _______________________ Date: _______________________

Workstation Location: _______________________

User: _______________________

Phone Number: _______________________ Ext.: _______________________

Workstation Type: _______________________

Operating System: _______________________ Version: _______________________

Installed Memory: _______________________ (in MB)

Extended ❑   Amount: _______________________ (in MB)

Expanded ❑   Amount: _______________________ (in MB)

Memory Management: _______________________ Type: _______________________

Network Adapter: _______________________

Network Drivers: _______________________ Version: _______________________

Network Protocols: (Check all that apply)

IPX/SPX	❑	NetBIOS	❑
TCP/IP	❑	EtherTalk	❑
NetBEUI	❑	TokenTalk	❑

Intranet Services to be Accessed: (Check all that apply)

Web Services	❑	News Reader	❑
E-mail	❑	Video Services	❑
FTP Services	❑	Audio Services	❑
Telnet	❑	Database	❑

Internet Client Software Installed?   Yes ❑   No ❑

If Yes, which one:

Netscape Navigator	❑	Version: _______________________
Microsoft Internet Explorer	❑	Version: _______________________
NCSA Mosaic	❑	Version: _______________________
Other	❑	Version: _______________________

Your inventory software should support the various workstation types and operating systems present in your intranet target area. If you have Macintosh clients as well as Windows, Windows 95, OS/2, and UNIX workstations, you will want to find an inventory package that supports most, if not all of these environments. You also want to control when inventory information is collected. If you do not have the time, manpower, or desire to perform this inventory manually, you might consider using a tool such as network inventory software.

Table 2-3 lists several good LAN-based automatic inventory packages and the clients they support.

Table 2-3. LAN Inventory Packages

Inventory Packages	DOS	Windows	OS/2	Macintosh
Intel LANdesk	√	√	√	√
McAfee Brightworks	√	√	√	√
Cheyenne Monitrix	√	√	√	√
Symantec Norton Administrator for Networks	√	√	√	√
Microsoft SMS	√	√	√	√
Seagate LAN Directory	√	√	√	√

When selecting an inventory package, you also want to consider the following:

- What client operating systems does the package support?
- Are there add-on software modules for additional clients or server operating systems?
- What network operating systems does the software support?
- Does the software support remote or mobile computers?
- What reporting options does the software provide?
- Can you generate custom reports?
- Can you schedule how and when the information is collected?

- What administrative tools does the software provide?
- Can the software be integrated into your current network management system?
- Is the software licensed per workstation or per concurrent user?
- Does the software allow you to perform electronic software distribution?
- Will the software collect system and initialization files, and can you display the contents of these files?

Once you have a better understanding of your client and server environment, you can make a better determination of what you need to provide for intranet services.

Once you have a good idea of what you have installed and the software and protocols that are required for your intranet clients, you need to implement the client software on your network. Many LAN inventory packages can also be used to "distribute" software to workstations. In addition, a good distribution package should have advanced reporting capabilities so you can find out how the installation went and where it broke down. Table 2-4 lists several LAN-based software distribution packages and the clients they support. Notice that several of the packages listed in this table can also be found in the LAN inventory package table. You should also notice the clients supported by these packages in the inventory section may not be supported in the distribution section.

Table 2-4. LAN Software Distribution Packages

Software Distribution Packages	DOS	Windows	OS/2	Macintosh
Intel LANdesk	√	√		
McAfee Brightworks	√	√		
Symantec Norton Administrator for Networks	√	√		
Microsoft SMS	√	√	√	
Seagate SUDS/ MacSUDS	√	√	√	√

Protocol Support	For the most part, intranet applications and services require TCP/IP as the transport protocol. However, you may not have the necessary memory available at some of your older client workstations to be able to support a dual or multiprotocol stack. Multiprotocol stacks permit several different LAN protocols, such as IPX and TCP/IP, to be simultaneously bound to the same network adapter. Older PC-class workstations with 80386-class processors may not have the memory management capability to support multiple protocols and sufficient memory remaining to run existing applications.

Web servers and other Internet/intranet services (which we will talk about later) require TCP/IP to communicate. If your intranet client does not natively support the TCP/IP, you will require a TCP/IP Gateway. A TCP/IP gateway consists of a protocol stack converter that resides on a server or a dedicated machine. Examples of TCP/IP Protocol gateways include IwareConnect and Novell's IPX-to-IP gateway. These products allow you to implement TCP/IP on your network, without needing to install and configure TCP/IP on each workstation. Most TCP/OP gateways provide services to let you assign static IP addresses or dynamically share a group of IP addresses among users.

The disadvantage of these gateways is that the gateway often becomes the performance bottleneck on the network. In a large network environment, you may want to use multiple TCP/IP protocol gateways. In the event of a gateway failure, your TCP/IP network will not collapse.

TCP/IP	TCP/IP is not required for an intranet, but it is an ideal protocol for provisioning intranet services and is a reliable transport mechanism. For the duration of this book, the products and services we will be covering are based on TCP/IP. With this in mind, you need to decide on a TCP/IP addressing scheme. You also want to consider applying to the InterNIC for a range of TCP/IP addresses. Why do you need addresses if you want only intranet services? Someday, you might want to connect your intranet to the Internet. Having a registered range of IP addresses

will give you a better chance of avoiding address conflicts when and if you connect to the Internet. Of course, you could always use a router to perform the address translation and network isolation for you, but that can be complicated and costly.

IP Addressing Scheme

There are three major classes of TCP/IP addresses: Class A, B, and C. The classes of address dictate the total number of devices that can be supported, as well as the format of the TCP/IP address.

The IP address consists of four binary octets, which are represented by decimal numbers. These numbers define the network and the host addresses for the network adapter. For each class of IP address, the network ID is always the first part of the IP address. The IP address class can be identified by the size of the network ID. Figure 2-4 indicates the respective sizes of the network and host IDs, as they relate to the binary octets.

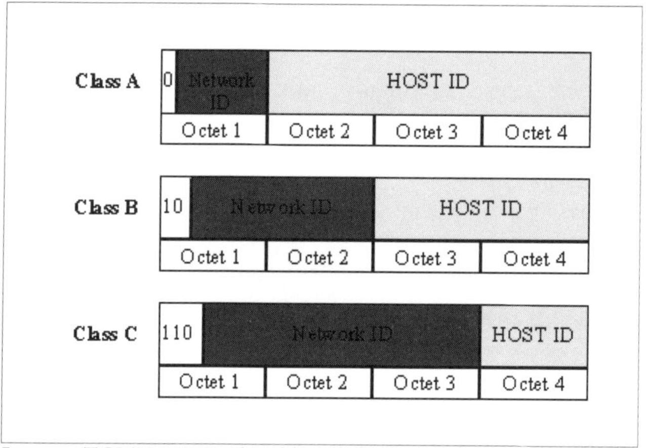

FIGURE 2-4 *TCP/IP Network Address Schemes*

There are two other classes of IP addresses: Class D and E. Class D is a multicast address and starts with 1110 in the first octet. Class E starts with 1111 in the first octet and is reserved for experimental purposes. Neither Class D nor Class E addresses are assigned.

Table 2-5 shows the number of network hosts allowed by the different Address classes.

Table 2-5. TCP/IP Address Classes

Address Class	1st Octet Start	Address Range	Subnet Mask
A	0	1–127	255.X.X.X
B	10	128–191	255.255.X.X
C	110	192–254	255.255.255.X

The Class C address is the most common and the address you will most likely be working with. A Class C address allows a possible two million networks with as many as 254 hosts. If you need more devices, you need to divide your network into subnets. Subnets are achieved by using the subnet mask, which divides the host portion of the network address and reassigns a portion of the host address to the network address.

For example: You have a network with an IP address of 198.22.192.1. You need to divide this network into three subnets: Subnet 1 will use host numbers between 32 and 95; subnet two will use hosts between 96 and 160; and subnet three will allow hosts between 161 and 223. For a Class C address, you have four bits in the host address field you can use for your subnet. By masking the first four bits in the host address, you get a subnet mask of 255.255.255.240 (1111 1111.1111 1111.1111 1111. 1111 0000). Because a subnet must physically occupy a different LAN or WAN segment on the wire, your first network could have an IP address of 198.22.192.32; your second segment could have an address of 198.22.192.96; and your third LAN segment could have an address of 198.22.192.161. All host devices within these segments must have unique IP addresses that start above these IP addresses.

To calculate your subnet number:

1. Convert the dotted decimal address into a binary number.
   193.22.192.32 = 1100 0110 0001 0110 1100 0000 0010 0000

2. Convert the subnet mask into a binary number.
   255.255.255.240 = 1111 1111 1111 1111 1111 1111 1111 0000

3. Logically AND the two binary numbers.
   1100 0110 0001 0110 1100 0000 0010 0000
   1111 1111 1111 1111 1111 1111 1111 0000

   1100 0110 0001 0110 1100 0000 0010 0000

4. Convert the result to dotted decimal.
   1100 0110 0001 0110 1100 0000 0010 0000 = 198.22.192.32

This result is the subnet number used to represent the wire itself and cannot be used as an interface address. All valid addresses on this subnet must be greater than this number.

INTRANET SERVICES

As we've discussed, there are several services you may want to provide on your intranet.

Mail Services

Your current network environment might already have a method of sending messages between workstations and workgroups within your organization. If not, this is the perfect opportunity to provide them. You may want to select a mail package that supports Internet browser-based e-mail, such as Eudora or Pegasus. If you select a commercial mail package, such as cc:Mail or Microsoft Mail, you may need to install a Simple Mail Transfer Protocol (SMTP) gateway to exchange mail between your network and Internet clients. These services will need to be hosted on shared or dedicated server platforms. Server requirements are discussed in Chapter 5.

File Services	If you have a network and a file server, you are already providing some level of file services. However, this might be the time to consider adding software to your servers so they can provide FTP-based file services. This could involve adding a TCP/IP protocol stack and additional software to your existing file servers. For example, if you want to use your existing NetWare server as your intranet server, you need to add support for the TCP/IP protocol and add support for FTP.
Web Services	The World Wide Web is the newest service to be provided on the Internet and is the service that started the intranet commotion. You need to decide if your Web services will be provided from a dedicated Web server or from an existing file server. You need to select a Web server package, and your choice of servers dictates which packages you can choose from. For example, if you want to use your NetWare server as your intranet server, you must add a NetWare-compatible Web server package, such as Purveyor Web Server for NetWare or Novell's NetWare Web Server. You may even need to add disk space as well as server memory. You must also consider that other programs or NetWare Loadable Modules (NLMs) may affect the performance and operation of the server. Any process that abends (an abnormal end to a server process) will bring down your file and intranet servers.
Audio Services	One advantage an intranet provides is reliable and available bandwidth. Because of this, you may consider providing intranet services that you might not have made available over the Internet. Audio over your intranet is one such service. Audio services can include music, sample client copy of advertisements, and even excerpts from corporate announcements or speeches. If you provide a "What's New" page on your intranet, you might have an audio clip from a product manager describing a new product your company is introducing to the marketplace.

Your audio server dictates the hardware and operating system it can be run on. Thus, if audio services are important to your intranet, you may need to re-think your intranet server selection or add a dedicated server for audio services.

Video Services	Video service is not limited by the Internet's bandwidth constraints. Video servers can provide multiple video streams, which allow a single Web page to simultaneously show several different video clips. Video clips can be of client commercials, new products, product technical information, and sales training.

Video servers require more horsepower than traditional Web servers and should be implemented on a dedicated machine. Storage capacity on your video server will also be a consideration because video clips themselves are large files. As with the audio server, a video server dictates the hardware and operating system it can be run on. If video services are important to your intranet, you may need to re-think your intranet server selection or add a dedicated server for video services.

PLANNING FOR GROWTH

Just as the Internet is a dynamic entity, you should plan for growth on your intranet. For the intranet, growth may come in the form of additional applications being provided on your Web servers. Keep in mind that HTML documents and their graphic files have a way of growing very large, especially because your network's bandwidth will facilitate larger files without suffering from load-time degradation at the client workstation.

Because the bandwidth of your network is greater than what you can expect from the Internet, deploying video and audio servers and applications on your intranet should also be anticipated. These applications are bandwidth-intensive, so if you do plan on implementing these types of services, you may wish to examine your current network access method and infrastructure.

3 Planning Your Company Intranet

CONTENTS

You know what an intranet is and some of the basic service classes you can provide to your users. Now, you need to start planning how you will implement these services. Setting up an intranet does not just consist of installing a Web server. You need to consider who will provide the content for your intranet, how the content will be converted into HyperText Markup Language (HTML), and how the content will be kept current and fresh. In addition, you may have to sell your intranet dream to upper management to get approval for the funding and staffing required to get the project off the ground. If this is the case, read on.

Setting up a company intranet is trivial, compared to the challenge of maintaining its content and keeping current with changes in corporate information. The ability to deploy corporate publishing and conferencing services using the Web and intranet as the core technologies for distribution of information is what is really needed. Several products, such as Microsoft's Front Page and products from Attachmate and Forman Interactive, enable "out-of-the-box" Internet conferencing and publishing. Other products handle content delivery, Web publishing, and document searching. To be truly useful for corporate use, new products are needed that allow mainframe-based data to be easily accessible via Internet-like tool sets, such as Attachmate's Emissary.

IS departments are filled with people who know how to maintain information and can quickly assume the role of mentoring content providers and members of the intranet team throughout the organization. Each of these factors is critical for the success of the intranet and for the successful involvement of IS departments in the transition from legacy mainframe systems. Note that many of these issues are not technical, but political. Indeed, many of our sources within corporate IS departments have told us they are wrestling with these issues just as they once wrestled with issues surrounding PC ownership and configuration. Hopefully, we have learned from the mistakes of the past ten years and will not repeat them.

SHOW, DON'T TELL

Top-down sponsorship from upper management will be a critical factor in developing your company's intranet. You'll see that once you've obtained executive support, the intranet project will take off. The key to winning executive support is often actions, not words.

To do so, find the "pain." Locate the departments where people are experiencing difficulties in getting information to different people or departments within the organization. These people will not only be your advocates, but will also provide you with your first real-world intranet applications.

You should sell the idea for your intranet to the senior managers responsible for that department. You must illustrate how the intranet can be an effective way to distribute information, and specifically address that department's needs. Create an intranet demo of mock Web pages and present these at a staff meeting to show how the intranet can be an information-sharing vehicle at a high level. Remember: People won't accept the idea without seeing what's in it for them. If you don't have the expertise in-house, you may need to solicit assistance from another department or an outside contractor. "Killer data," information that needs to be shared routinely with all employees, often spurs an intranet's creation and will often turn into your first practical intranet application.

For example, at a 50-employee municipal planning department in Durham, Ontario, the niche application was zoning policies and maps. Once management was shown how an existing server could enhance collaboration, the project was approved. Today, a $5,000 budget has been devoted to the project.

For Turner Home Entertainment, the killer data was the Nielsen ratings. Simple e-mail wasn't doing the job of communicating the data, and Turner's technology director proposed an intranet solution.

It is important that you don't sell a minimal intranet configuration because the maintenance involved in an intranet is an ongoing expense that shouldn't be ignored. When you are faced with the "How-much-is-this-going-to-cost?" question, be prepared. Factor in the cost of servers, software, and staffing. Chapter 4 deals with staffing issues in more detail.

RETURN ON INVESTMENT

Explain what you can do with the intranet. Company executives are not afraid to spend money if they see there will be a return on investment.

Don't make the case that an intranet will make money for your company because this is often not the case. Improvements in communications will make an impact in efficiency, but it does not always make an immediate and measurable impact on the bottom line. Don't overstate the intranet's advantages by weighing benefits against other options. It's better to make a case for the usefulness of the intranet as the least common denominator for sharing information than to compare it to existing groupware applications.

There are cost savings from using Web-enabled applications and additional savings from having a focused intranet effort.

BY USING WEB-ENABLED APPLICATIONS, YOU WILL SEE:
- reduced costs — printing, paper, software distribution, mailing, and order processing;
- reduced telephone support expenses;
- easier, faster access to technical and marketing information;
- easier, faster access to remote locations;
- increased access to competitive information;
- a more thorough research base;
- easier access to customers and partners;
- increased accuracy and timeliness of information;

- a consistent interface to learn and use;
- just-in-time information; and
- just-in-time training.

From Focused Intranet Work, You Will See:

- easily accessible information;
- reduced information searching time;
- sharing and reuse of tools and information;
- reduced setup and update time;
- simplified, reduced corporate licensing;
- reduced documentation costs;
- reduced support costs;
- reduced redundant page creation and maintenance;
- faster, cheaper creation;
- one-time archive development costs; and
- sharing of scarce resources and skills.

This is a challenge. There will be specific cost savings from using an intranet and Web-based applications, such as reductions in printing and distribution costs, but one of the largest benefits is the increased access to information. This is very difficult to quantify.

If at all possible, avoid getting involved in return on investment (ROI) issues until people can see the capabilities of the intranet. If you get caught up in ROI issues, you may get started with the intranet project, but the hatchet will eventually fall on you.

The onus is on departments to create engaging, worthwhile, and even fun content. Part of the challenge in establishing an intranet is to serve as a middleman between technology workers, the content providers, and users of the intranet.

But before content development gets rolling, the battle for intranet adoption goes on within corporate walls.

Perhaps the best place to start is to focus on the business problem or issue you are trying to solve, rather than trying to identify how you can use intranets in your company (i.e., find a problem that needs a solution rather than a solution looking for a problem). The "why" for this statement is simple: By articulating the business issues you are trying to solve, you will have a much stronger foundation from which to identify and select your solution. You may find that the solution you need is not an intranet, but rather some other technology, if any technology at all. If you can successfully articulate the business value of a given solution, you will have a much easier time developing a "business case" rather than a "business excuse."

If you have a solid business case and it makes financial and technological sense, you should be one step closer to getting the "green light" for your intranet project.

NEW MANAGEMENT ISSUES

Intranets create new challenges for technology managers. Should a company's intranet have a consistent look and feel dictated by top management, or should employees be given freedom to create Web pages as they see fit? Companies wrestle with this issue. On one hand, you want to let employees create distinctive Web pages, yet somehow maintain a consistent look with other company sites.

One approach is to maintain tight, central control. Others think that because the 'Net's decentralized, democratic culture should be allowed to flourish within corporate walls. Much like the Web itself, intranets shouldn't be dictated by guidelines. Other questions this new technology raises are:

- Should users be able to chat online anonymously?
- Which applications are best suited for the Web?

Perhaps the most profound change brought about by corporate intranets will be social, not technological. Intranet technology has given us a new tool to command political influence that will change the organization as a whole. The technology is trivial; the hard part is the community it provides.

A PHASED APPROACH TO IMPLEMENTATION

Most users express a preference for a system that is constantly being changed and updated, rather than "dead" static documents that never change as it gives the user an idea that they might find newer, more up-to-date information each time they view the system. Because conversion to the new technology cannot happen overnight, use a phased approach in which various components of the system are brought online gradually.

Recommended Steps

To bring a system online in phases, take the following steps:

- Plot the initial design completely, and use a flowchart or storyboard for easier visualization of the hypertext flow. Collaborative design can be done through online flowcharts or wall displays.
- Implement a "demonstration project" that brings online small pieces of the eventual system to demonstrate the potential of the technology to managers and concerned user groups.
- Take special care to design a front end (home page and opening menus) that is intuitive and quick to access.
- Provide sophisticated color graphics with gimmicks (such as a sound bite from the company president or a video) to give the front end a professional and impressive effect.
- Develop graphic icons and visual/color motifs to give a consistent look to the interface or to indicate a transition to different domains.
- Test embedded graphics on high- and low-resolution monitors. Text is automatically re-sized to user preferences; graphics are not.

- Design home pages tailored to specific departments or work groups.

- Provide access to the correct home page through customization of resource files or menus.

- Plan which elements should go online first, second, and third. Management will have its own priorities you need to take into account.

- Immediately bring online crucial data, such as computer reports, by simply dumping it to a formatted ASCII file and making a hypertext link directly to the file.

- Quickly bring online published information, such as Microsoft Word or FrameMaker documents, by linking them through MIME types to their original authoring tool or to convenient and inexpensive external viewers such as Adobe Acrobat. Ideally, however, you should convert all content to HTML format for easier browsing over the network.

- Scan and present sales brochures as solid blocks of graphics. This is not a good idea if some users are using dial-in access over modems, if disk space is at a premium, or if these images cause intolerable slowdowns in network traffic. However, it is a good way to make highly visual content available quickly. For quicker access, make all links to the current location of the source document by pointing to a specific network node and path name. It is not necessary to retrieve all the online files and store them in a central location, though this may eventually be desirable for control purposes. If files are not centralized, you should develop some plan for making sure linked information does not move without notification. You may ask each department to maintain a centralized set of browsable files. The same person or group that planned and designed the system should also continue to develop it until a consistent style has been established or a critical mass has been reached.

- Develop templates and scripts to make it easier to add components to the system. Write a style guide or detailed instructions to ensure that consistent methods are used even after the initial developers depart.

Once you have the system installed and working, put procedures in place for keeping the system updated and for dealing with user problems or bugs in the system design. Typically, you should appoint a "Webmaster" to perform these duties. You may also need a support group if ongoing content authoring is required. However, Web publishing tools are becoming so easy to use that many departments can now write and update their own materials.

In some cases where there are large groups of authors you don't want to retrain, you may want to consider having automatic conversion tools that take the daily output of the group and convert it automatically to the Web environment. For instance, a tool such as HTML Transit automatically takes a set of source files in Microsoft Word, converts them to HTML, extracts all the graphics and stores them as GIFs, builds a hyperlinked table of contents and index, adds navigation buttons at the top and bottom of each page, and moves the finished HTML/GIF output files to a production site under the Web server. Sophisticated site management tools such as Adobe Sitemill and Netscape Livewire also provide easy ways to manage the content at a site, check and repair broken links, and perform other content management chores.

The Web Is Like a Magazine...

The intranet Web server is like a magazine your employees will access and cull for the information they need. It's like the joke that *Playboy* wants to create a special magazine for married men: It will have the same girls in it every month. The point is, you need to find content from different sources and keep your Web pages current, or your organization will lose interest in this tool you have worked so hard to establish.

The intranet is an ideal solution for virtually any organization. It's an appropriate fit for any business that needs a cost-effective way to disseminate constantly fluctuating information on demand to its employees.

Functional areas within an organization that can benefit from intranet technology include:

- Human Resources
- Training
- Sales and Marketing
- MIS
- Manufacturing
- Facilities
- Finance
- Corporate Communications
- Research and Development
- Technical Documentation

A human resources department will find the intranet a highly effective way to enhance communications and increase staff productivity while reducing costs. The use of an internal WWW server provides employees worldwide with easy and convenient access to standard HR material, including information about benefits, stock purchase plans, policies and procedures, job postings, employee newsletters, and organizational charts. Your HR staff can focus its efforts on critical organizational needs, rather than on repetitive, routine requests. With the average cost of an employee handbook at $10 to $15 per copy, the cost savings and budget payback alone are well worth the effort.

For training departments, a continual challenge is to keep training materials up-to-date despite changes to the product suite, sales direction, or market focus. An internal WWW site is a convenient way to tackle this problem, provide your employees access to the most current training materials incorporating video and audio, and allow employees to learn at their own pace. For example, a new sales employee may want to simply review the "Solutions Selling" portion of the new employee training class. At the touch of a button and at his or her convenience, the new employee simply clicks on the right spot instead of poring through reams of paper.

Marketing must support sales with a wide variety of material: customer presentations, pricing, special promotions and incentives, trade show and user group schedules, competitive market data, product literature, catalogs, sales guides, customer testimonials, boilerplate proposal descriptions, and order forms.

With the intranet, the marketing department can be confident that the sales force always has access to the latest information — wherever and whenever they need it. For example, by storing PowerPoint presentations on your internal WWW server, you can be sure the same information is being presented consistently. Depending on their needs, sales personnel can use their notebook PCs to download the entire presentation or extract only the slides they need. Instant access to the intranet saves significant time, reduces costly publishing charges, and eliminates the last-minute, frantic rush to photocopy and special express a package to a remote sales location.

The Seven "C's" of Web Page Design

The following guidelines for good Web page design are based on these elements:

- Captivating: Your opening Web page must be intriguing enough for users and visitors to want to learn more about your company and the services you offer. A user or visitor should feel interested enough to view your entire Web site, not just the home page.
- Content: The information and resources contained within or linked to by your Web site must have relevance to your company.
- Current: The information in your Web pages must be updated regularly.
- Communicated: Your Web site needs to be advertised, through commercial and Internet sources.
- Concise: The content of your Web pages should be brief and to the point.
- Consistent: The pages of your Web site should bring across the focus or core competencies of your orginization.
- Cool: Your use of graphics, clickable maps, and other forms of Web technologies should be useful, interesting, and fun.

INCLUDE THE DATA PRODUCERS

By now, you have reached the conclusion that there are plenty of ways your organization could use an intranet to distribute corporate information. However, the trick is to make sure you and your IS staff don't end up in the Web-publishing business.

To avoid that, draw up a list of the information you think your company will want on your internal Web. Find out which departments are responsible for creating that data, so you can recruit people there to help get data onto your internal Web.

Most word-processing and publishing vendors, including Adobe, Frame Technology, Microsoft, and Novell (via Corel's WordPerfect), are now shipping products that can convert their document formats to HTML. You should investigate the time and resources required for each business unit or their production subcontractors to deliver Web-ready documents. On-the-fly HTML tools are getting mixed reviews from some early users, so you may find yourself debugging and editing documents created by these departments. The plus side is that these conversion programs let non-IS staff create simple, quick-to-publish documents. The downside is that, without an intranet publishing policy, you lose the consistent look of your site.

INTRANET PUBLISHING POLICY

But before you let everyone in the company produce his or her own material, consider setting some company-wide policies aimed at standardizing the look of the documents. This will pay off if you set standards for intranet documents that make it possible to put them on your Internet Web site without having to create them over again. Policies need to be established to determine which links to other documents should be embedded in the material, who should get access to the intranet material, and what type of material will be suitable for the Internet.

With the way the intranet is exploding, you will probably get lucky in this regard. Companies are finding that their own personnel look for ways to use the intranet. In the case of Federal Express, the personnel came to the IS staff looking for ways to save the cost of publishing and updating their manuals. For Federal Express, the cost for printing, shipping, and updating manuals for 30,000 employees was not a trivial matter. The concern was to retain the look of its paper manuals because the personnel didn't want boring text.

Members of the Federal Express personnel department took the initiative to look for a technical solution and found a Web conversion tool that would retain much of the original document formatting, as long as all users had a special viewer. The project, currently in the final stages of beta with about 50 employees, has worked so well with so little desktop overhead that it is expected to be in full deployment in the spring of 1997.

Browser Wars

Adopting a universal intranet client has helped establish the same desktop look for everyone throughout the company. The next step is to define the kind of access, authoring, and authentication components you'll want at the user's workstation. Currently, a handful of application vendors appear to give your users a universal front-end to most of your intranet static data. This number is growing every day.

Netscape, Microsoft, Attachmate, and InterCon are among the intranet players trying to convince you that your smart intranet or Internet browser could become your universal front-end, allowing employees to reach all manner of applications.

Microsoft is pushing the "Explorer" paradigm for Windows 95 to give you a schematic view of intranet Web documents without blindly clicking through pesky HTML links. With just one click to the side of the user interface, you'll go right to the page you want within that linked family. Microsoft Office, with its popular Word and Excel applications, will also be intranet-enabled by mid-year, letting users publish directly to the Web.

Netscape, in addition to adding e-mail features to its browser, hopes to provide a platform for collaborating with users of traditional productivity applications by incorporating recently acquired technology from Collabra Software. Attachmate is making headway in providing access to mainframe resources over the intranet by merging its emulation technology with Emissary's object-based front end. Lotus/IBM has reduced the cost of its Lotus Notes client and is developing a host of Notes-to-Internet access tools to combine static read-only and collaborative computing. One such product to pay close attention to is the Notes HTTP server, named "Domino."

WEB MANAGEMENT

Unless you plan for growth and expansion, the bigger your intranet gets, the closer you'll get to a ticking time bomb. One of the biggest problems facing the explosive growth of the intranet is that current intranet technologies are not designed to help you quickly and easily solve management problems such as updating or changing expired links in your pages, setting up a directory of your users and accessible files, or managing documents and setting version controls for routing. Netscape's LiveWire extensions to its Web server is expected to be the first entry in this area in the spring of 1997. IBM, Microsoft, and others are slated to follow with beta projects or "what-to-watch-for" announcements later this year.

Microsoft has recently previewed Office 97, a new version of its leading suite of desktop applications, which will include Web technology to make it easy for business users to create, analyze, and publish content on intranets. Microsoft also previewed Microsoft Outlook, an innovative new desktop information management application that helps users organize, communicate, and collaborate on intranets.

Microsoft has just shipped its next-generation Web browser, Microsoft Internet Explorer 4.0, and the Windows Active Desktop technologies. By integrating Microsoft Internet Explorer with the Windows operating system, the Active Desktop provides seamless access to information of all types, regardless of location. Furthermore, it notifies the user when priority information is updated on an intranet or the Internet.

Microsoft is updating the Windows NT Server 4.0 to include Microsoft FrontPage, its innovative Web publishing and site-management product, and Search Server for document searching. These features, along with the Internet Information Server, the high-performance Web server already incorporated in the product, make Windows NT Server one of the most capable intranet operating systems available.

With this new onslaught of Internet/intranet offerings, Microsoft will continue to develop its next-generation Windows NT Directory Server, designed to seamlessly integrate Internet and intranet environments. The next-generation Directory Server combines the best of DNS (domain name server) and X.500 in a seamless upgrade to Windows NT Server 4.0. Microsoft anticipates having the Directory Server available for preview in the second half of 1996.

Netscape LiveWire and LiveWire Pro are visual tool suites designed for managing Web sites and creating live, online applications. With LiveWire and LiveWire Pro, developers can create and manage Web content, sites, and applications. Netscape LiveWire and LiveWire Pro let novice users create and manage Web content, Web sites, and live online Web applications for intranets and the Internet, while offering experienced application developers the power to manage highly complex Web sites and applications.

Netscape has developed LiveWire Site Manager, a visual site-management tool for creating and managing Web sites with drag-and-drop ease. LiveWire helps application developers create server-side programs that enable Netscape Navigator and other Web clients to browse, search, and update relational databases on intranets and the Internet. The LiveWire Database Connectivity Library enables direct SQL connections to databases from Oracle, Sybase, Informix, and Illustra; and Open Database

Connectivity (ODBC) connections to dozens of other databases, from desktop to mainframe.

For rapid development of client- and server-side applications without requiring extensive programming experience, Netscape and Sun Microsystems developed JavaScript. JavaScript has been widely adopted as the standard scripting language for adding "intelligence" to Web pages. With LiveWire, Netscape brings JavaScript to Web servers. Netscape's FastTrack 2.0 and Enterprise 2.0 Web Servers include the capability to run compiled JavaScript applications. The LiveWire JavaScript Compiler enables application developers to quickly and easily convert JavaScript applications and HTML pages incorporating JavaScript code into platform-independent byte codes ready to run on any Netscape 2.0 server. A simplified version of the JavaScript compiler is also built into the LiveWire Site Manager for one-button compiling.

Novell has been touting how it will enable users to grandfather its Novell Directory Services (NDS) technology into an intranet. Novell has released the latest version of its network operating system, IntranetWare, which includes NetWare Web Server, version 2.5. The NetWare Web Server is the only Web server that enables you to access information on the Internet or an intranet through NDS, a distributed database that presents all network users and resources as objects that can be located, viewed, and managed from a single location. The new directory-enabled NetWare Web Server improves productivity and simplifies network management by enabling you to access information stored in the NDS tree. This information, such as usernames, e-mail addresses, Uniform Resource Locators (URLs), and listings of computers, applications, and other resources, can be stored securely in NDS and made accessible to appropriate users through their Web browsers.

Novell's ManageWise PC LAN management solution will become platform-independent in the next year through support of Java technology and the Internet infrastructure. These enhanced products, part of Novell's Internet vision, will enable network administrators to perform management tasks from any intranet or Internet location through Web-based management consoles.

Novell's ManageWise will provide increased scalability through integrated support for NDS, Novell's industry-standard global directory services. NDS support will allow users to consolidate management information for easier site-level administration and reporting.

Future versions of ManageWise solutions will be based on Java technology, simplifying PC LAN management by enabling network administrators to quickly and easily connect to network information through any desktop Web browser. ManageWise applications performing management tasks, including traffic monitoring and real-time server statistics gathering, will be written in Java and stored as applets so users will be able to access them from any server. These platform-independent tools will not only improve the efficiency of in-house network administration, but will also enable service providers to remotely manage networks over secure Internet services.

Future Java-based versions of ManageWise will significantly speed the collection of and access to cross-platform network information by providing integrated support for NDS. As a common framework unifying access to NetWare, UNIX, and Windows NT servers, NDS will serve as a central business object repository for all network resources and devices. ManageWise will populate this data store with hardware and software inventory, as well as topology information. Through the Java-based infrastructure, multiple users will be able to easily access this information and related fault conditions through any management console regardless of platform.

Novell previously shared ManageWise development with Intel, but is now moving ManageWise forward by licensing Intel's most recent desktop management technology, including remote control, hardware and software inventory, file transfer, chat, and virus protection capabilities historically found in ManageWise. Novell will continue to advance these features in future versions of ManageWise and will provide even tighter integration among the product family's range of management capabilities.

By mid-year, users will see lots of approaches from these and smaller companies, and they're all likely to have in common features to help manage collaborative authoring (multiple read/write privileges), document version control, and signoff. For the most part, the paradigm will be document-based, much like what Lotus Notes uses now.

FULL, NOTES-LIKE COLLABORATION

Lotus will rapidly evolve its Domino technology to deliver a Web server based on Internet-only standards, as well as a line of specialized Web servers, clients, and tools that exploit core Lotus Notes technologies. The Notes product line will continue to support a superset of heterogeneous protocols that is inclusive of those supported by Domino II. Key elements of the plan include a line of Domino II Servers, built entirely on Internet-only standards and protocols, as well as the HTML data format. The first in this line of Domino II Servers will feature the Notes-based object store, enabling high-performance storage and retrieval of objects, including HTML pages, MIME and S/MIME messages, JPEG and GIF images, Java and Lotuscript applets, forms, views, folders, and other application-defined objects. A native, open programming interface will be provided through support for the Common Object Request Broker Architecture (CORBA), a standard and distributed method for accessing object services from a choice of programming languages such as Java, C++, and C. Distributed access to CORBA services is provided via IIOP, the Internet Inter-Orb Protocol.

Other Domino-series servers will include specialized servers for mail and directory services. Lotus will make the Domino II Server's object services available for trial to prospective customers and partners via the Lotus Web site later this year.

Key to the Domino II product line will be an Interactive Application Designer package, to be tightly integrated with the Domino II Servers. The Designer client offers a range of rapid application development tools for the Internet — from collaboration templates such as those introduced to first-time Web users with Domino to tools aimed at aiding developers in delivering next-generation, mission-critical business applications for the Web.

Lotus will ship a new Mobile Web Information Manager, also built entirely on Internet standards and protocols. This Web client leverages Notes' unique support for mobile users, world-class messaging, and industry-leading collaboration applications, and will feature a new class of Web personal information management tools leveraging Lotus agent technology. It will also offer integration with desktop applications, as well as ActiveX/OCX components. The first products in the Domino II product line will be available on the Lotus Web site (*www.lotus.com*) by the end of this year.

Lotus has also announced and demonstrated Net.Presence, one of its forthcoming Net.App solutions, which will be shipping in the second half of 1996. Net.Apps is a set of interactive Notes applications that build on the new Domino services. Net.Apps can be used "out-of-the-box" as Web applications that support Web browsers as well as Notes clients. They can also serve as extensible templates with which customers and Lotus Business Partners can build customized applications.

Net.Presence is designed specifically to allow customers to create a Web site intranet presence in about an hour.

Don't expect the existing third-party intranet to offer a full suite of Notes-like features soon. Intranet and Internet authoring tools, such as Sun Microsystems' Java and Microsoft's ActiveX, will begin to enable well-trained software developers to exploit some features of objects and live linking for Web documents. Audio and video clips will be enabled, provided you have enough bandwidth. Most vendors expect IS managers to be deploying intranets on at least 10Mbps Ethernet LANs. Even with enough bandwidth, you'll likely need browser upgrades or special readers.

Analysts are wary about the intranet's capability to provide full, live, two-way (much less multiuser) collaboration. There's not enough infrastructure, even with a document model, for the intranet right now to let you share documents, edit them in a group, and pass them along the way Notes can. It may get there some day, but there's no way to tell just how long it will take, if it can be done at all.

Beyond Basic HTML

The cost of creating a World Wide Web presence, whether it be on the Internet or on a corporate intranet, is escalating dramatically. Custom application development is topping the list of expenses. Corporate

World Wide Web and intranet sites have moved beyond static Hypertext Markup Language (HTML) pages to embrace multimedia technologies for use in commercial applications.

According to an International Data Corp. (IDC) report, companies building commercial Web sites can expect hardware and software to consume 20 percent of a Web site's overall budget; the remaining 80 percent goes to software development and integration.

Almost anyone can create a basic Web page, but custom development is required if you want to link the Web back to a billing system or an inventory database. The cost of the Web server is only the tip of the iceberg. Companies participating in a recent IDC survey said they spent $840,000 to $1.5 million establishing Web sites.

Though Web sites with financial transaction capabilities are complex, companies with less ambitious goals can face hefty programming costs for features such as connectivity to an SQL database.

The basic Web server is a relatively small part of the equation. As soon as you start writing Perl scripts, things can get complicated. Unlike programming, people go into Web development with more open-ended projects. Because the bulk of Web commerce applications and other advanced Web applications are custom-designed today, projects can get very expensive.

Integrating any sort of live information into Web pages from back-office applications is a significant investment. Although there are numerous companies that claim they can undertake such a task, the people who can actually do that work well are very expensive. It takes little effort to put up an intranet Web server; however, the content will most likely be static. The bar has been raised for sites that want to make a mark on the Web by offering compelling services. True Web and intranet application development is a lot less design and more akin to SQL programming.

4

The Webmaster

CONTENTS

The corporate intranet saves costs, increases productivity, and provides organizations with a competitive edge. However, widescale and effective use of the corporate intranet will not happen without planning, ongoing care, and support. Initial use and growth could, and often will, happen at an explosive rate. Over time, management and support issues for the intranet become more complex and interrelated. To effectively design, deploy, and support an intranet within an enterprise, you must have:

- a clear understanding of the challenges involved;
- a cross-organizational plan for its use;
- a technical strategy in support of this plan;
- a client and information deployment strategy; and
- support tools and services.

These tasks and objectives define the role of the individual known as the "Webmaster."

SO, WHO IS THIS PERSON?

The overall responsibility for the creation and maintenance of intranet servers and services belongs to the Webmaster. "Webmaster" is a buzz word coined during the recent surge of Internet popularity and refers to the individual or individuals who set up and maintain the company's internal or external Web site. This classification of Internet, computer system administrators has sprung into popularity overnight, even though the Internet has been around for many years.

The Webmaster typically maintains the functionality of the intranet services provided. In addition, the Webmaster is responsible for updating the content of the Web sites as well as keeping up-to-date on current Web technologies and services. After all, if the content of the site never changes and there is nothing new and different to look at on the site, site browsers will stop visiting.

What Are the Webmaster's Roles and Responsibilities?	For the intranet, the Webmaster is typically the individual or group of individuals who sets up the initial Web site and related intranet services. This includes electronic mail services, FTP services, news services, audio and video services, and other specialized services. It takes energy, desire, and enthusiasm to sell a Web project to top management, and to the rest of the organization as well. In addition, the Webmaster must possess a thorough understanding of the organization's business, have a touch of marketing ability, be familiar with the Internet, and have a solid understanding of programming languages and technology.

A grasp of programming languages and technology is more important for intranet planning vision than for anything else. HTML page layout and CGI programming chores can be delegated to one or more members of the IS staff, but the Webmaster must understand the bigger picture to see the site's present and future goals. The Webmaster must keep up with and recognize the significance of emerging technologies and business models and be able to educate the rest of the organization about them.

Perhaps the Webmaster's most important skill is the ability to work well with members of the company's intranet committee. This committee should include representatives from all corporate business units contributing to the site, including legal and public relations departments. Most importantly, the committee must be commissioned and supported by upper management to be effective.

The selection of a Webmaster should be determined by his or her skills with the client and server operating systems, network operating systems, and hardware and software platform requirements. If the Web server platform is based on the Apple Macintosh computer, the Webmaster should be familiar with the workings of Macintosh software and hardware. Likewise, if a UNIX- or Intel-based hardware platform has been selected, the Webmaster should be familiar with these. More often than not, the mix of Web-based intranet services may dictate a mixture of hardware and software. In this case, a more diversified skill set will be required, which may require additional staffing. The services offered will also dictate the skills required of the Webmaster. Often, a new software package or service will need to be installed on the intranet. The Webmaster needs to be comfortable with installing, testing, and rolling out this service to users over the intranet. If the individual or individuals responsible for the intranet do not possess the necessary skills, these skills need to be learned, acquired, or outsourced.

Skill sets can be learned, providing the individual and organization have the time to invest and the desire to gain the new skills. Books (such as this one), magazine articles, and even user groups are an excellent way to pick up new tips, tricks, and techniques. In addition, as with every new industry that comes into popularity, training centers and instructors are soon to follow. Courses for Internet server management will soon be modified to cover intranet server management. Even if such a course is never available, virtually any Internet server management course can be used, and the techniques learned can be applied to your intranet.

If there is no time, ability, or desire to learn a new skill, the needed expertise can be acquired. Sometimes, this comes from hiring a new person if your budget permits.

If you cannot expand your present staff, you need to outsource the required skill sets. An increasing number of companies are offering Web page and intranet development services. (See Appendix B for an example of this type of service.)

That Artistic Flair	Beyond the technical requirements of a Webmaster, a certain degree of creative ability goes a long way. The Webmaster is often responsible for the content and graphics of Web pages, so an artistic flair can make the difference between a Web page that just provides information and a page that reads and looks like a newsletter. However, most technically inclined individuals are not necessarily artists. For that matter, most technical

individuals aren't great copywriters, either. For these reasons, among others, appointing a virtual Webmaster (which is a team of several individuals, including graphic artists and copywriters/editors) to work in conjunction with the intranet committee is often the best solution.

Physical and Logical Administration	The role of the Webmaster can be divided into physical administration and logical administration. Physical administration involves the Web server hardware and the related tasks required to keep the Web servers and services running. It also applies to the infrastructure of the intranet as well, including the intranet client workstations and any other gateway services (hosts and Internet access devices). Logical administration involves the security of the intranet and the Web site creation and content. This includes all HTML documents, graphic files, audio clips, and video files. The TCP/IP addressing scheme and protocol management are also part of these responsibilities.

WEBMASTER SELECTION

The Webmaster must consider the needs of users, providers, and developers, and the impact of intranet applications on the enterprise's infrastructure, while dealing with the concerns of management. This requires different skills.

In a small organization, the Webmaster is typically one individual. More often than not, this person is also responsible for the overall maintenance of the LAN. Although this may be the logical choice, it is not necessarily the best selection. The LAN administrator typically is wearing several hats already. Between day-to-day LAN administration and the applications' help-desk functions your system administrator already performs, adding Web administration and Web page creation to the list of tasks will only be to your site's detriment. If the LAN administrator is already overburdened, the quality of your Web pages will suffer, and the content may become dull and repetitive. You want your intranet to be proactive and provide users with current company information. Small company LAN administrators are all too often in a reactive mode, having just enough bandwidth to react to problems as they occur.

For larger organizations, the MIS group is often given the charge to host and maintain intranet Web services. Again, the same danger exists in assigning Webmaster duties to an overburdened network administrator or IS professional. Just because a department has more people doesn't mean it has more time (or talent!).

In larger corporations, several people, usually from different departments, may collectively act as the Webmaster or as an intranet team. It may be appropriate for your organization to cultivate a core team of experts that can quickly and effectively get your users and content providers online. The services you offer over your intranet will evolve to reflect the needs of your users and the company. The maturity of these services often reflects your corporate culture, needs, and phase of intranet adoption. A core service group, or intranet team, will provide a way for you to share scarce talent across the larger organization.

When selecting your intranet team, let departments do what they do best. The IS group determines the best methods and tools for applying technology to business needs. Departments such as public relations and marketing that are responsible for press releases, publications, and anything that goes in a corporate database, should manage that information. By all means, get the human resources department involved to handle staffing and support throughout the development, implementation, and operational phases of the intranet project. Create an oversight committee for cross-functional issues and to fill in gaps that are not covered by a specific skill set.

The department that plays a leading role over your intranet site depends on your organization's mission and the goals you want the site to accomplish. Your intranet site may include search engines, transaction capabilities, and downloadable software; in those cases, the technical information services arm of your organization should take the lead.

In either instance, the best alternative is to look outside the MIS department and solicit assistance from the rest of the organization. By distributing the responsibilities, one individual won't be overwhelmed and your page content will remain fresh.

The first objection to this plan will be that you don't want to turn the asylum over to the inmates. Don't turn over the logical server administration to your LAN users, but let the users generate the Web page content. There are many HTML conversion tools that allow you to turn a word processing document into HTML. Without such a tool, converting a document to HTML can be a time-consuming task. Even with such a tool, converting multiple documents into HTML can still take time — time that an over-burdened LAN administrator does not have. However, if each department had all its documents converted into HTML before submitting them for publication on the intranet, the Webmaster would be a much happier camper.

Develop a staffing plan for your intranet that includes current employees' responsibilities and job descriptions for any new hires. Without such a plan, you run the risk of your intranet being ineffective and the operations and management costs outweighing the benefits.

GROWING YOUR STAFF

No matter how your organization is structured, if you are moving forward with an intranet project, you will need resources. Those bodies need to come from within your existing staff or an outsourcing talent pool, or you need to hire someone. Deciding to hire new people for a project that may not be generating revenue is not easy; neither is overworking your existing technical staff. Your staffing requirements depend on the size of your intranet undertaking. Keep in mind that in addition to appointing a Webmaster, you will probably have to fill several other technical positions. In addition, you may need to add some editorial and

Table 4-1. Intranet Support Staff Positions

Position	Primary duties	Skill
Webmaster	Analysis, design, maintenance, and programming of intranet	Technical and interpersonal skills, network administration, and knowledge of programming languages
Web developer and programmers (various levels)	Systems design and programming	Knowledge of HTML, Java, and Visual BASIC, and ability to work with Webmaster
User support	Training, help design, and documentation	Strong interpersonal and communication skills
Network/ systems administrator	Network configuration, installation, and support	Knowledge of UNIX, Netscape, or other server software
Project manager	Manage non-technical tasks related to site development and maintenance	Excellent writing and communication skills and ability to take charge, make decisions, and control projects

Source: *Webmaster Magazine*, May, 1996

customer service staff if your intranet site requires a steady supply of original material, feedback, or transactional capabilities.

HOW MUCH SHOULD WE PAY?

Depending on the staff you require, pay scales for those positions vary with experience and skill sets. You should expect to pay more for technical staff who can talk to business people. Customer service-oriented people are a valuable addition to any technical staff, and you should expect to pay more for these individuals. As you interview for your intranet staffing positions, look for people who can work together with others in your organization. Don't be swayed by industry salary ranges, but base salaries on your organization's predefined wage scales.

Colleges and universities are a good place to start if you are looking to hire intranet technical staff. You can probably hire a decent candidate straight out of college who has some good technical experience for $25,000 to $30,000. An experienced Webmaster with real-world business experience would command a much higher salary. Expect to pay this individual $70,000 to $80,000 if he or she brings considerable technical, marketing, management, and organizational expertise to the table. While expensive, if you expect the intranet to become a critical component of your business, these candidates are worth every penny you spend.

In the final equation, of course, the size and make-up of your Web staff depends on your organization's culture, budget, and mission. Include all parts of the organization from the very beginning of the intranet project and clearly assign roles and responsibilities. This will prevent any one part of the organization from feeling alienated, and will make the entire experience more productive, functional, and enjoyable for all involved.

WEBMASTER ALTERNATIVES

A new industry of consultants is emerging to help companies set up shop or establish a presence on the World Wide Web. These start-up companies, known as Web Service Providers, are working with businesses large and small to help them create, publish, and maintain home pages on the Web. Large corporations seeking to tap the marketing potential of the Internet are fueling this breed of company, offering technical know-how and graphical design savvy in short order. Corporate giants, such as VISA and GE Plastics, are finding they need help in designing appropriate content, coding the Web's standard Hypertext Markup Language (HTML), and choosing a server platform.

Most Web initiatives are entrepreneurial, cross-functional projects that need to move quickly. Most companies find they do not have the in-house expertise to spearhead such a project. In fact, it may be more cost-effective to outsource the project to a company that has such expertise. Certainly, many companies have constructed their own home pages and run in-house servers. But others find it's not worth the cost and hassle to assemble a staff to convert corporate documents into HTML, choose among the dizzying array of Web applications and security software, and maintain a home page on a dedicated server.

Faced with today's limited marketing budgets, most small to midsize companies cannot afford the initial cash outlay required just to get a corporate presence on the Internet. In less than two years, the Web has attracted more than 12,000 companies that have created home pages at an average cost of $20,000. The marketing potential of the Web is available to all, but the start-up costs in some cases make it prohibitive for smaller companies. The start-up costs associated with an intranet are somewhat smaller than an Internet presence because a leased line, router, and CSU/DSU are not required. However, companies without a dedicated Webmaster, the time, or the artistic flair required for putting up a quality intranet site may need outside assistance.

What's interesting is that because the RBOCs (Regional Bell Operating Companies) can now offer Internet connection services, most traditional Internet Service Providers (ISPs) are now offering Web hosting and consulting services.

Finding good outsourcing services to assist with your intranet can be difficult. Virtually every consultant and systems integrator is using the intranet buzzword, but relatively few of them have any experience. Realistically, intranets are a new and growing business, so you will probably be hard-pressed to find any one organization that has been building intranets for any lengthy period. However, you should look for partners with LAN/WAN expertise, Internet integration experience, and some solid HTML page layout and design experience. You will also want to partner with individuals or organizations that have database development and integration experience if your intranet applications need to interface with your existing database and legacy systems. Strong CGI and programming skills will also be a definite plus.

5

The Intranet Web Server

Spinning Your Own Web

CONTENTS

In previous chapters, you've learned of Web services and how to go about planning your intranet. Now, you can get down to the nitty-gritty of setting up the hardware and software for your intranet. In this chapter, you'll take a closer look at the hardware required to serve up those intranet services to your user community.

To set up your own intranet, you'll need several pieces of hardware and software.

WEB SERVER HARDWARE

A dedicated workstation is the preferred intranet Web server. You can use an existing file server, but overall performance may suffer. Although UNIX workstations such as Sun, Silicon Graphics, and Hewlett-Packard have traditionally been the Web servers of choice, Windows NT, NetWave and Linux Web server software permits Intel Pentium-based machines to function quite well as dedicated Web servers. You can also use a Macintosh as a Web server.

A typical Web server hardware platform might consist of an Intel Pentium-based EISA or PCI workstation (100Mhz or better), with 64 megabytes (MB) of RAM, a two-gigabyte (GB) hard disk drive, a 16- or 32-bit Ethernet adapter, keyboard, mouse, and SVGA monitor. You will also need to connect your intranet Web server to your existing network. If you want to connect your intranet to the Internet, you may also need a router and CSU/DSU.

We will be using Intel-based server platforms for Web servers throughout this book. This should not infer that the Intel processor makes the best Web server; other server platforms can be just as good, if not better.

Depending on the level of service you intend to offer, a good Intel-based Web server should contain at a minimum:

- an Intel Pentium processor, 75MHz or faster (EISA or PCI bus);
- 32MB of RAM;
- a 2GB hard disk drive;

- an SVGA monitor; and
- a 32-bit Ethernet adapter (or token-ring adapter if your intranet is running on a token-ring network).

Various hardware manufacturers are beginning to develop dedicated intranet server products. Sun Microsystems, for example, has released an entire line of Web servers based on the Sun SPARC technology. Hewlett-Packard has released a line of Web servers, as well.

SOFTWARE

Your Web server also requires a network operating system, such as Windows NT v3.5, Novell NetWare (v3.12 or higher), or Linux. In addition, you may require a copy of MS-DOS. You will need a TCP/IP stack (if it doesn't come native with your network operating system) and Web server software. If you intend to provide other services, such as video or audio, you may need to install additional software and hardware.

The Web server software you select will dictate the hardware platform and operating system of your Web server, or be dictated by your choice of hardware platform and network operating system. Table 5-1 on page 82 lists some commercially available Web server software and the network operating systems they support.

OPERATING SYSTEMS

Depending on the software you select, the Web server needs operating system software. Table 5-2 on page 82 shows you the operating systems or environments available for the platform you choose.

Table 5-1. Commercial Web Server Packages

Web Server Software	Windows	Windows 95	Windows NT	NetWare	Macintosh	UNIX
American Internet SiteBuilder				√		
Quarterdeck WebStar		√			√	
Mac HTTP					√	
Netscape Netsite Commerce Server			√			√
Glaci-HTTPD				√		
Process Software Purveyor			√	√		
O'Reilly WebSite		√	√			
EMWAC HTTPS			√			
NetWare Web Server				√		

Table 5-2. Web Server Operating Systems

Operating System	Platform
Microsoft DOS	Intel
Microsoft Windows	Intel
Microsoft Windows 95	Intel
Microsoft Windows NT	Intel, Digital, HP
Novell NetWare	Intel
Apple System Software	Macintosh
Linux	Intel
Solaris	Intel, Sun
HPUX	HP

MEMORY AND STORAGE

The amount of RAM your intranet server requires varies, depending on your server selection, hardware platform, and network operating system. All major Web server software providers have a recommended minimum amount of RAM you should install. However, if you are going to run other services on your intranet server, you may require more memory than the minimum suggested amount.

A good rule of thumb is that there is no such thing as too much memory. Unfortunately, the converse is also true; too little memory is often the source of performance problems. When in doubt, start with 32MB of RAM or more. This number should be sufficient for most Intel-based operating systems, depending on the size of your disk drives and other factors, such as network adapters installed and server processes running on your network.

Some operating systems, such as Novell's NetWare, have formulas for calculating the minimum required server memory. An Excel spreadsheet template is included on the companion CD-ROM in the back of this book for calculating the required server memory if you use a NetWare server as your intranet server.

Whatever operating system you use, the following information will provide you with a starting point for defining server memory:

1. Take the minimum recommended memory configuration for your server platform.
2. Round that amount up to the nearest 4MB increment.
3. Add the minimum recommended memory configuration for your Web server.
4. Round up that result to the nearest 4MB increment.
5. Add the required memory configuration for any additional server processes.
6. Round up that result to the nearest 4MB increment.

For example:

1. Your server needs a minimum of 24MB of RAM.
2. You round up to 28MB of RAM.
3. Add to this the 4MB of RAM required for your Web server (minimum 32MB).
4. Rounding up to the nearest 4MB, gives you 36MB of RAM.
5. You are not running any additional server processes.
6. Depending on how your system accepts memory, you will most likely need a total of 40MB of RAM.

Hard Disk Storage

Your network operating system and your Web server software each have recommended minimum disk space requirements. When you are determining the storage space you will need, keep these things in mind:

- Operating systems sometimes use disk space as swap space, so you should always have more than just the minimum amount of disk space required.
- Your Web pages will consist of graphic files, video files, and audio clips that can each exceed 1MB in size. The more elaborate your pages, the more storage you need.
- Plan for growth. If your disk drive isn't large enough, make sure your system is modular to allow you to add storage as required.

Another consideration for the configuration of your intranet server's storage is security. You may want to make your intranet server volume something other than the root partition or the boot drive. This may entail adding a second disk drive and making this drive your intranet server volume. Doing so will let you isolate the intranet file I/O from any network operating system functions.

Use the fastest network adapter your topology and server bus will support. Keep your networking rules in mind when adding your adapter cards to your intranet servers. Here are some simple rules of thumb to use when selecting a network interface card for your intranet server:

1. Use the fastest bus speed your server will support. If your server has both a PCI and a ISA bus, use a PCI bus network adapter.
2. Use the widest bus interface width supported by your server platform. If you have a choice between a 16 and a 32-bit network adapter, use a 32-bit adapter.
3. Get the latest drivers from the network adapter manufacturer. Improvements in network driver software often translate into performance increases.

The Universal Client

Each workstation will also need Internet browser software and possibly a TCP/IP protocol stack.

Operating Systems

Depending on the software you select, the intranet client needs operating system software. Table 5-3 shows you the software you might select.

Table 5-3. Web Server Operating Systems

Operating System	Platform
Microsoft DOS	Intel
Microsoft Windows	Intel
Microsoft Windows 95	Intel
Microsoft Windows NT	Intel, Digital, HP
Apple System Software	Macintosh

TCP/IP WINSOCK APPLICATION

All Internet communications use the Transmission Control Protocol/ Internet Protocol (TCP/IP). To use any of the Internet browsers and tools to manage your Web servers, you need to install a TCP/IP protocol stack on your workstations. Following is a partial list of TCP/IP software packages.

Table 5-4. Commercial TCP/IP Protocol Stacks

Manufacturer	Software	Platform
Novell	LAN WorkPlace	DOS, Windows, Macintosh
NetManage	Chameleon NFS	DOS, Windows
Trumpet	Winsock	Windows, Windows 95
Frontier Technologies Corp.	SuperTCP Pro	Windows, Windows 95
WRQ	Reflection	DOS, Windows, Macintosh

THE WEB BROWSER

A browser is software that can exchange and interpret HTML documents with an HTTP server. Common Web browsers include Mosaic, Netscape Navigator, and Microsoft's Internet Explorer.

You need to select the intranet client browser that will serve as your universal client front end. You should pick your client software so a single interface style fits your client mix. This will simplify the overall support for your intranet, as well as provide a more consistent look across all client platforms.

Some browsers have unique features that extend the HTML document specifications or support third-party plug-in modules. You may want to use such features as frames, Object Linking and Embedding (OLE) support, and Java within your intranet applications. If this is the case, your browser should reflect these feature sets.

Table 5-5. Internet Client Software

Browser	Windows	Windows 95	Windows NT	Macintosh	UNIX
Netscape Navigator	√	√	√	√	√
NCSA Mosaic	√	√	√	√	√
Microsoft Internet Explorer	√	√	√	√	
AttachMate	√	√	√		
QuarterDeck InternetSuite	√	√	√		

Some of today's commercial browsers support more than just World Wide Web access. These tools support electronic mail, FTP, Telnet, and Usenet, among others. Sometimes these features are incorporated into the browser software, and other times, the browser is bundled with a suite of products. If you have multiple client types (Macintosh, Windows, and UNIX machines), you might want to consider using an integrated client as opposed to the client suite. Suites tend to be developed for specific market platforms, such as Windows or Windows 95, and often do not cover the gamut of client platforms. (Lotus Notes performs many of the same functions as a Web server and browser. It is even a satisfactory product for hosting your company's intranet. For further information on Lotus Notes, see Appendix A.)

WEB AUTHORING WORKSTATION

Keep in mind that you need to create your HTML documents and CGI scripts, as well. In some Web server environments, the server can also function as a client. However, it really is better to have a separate machine for this function.

A Web authoring workstation can also be useful in testing the client/server functionality of your intranet. This machine can consist of any type of machine, as long as you can use it to communicate with your intranet services — it needs to contain your browser software, a TCP/IP stack, and sufficient disk space and memory for the HTML document editors and graphics programs you are running.

The Web authoring station, in addition to having operating system software and a TCP/IP stack, requires a variety of graphic utilities and converters. You should have graphics programs capable of translating files into GIF or JPEG format. You may also want a program capable of creating image map files. If you plan to create forms on your server, you will also need to learn some CGI programming, WebBasic, and a shell language, such as Perl. Your server should be capable of supporting these languages.

6

What Is HTML?

CONTENTS

T he HyperText Markup Language (HTML) is a collection of platform-independent styles, indicated by markup tags, that define the various components of a World Wide Web document. It was invented by Tim Berners-Lee while at CERN, the European Laboratory for Particle Physics in Geneva. HTML documents are plain-text (also known as "ASCII") files that can be created using any text editor (such as vi on UNIX workstations or Notepad on a Windows PC). You can also use word-processing software if you remember to save your document as "text only with line breaks." Specialized software, called HTML editors, is available.

AUTHORING TOOLS

WYSIWYG (What You See Is What You Get) editors, such as HotMetal Pro, Front Page, and Adobe PageMill, are plentiful. You may wish to try one of them after you learn the basics of HTML tagging. It is useful to know enough HTML to code a document before you determine how useful a WYSIWYG editor is. Once you start using a WYSIWYG editor, you might want to just use a word processor for all your HTML coding. If you haven't already selected your software, refer to Table 6-1 on page 93 for a list of HTML editors (organized by platform) to help in your search for appropriate software.

TAG (YOU'RE IT!)

Each HTML contains several structural components or elements that are defined by tags. Examples of elements include headings, tables, paragraphs, and lists. Elements can contain plain text, other elements, or both.

HTML tags consist of a left angle bracket (<), a tag name, and a right angle bracket (>) that are usually paired (e.g., <p> and </p>) to start and

Table 6-1. Web Authoring Tools and HTML Editors

Company	Software	Environment	Function
Microsoft	Front Page	Windows, Windows 95, Windows NT	HTML page design
SoftQuad	HotMetal PRO	Windows, Windows 95, Windows NT	HTML page design
Quarterdeck	WEB Author	Windows, Windows 95, Windows NT	HTML page design
Adobe	PageMill	Macintosh	HTML page design
Adobe	Acrobat	Windows, UNIX, Macintosh	.PDF file viewer
JASC	Paint Shop Pro	Windows, Windows 95	Graphics program
Thomas Boutell	Map Edit	Windows, Windows 95	Image map program
Sun Microsystems	Java	Windows, Windows 95, Windows NT, Macintosh, UNIX	Object-oriented programming language
Macromind	Shockwave	Windows, Windows 95, Windows NT, Macintosh	Web-based animation or video

end the tag instruction. The end tag looks like the start tag except a slash (/) precedes the text within the brackets.

Some elements may also include an attribute, which is additional information inside the start tag. For example, you can align images (top, middle, or bottom) by including the appropriate attribute with the image source HTML code.

Note: HTML is not case-sensitive. <TITLE> is equivalent to <title> or <TiTlE>. A few exceptions are used in escape sequences.

Not all tags are supported by all World Wide Web browsers. If a browser does not support a tag, it usually just ignores it.

The Minimum Elements	Every HTML document should contain certain standard HTML tags. Each document consists of a head and body text. The head contains the title of the document and the body contains the text, which is made up of paragraphs, lists, and other elements. Browsers expect specific information because they are programmed according to HTML and Simple General Markup Language (SGML) specifications.

A bare-bones document requires the following HTML tags:

```
<html>
<head>
<TITLE>Minimal HTML Example</TITLE>
</head>
<body>
<H1>Heading 1</H1>
<P>This is the first paragraph.</P>
<P>This is the second paragraph.</P>
</body>
</html>
```

In the previous example, the only required elements are the <html>, <head>, <title>, and <body> tags and their corresponding end tags. You might want to create a template file with these tags included because you should include these tags in each HTML file.

To see a copy of the file your browser uses to generate the information in your current window, select View Source (or the equivalent) from the browser menu. The file contents, with all the HTML tags, will be displayed in a new window.

This is an excellent way to see how HTML is used and to learn tips and constructs of HTML programming. Of course, the HTML might not be technically correct. Once you become familiar with HTML and check the many online and hard-copy references on the subject, you will learn to distinguish between "good" and "bad" HTML.

<HTML>

This element tells your browser that the file contains HTML-coded information. The file extension .html also indicates this is an HTML document and must be used. (If you are restricted to 8.3 filenames [eight characters and a three character extension, such as brightid.htm], use only .htm for the file extension.)

<HEAD>

The <head> element identifies the part of your HTML-coded document that contains the title. The title is shown as part of your browser's window.

<TITLE>

The <title> element contains the document title and identifies its content in a global context. The title is displayed somewhere on the browser window (usually at the top), but not within the text area. The title is also the name that is displayed on the browser's hotlist or bookmark list and should be descriptive, unique, and short. The title is also used during a WAIS search of a server. You should keep titles to 64 characters or less.

<BODY>

The largest part of your HTML document is the <body>, which contains the content of your document. This portion of your HTML code is displayed within the text area of your browser window. The following tags are used within the body of your HTML document.

HEADINGS

HTML has six levels of headings, numbered 1 through 6, with 1 being the most prominent. Headings are displayed in larger and bolder fonts than normal body text. The first heading in each document should be tagged <H1>.

The syntax of the heading element is:

```
<Hx>Text of heading </Hx>
```

in which x specifies the heading level between 1 and 6.

As in an outline, do not skip levels of headings in your document. For example, don't start with a level-three heading (<H3>) and then next use a level-one (<H1>) heading.

PARAGRAPHS

Unlike documents in most word processors, carriage returns in HTML files aren't significant. You don't have to worry about how long your lines of text are, although it is better to have fewer than 72 characters per line. Word-wrapping occurs at any point in your source file, and multiple spaces are collapsed to a single space by your browser.

A sample paragraph may look like this:

```
<P> Winc. specializes in assisting organizations, no matter what
the size, in establishing a presence on the Internet. We have
assembled a dedicated team of professionals and technical writ-
ers, graphic artists, and programming specialists, to bring you
the highest caliber WWW page-design and layout talent.

We also pride ourselves in our depth of knowledge in being able
to make the World Wide Web a viable marketing vehicle to meet
today's business requirements. </P>
```

In the above source file, a line break occurs between the sentences. A Web browser ignores this line break and starts a new paragraph only when it encounters a second <P> tag. Thus the above will appear as a single paragraph.

Note: You must indicate paragraphs with <P> elements. A browser ignores any indentations or blank lines in the source text. Without <P> elements, the document becomes one large paragraph. The exception to this is to use text tagged as "prefor-matted," which is explained below.

To preserve readability, put headings on separate lines, use a blank line or two to identify the start of a new section, and separate paragraphs with blank lines (in addition to <P> tags). These conventions will help you when you edit your files (the browser will ignore the extra spaces because it has its own set of rules on spacing that do not depend on the spaces you put in your source file).

Note: The </P> closing tag can be omitted if you wish because browsers under-stand that when they encounter a <P> tag, it implies that there is an end to the paragraph.

Using <P> and </P> as a paragraph container lets you center a paragraph by including the ALIGN= alignment attribute in your source file, as shown:

```
<P ALIGN=CENTER>
This is a test of a centered paragraph.
</P>
```

will display as:

```
This is a test of a centered paragraph.
```

LISTS

HTML supports unnumbered, numbered, and definition lists. You can nest lists, too, but use this feature sparingly because too many nested items can be difficult to follow.

UNNUMBERED LISTS

To make an unnumbered, bulleted list:

1. Start with an opening list <UL> (for unnumbered list) tag.
2. Enter the <LI> (list item) tag followed by the individual item; no closing </LI> tag is needed.
3. End the entire list with a closing list </UL> tag.

Below is a sample three-item list:

```
<UL>
<LI> Moe
<LI> Larry
<LI> Curly
</UL>
```

which displays as:

Moe

Larry

Curly

<LI> items can also contain multiple paragraphs. Indicate the paragraphs with <P> paragraph tags.

```
<ul>
<li>Drill Drawing Requirements<br>
<ul>
<li>Board outline with dimensions<br>
<li>Hole diameters and tolerances<br>
<li>Indication of plated or non-plated holes<br>
<li>Manufacturing tolerances
</ul>
<p>

<li>Drill Drawing Notes should contain:<br>
<ul>
<li>Material type and thickness (i.e. .062 FR4 1/1)<br>
<li>Minimum conductor width and spacing<br>
```

```
<li>Minimum annular ring<br>
<li>Copper plating requirements<br>
<li>Finish requirements (i.e. PB/SN or NI/AU)<br>
<li>Soldermask and/or marking requirements
<ul>
<li>color<br>
<li>type<br>
<li>location<br>
</ul>
<li>Vendor ID marking (if required)<br>
<li>Datecode format and location (if required)<br>
<li>Multilayer  layout (if applicable)
</ul>
<p>
<li>Artwork<br>
<ul>
<li>Board artwork supplied in gerber format aperture listing (i.e
.rep .usr .gap)<br>
<li>Absolute, 2,3 leading zero suppression, english<br>
<li>Drill information supplied in ASCII text format<br>
<li>A readme file explaining files and PO# and part#
</ul>
</ul>
```

NUMBERED LISTS

A numbered list, also known as an ordered list (from which the tag name is derived), is identical to an unnumbered list, except it uses the <OL> tag instead of <UL>. Items are tagged using the same <LI> tag. The following HTML code:

```
<OL>
<LI> Moe
<LI> Larry
<LI> Curly
</OL>
```

produces this formatted result:

1. Moe
2. Larry
3. Curly

DEFINITION LISTS

A definition list (coded as <DL>) usually consists of alternating a definition term (coded as <DT>) and its definition (coded as <DD>). Web browsers generally format the definition on a new line.

The following is an example of a definition list:

```
<DL>
<DT> NCSA
<DD> NCSA, the National Center for Supercomputing Applications,
is located on the campus of the University of Illinois
at Urbana-Champaign.
<DT> Cornell Theory Center (CTC)
<DD> CTC is located on the campus of Cornell University in Ithaca,
New York.
</DL>
```

The result looks like:

NCSA

NCSA, the National Center for Supercomputing Applications, is located on the campus of the University of Illinois at Urbana-Champaign.

CORNELL THEORY CENTER (CTC)

CTC is located on the campus of Cornell University in Ithaca, New York.

The <DT> and <DD> entries can contain multiple paragraphs (indicated by <P> paragraph tags), lists, or other definition information. Definition lists contain the COMPACT attribute, which can be used routinely if definition terms are very short. If, for example, you are showing computer options, the options may fit on the same line as the start of the definition.

```
<DL COMPACT>
<DT> -i
<DD>invokes NCSA Mosaic for Microsoft Windows using the
initialization file defined in the path.
<DT> -k
<DD>invokes NCSA Mosaic for Microsoft Windows in kiosk mode.
</DL>
```

The output looks like:

-i invokes NCSA Mosaic for Microsoft Windows using the initialization file defined in the path.
-k invokes NCSA Mosaic for Microsoft Windows in kiosk mode.

DL tags create glossary-like entries on a Web page. Used with the <DT> and <DD> tags, the resulting HTML file includes bolded and

indented entries. The same effect can be achieved with the unordered list
<UL> tag, but would require much more effort and coding. If you need
the formatting of the glossary list, use the <DL> tags.

NESTED LISTS

Lists can also be nested. You can have a number of paragraphs, each containing a nested list, in a single list item. Here is a sample nested list:

```
<UL>
<LI> The Three Stooges:
<UL>
<LI> Moe
<LI> Larry
<LI> Curly
</UL>
<LI> Laurel and Hardy:
<UL>
<LI> Stan Laurel
<LI> Oliver Hardy
</UL>
</UL>
```

The nested list is displayed as:

The Three Stooges:

Moe

Larry

Curly

Laurel and Hardy:

Stan Laurel

Oliver Hardy

PREFORMATTED TEXT

Use the <PRE> preformatted tag to generate text in a fixed-width font.
This tag also makes spaces, new lines, and tabs significant (multiple
spaces are displayed as multiple spaces, and lines break in the same locations as in the source HTML file). This is useful for program listings,
among other things. For example, the following lines:

```
<PRE>
#!/usr/bin/perl — -*- C -*-
$mailprog = 'mail';
$recipient = 'ciminoj@bright-ideas.com';
print "Content-type: text/html\n\n";
```

```
print "<Head><Title>Bright Ideas Software</Title></Head>";
print "<Body><H1>Thank you for signing the Guest Book . . . </H1></Body>";
</PRE>
```

displays as:

```
#!/usr/bin/perl — -*- C -*-
$mailprog = 'mail';
$recipient = 'ciminoj@bright-ideas.com';
print "Content-type: text/html\n\n";
print "<Head><Title>Bright Ideas Software</Title></Head>";
print "<Body><H1>Thank you for signing the Guest Book . . . </H1></Body>";
```

The <PRE> tag can be used with an optional WIDTH attribute that specifies the maximum number of characters on a line. WIDTH also signals your browser to choose an appropriate font and indentation for the text. Hyperlinks can be used within <PRE> sections. You should avoid using other HTML tags within <PRE> sections, however.

Note: Because <, >, and & have special meanings in HTML, you must use their escape sequences (<, >, and &, respectively) to enter these characters. See "Escape Sequences" for more information.

EXTENDED QUOTATIONS

Use the <BLOCKQUOTE> tag to include lengthy quotations in a separate block on the screen. Most browsers change the margins for the quotation to separate it from surrounding text.

In the example:

```
<BLOCKQUOTE>
<P>The Threat of Computer Viruses</P>
<P>The only truly secure system is one that is powered off,

- and even then, I have my doubts.</P>
-Eugene H. Spafford
</BLOCKQUOTE>
```

the result is:

The Threat of Computer Viruses

The only truly secure system is one that is powered off, cast in a block of concrete, and sealed in a lead-lined room with armed guards — and even then, I have my doubts.

—Eugene H. Spafford

ADDRESSES

The <ADDRESS> tag specifies the author of a document, a way to contact the author (such as an e-mail address), or a revision date. It is usually the last item in a file.

For example, a sample address tag might look like this:

```
<ADDRESS>
To contact the author, send e-mail to: ciminoj@bright-ideas.com
</ADDRESS>
```

The result is:

To contact the author, send e-mail to: ciminoj@bright-ideas.com

Note: <ADDRESS> is not used for postal addresses.

FORCED LINE BREAKS/POSTAL ADDRESSES

The <BR> tag forces a line break with no extra space between lines. Using <P> elements for short lines of text such as postal addresses results in unwanted additional white space. For example, with <BR>:

```
Bright Ideas Software, Inc.<BR>
P.O. Box 6932<BR>
Edison, NJ 08818-6932<BR>
```

the output is:

Bright Ideas Software, Inc.
P.O. Box 6932
Edison, NJ 08818-6932

HORIZONTAL RULES

The <HR> tag produces a horizontal line the width of the browser window, which is useful to separate sections of your document. For example, many people add a rule at the end of their text and before the <ADDRESS> information. You can vary a rule's size (thickness) and width (the percentage of the window covered by the rule). Experiment with the settings until you are satisfied with the presentation. For example:

```
<HR SIZE=4 WIDTH=50%>
```

would display a line that extends half-way across the screen and would be four times the size of a normal horizontal rule line.

Logical and Physical Tags

HTML has two styles for individual words or sentences: logical and physical tags. Logical styles tag text according to its meaning, while physical styles indicate the specific appearance of a section.

For example:

```
<DFN>Logical styles </DFN>tag text according to its meaning, while
physical styles indicate the specific appearance of a section.
```

displays as:

Logical styles tag text according to its meaning, while physical styles indicate the specific appearance of a section.

Note: Some browsers don't attach any style to the <DFN> tag, so you might not see the indicated phrases in italics. The same effect (formatting those words in italics) could have been achieved via a different tag that tells your browser to "put these words in italics."

LOGICAL VERSUS PHYSICAL STYLES

If physical and logical styles produce the same result on the screen, why do both exist? In the ideal SGML universe, content is separate from presentation. Thus, SGML tags a level-one heading as a level-one heading, but does not specify that the level-one heading should be, for instance, 24-point bold Times centered. The advantage of this approach (it's similar in concept to style sheets or templates in many word processors) is that if you decide to change level-one headings to 20-point left-justified Helvetica, all you have to do is change the definition of the level-one heading in your Web browser. Indeed, many browsers today let you define how you want the various HTML tags rendered on-screen.

Another advantage of logical tags is that they help enforce consistency in your documents. It's easier to tag something as <H1> than to remember that level-one headings are 24-point bold Times centered. For example, consider the <STRONG> tag. Most browsers render it in bold text. However, it is possible a reader would prefer these sections be displayed in red, instead. Logical styles offer this flexibility.

If you want something to be displayed in italics and do not want a browser's setting to display it differently, use physical styles. Physical styles offer consistency, so text you tag a certain way will always be displayed that way for readers of your document.

Try to be consistent about which type of style you use. If you tag with physical styles, do so throughout a document. If you use logical styles, stick with them within a document. Keep in mind that future releases of HTML might not support physical styles, which could mean browsers will not display physical-style coding.

LOGICAL STYLES

Logical styles use several tags, shown in Table 6-2.

Table 6-2. Logical Tags and Their Uses

Tag	Used for	Displayed as	Example
<DFN>	Used for a word being defined	Typically displayed in italics	*NCSA Mosaic* is a World Wide Web browser.
<EM>	Used for emphasis	Typically displayed in italics	*Consultants cannot reset your password unless you call the help line.*
<CITE>	Used for the titles of books and films	Typically displayed in italics	*A Beginner's Guide to HTML*
<CODE>	Used for computer code	Typically displayed in a fixed-width font	The <stdio.h> header file
<KBD>	Used to prompt the user to enter a command	Typically displayed in plain fixed-width font	Enter passwd to change your password.
<SAMP>	Used for a sequence of literal characters	Typically displayed in a fixed-width font	Segmentation fault: Core dumped.
<STRONG>	Used for strong emphasis	Typically displayed in bold	**Note: Always check your links.**
<VAR>	Used for variables replace in which you will the variable with specific information	Typically displayed in italics	*rm filename* *deletes the file.*

Physical Styles

Physical styles are more limited than logical styles. They are shown in Table 6-3

Table 6-3. Physical Tags and Their Uses

Tag	Use
<B>	Used for bold text
<I>	Used for italic text
<TT>	Used for typewriter text, e.g., fixed-width font

Escape Sequences (Character Entities)

HTML uses escape sequences where necessary. Character entities have two functions:

1. For escaping special characters; and
2. For displaying other characters not available in the ASCII character set (primarily characters with diacritical marks for foreign expressions).

In addition, three ASCII characters — the left angle bracket (<), the right angle bracket (>), and the ampersand (&) — have special meanings in HTML and, therefore, cannot be used "as is" in text. (The angle brackets are used to indicate the beginning and end of HTML tags, and the ampersand is used to indicate the beginning of an escape sequence.) Double quotation marks may be used as is, but a character entity may also be used (").

To use one of the three characters in an HTML document, you must enter its escape sequence, as shown below:

- <   the escape sequence for <
- >   the escape sequence for >
- &   the escape sequence for &

Additional escape sequences support accented characters, such as:

- ö   the escape sequence for a lowercase o with an umlaut: ö
- ñ   the escape sequence for a lowercase n with a tilde: ñ
- È the escape sequence for an uppercase E with a grave accent: È

You can substitute other letters for the o, n, and E shown above.

Note: Unlike the rest of HTML, escape sequences are case-sensitive. You cannot, for instance, use < instead of <.

Linking

The chief power of HTML comes from its ability to link text and image to another document or section of a document. A browser highlights the identified text or image with color and underlines to indicate that it is a hypertext link (this term is often shortened to "hyperlink" or "link").

HTML's single hypertext-related tag is <A>, which stands for "anchor." To include an anchor in your document:

1. Start the anchor with <A (include a space after the A).
2. Specify the document you're linking to by entering the parameter HREF="filename" followed by a closing right angle bracket (>).
3. Enter the text that will serve as the hypertext link in the current document.
4. Enter the ending anchor tag: </A> (no space is needed before the end anchor tag).

Here is a sample hypertext reference in a file called about.html:

```
<A HREF="about.html">About Bright Ideas Software</A>
```

This entry makes the phrase "About Bright Ideas Software" the hyperlink to the document about.html, which is in the same directory as the first document.

RELATIVE PATHNAMES VERSUS ABSOLUTE PATHNAMES

You can link to documents in other directories by specifying the relative path from the current document to the linked document. For example, a link to a file level1.html located in the subdirectory HTMLTEST would be:

```
<A HREF="htmltest/level1.html">Path Test</A>
```

These links are called relative links because you are specifying the path to the linked file relative to the location of the current file. You can also use the absolute pathname (the complete URL) of the file, but relative links are more efficient in accessing a server.

Pathnames use the standard UNIX syntax. The UNIX syntax for the parent directory (the directory that contains the current directory) is "..".

If you were in the level1.html file and were referring to the original document test.html, your link would look like this:

```
<A HREF="../test.html">Test</A>
```

In general, you should use relative links because:

- they make it easier to move a group of documents to another location;
- they are a more efficient way to connect to the server; and
- there is less to type.

However, use absolute pathnames when linking to documents that are not directly related. For example, consider a group of documents that comprise a user manual. Links within this group should be relative links. Links to other documents (perhaps a reference to related software) should use full pathnames. This way, if you move the user manual to a different directory, none of the links would have to be updated.

URLs

The World Wide Web uses URLs to specify the location of files on other servers. A URL includes the type of resource being accessed (e.g., Web, Gopher, or WAIS), the address of the server, and the location of the file. The syntax is:

```
scheme://host.domain [:port]/path/filename
```

in which scheme is one of the following types:

- file   a file on your local system
- ftp   a file on an anonymous FTP server
- http   a file on a World Wide Web server
- gopher   a file on a Gopher server
- WAIS   a file on a WAIS server
- news   a Usenet newsgroup
- telnet   a connection to a Telnet-based service

The port number can generally be omitted in a URL. In fact, unless someone tells you otherwise, do not specify the port number.

For example, to include a link to the "New Jersey Lotus Notes Users Group" home page in your document, enter:

```
<A HREF="http://www.bright-ideas.com/njlnug/lnughp.htm">
New Jersey Lotus Notes Users Group </A>
```

This entry makes the text "New Jersey Lotus Notes Users Group" a hyperlink to this document.

LINKS TO SPECIFIC SECTIONS

Anchors can also be used to move a reader to a particular section in a document (either the same or a different document) rather than to the top, which is the default. This type of anchor is commonly called a "named anchor" because to create the links, you insert HTML names within the document.

Named anchors in one document can be used to facilitate both printing and browsing a document. Internal hyperlinks are used to create a "table of contents" at the top of a document. These hyperlinks move you from one location in the document to another location in the same document.

You can also link to a specific section in another document. That information is presented first because understanding that helps you understand linking within one document.

LINKS BETWEEN SECTIONS OF DIFFERENT DOCUMENTS

Suppose you want to set a link from document A (documenta.html) to a specific section in another document (documentb.html).

Enter the HTML coding for a link to a named anchor:

```
documentA.html:

<a href="support.html#GSA">GSA Contract</a>.
```

Think of the characters after the hash mark (#) as a tab within the support.html file. This tab tells your browser what should be displayed at the top of the window when the link is activated. In other words, the first line in your browser window should be the GSA Contract heading.

Next, create the named anchor (in this example, "GSA") in the support.html file:

```
<H2><A NAME="GSAGSA Contract</a></H2>
```

With both of these elements in place, you can bring a reader directly to the GSA reference in the support.html file.

Note: You cannot make links to specific sections within a different document unless you have write permission to the coded source of that document, or that document already contains in-document named anchors.

LINKS TO SPECIFIC SECTIONS WITHIN THE CURRENT DOCUMENT

The technique is the same as linking to separate sections, except the filename is omitted. For example, to link to the GSA anchor from within support.html, enter:

```
...More information about our<A HREF="#GSA">GSA Contract</a>
is available elsewhere in this document.
```

Be sure to include the <A NAME=> tag at the place in your document where you want the link to jump to (<H2><A NAME="GSA">GSA Contract</A></H2>).

Named anchors are particularly useful when you think readers will print a document in its entirety or when you have a lot of short information you want to place online in one file.

MAILTO LINKS

You can make it easy for a reader to send electronic mail to a specific person or mail alias by including the MAILTO attribute in a hyperlink. The format is:

```
<A HREF="mailto:emailinfo@host">Name</a>
```

For example, enter:

```
<A HREF="mailto:ciminoj@bright-ideas.com">Contact The Author</a>
```

to create a mail window that is already configured to open a mail window for the author of this book.

Inline Images

Most Web browsers can display inline images (that is, images next to text) that are in one of the following three formats:

- X Bitmap (XBM)
- GIF
- JPEG

Other image formats are being incorporated into Web browsers, such as the Portable Network Graphic (PNG) format and Fractal Image Format (FIF). Each image takes time to process and slows down the initial display of a document. Carefully select your images and the number of images in a document.

To include an inline image, enter:

```
<IMG SRC=ImageName>
```

in which "ImageName" is the URL of the image file.

The syntax for <IMG SRC> URLs is identical to that used in an anchor HREF. If the image file is a gif file, the filename part of ImageName must end with .gif. Filenames of X Bitmap images must end with .xbm; jpeg image files must end with .jpg or .jpeg; and Portable Network Graphic files must end with .png.

IMAGE SIZE ATTRIBUTES

You should include two other attributes on <IMG> tags to tell your browser the size of the images it is downloading with the text. The HEIGHT and WIDTH attributes let your browser set aside the appropriate space in pixels for the images as it downloads the rest of the file. (Get the pixel size from your image-processing software, such as Paint Shop Pro or Adobe Photoshop.) Specifying image attributes will also speed up the loading of the image because the client browser will not need to perform the image size calculations.

For example, to include a corporate logo image in a file along with the image's dimensions, enter:

```
<IMG SRC=corplogo.gif HEIGHT=100 WIDTH=65>
```

Note: Some browsers use the HEIGHT and WIDTH attributes to stretch or shrink an image to fit into the allotted space when the image does not exactly match the attribute numbers. Some browser developers don't think stretching and shrinking is a good idea.

Don't plan on your readers having access to this feature. Check your dimensions and use the correct ones.

ALIGNING IMAGES

You have some flexibility when displaying images. Images can be separated from text and aligned left, right, or centered. Or, you can have an image aligned with text. Try several possibilities to see how your information looks best.

ALIGNING TEXT WITH AN IMAGE

By default, the bottom of an image is aligned with the text. You can align images to the top or center of a paragraph using the ALIGN= attributes TOP and CENTER.

Note: The browser aligns only one line and then jumps to the bottom of the image for the rest of the text.

IMAGES WITHOUT TEXT

To display an image without any associated text (e.g., your organization's logo), make it a separate paragraph. Use the paragraph ALIGN= attribute to center the image or adjust it to the right side of the window.

```
<p ALIGN=CENTER>
<IMG SRC = "logo.gif">
</p>
```

For the above example, the image centered and any text that follows would start below it and be left-justified.

ALTERNATIVE TEXT FOR IMAGES

Some World Wide Web browsers, primarily those that run on VT100 terminals, cannot display images. Other users turn off image loading even if their software can display images. HTML provides a mechanism to tell readers what they are missing on your pages if they choose not to use graphics. The ALT attribute lets you specify text to be displayed instead of an image. For example:

```
<IMG SRC="corplogo.gif" ALT="Logo">
```

in which CORPLOGO.GIF is the picture of a corporate logo. With graphics-capable viewers that have image-loading turned on, you see the corporate "logo" graphic. With a VT100 browser or if image-loading is turned off, the word logo is shown in your window.

You should try to include alternative text for each image you use in your document as a courtesy to your readers.

Background Graphics

Newer versions of Web browsers can load an image and use it as a background when displaying a page. In general, if you want to include a background, make sure your text can be read easily when displayed on top of the image. Background images will not print if you decide to print the Web page.

Background images can be textured (linen-finished paper, for example) or an image of an object (a logo possibly). You create the background image as you do any other image.

However, you have to create only a small piece of the image. Using a feature called tiling, a browser takes the image and repeats it across the screen and down to fill your browser window. In summary, you generate one image and the browser replicates it enough to fill your window. This action is automatic when you use the background tag shown below.

The tag to include a background image is included in the <BODY> statement as an attribute:

```
<BODY BACKGROUND="filename.gif">
```

BACKGROUND COLOR

By default, browsers display text in black on a gray background. However, you can change both elements if you want. Some HTML authors select a background color and coordinate it with a change in the color of the text.

Always preview changes like this to make sure your pages are readable. For example, many people find red text on a black background difficult to read.

You change the color of text, links, visited links, and active links using attributes of the <BODY> tag. For example, enter:

```
<BODY BGCOLOR="#000000" TEXT="#FFFFFF" LINK="#9690CC">
```

This creates a window with a black background (BGCOLOR), white text (TEXT), and silvery hyperlinks (LINK).

The six-digit number and letter combinations represent colors by giving their RGB (red, green, blue) value. The six digits are actually three two-digit numbers in sequence, representing the amount of red, green, or blue as a hexadecimal value in the range 00-FF. For example, 000000 is black (no color at all), FF0000 is bright red, and FFFFFF is white (fully saturated with all three colors). These number and letter combinations are cryptic. Fortunately two online resources are available to help you track the combinations that map to specific colors:

- ColorPro Web server (http://www.biola.edu/cgi-bin/colorpro/), and
- Yahoo's links to documents on backgrounds (www.yahoo.com/Computers_and_Internet/Internet/World_Wide_Web/Page_Design_and_Layout/Backgrounds/).

External Images, Sounds, and Animations

You may want to have an image open as a separate document when a user activates a link on a word or a smaller, inline version of the image included in your document. This is called an "external image," and it is useful if you do not wish to slow down the loading of the main document with large inline images.

To include a reference to an external image, enter:

```
<A HREF="MyImage.gif">link anchor</A>
```

You can also use a smaller image as a link to a larger image. Enter:

```
<A HREF="BigImage.gif"><IMG SRC="SmallImage.gif"></A>
```

The reader sees the SMALLIMAGE.GIF image and clicks on it to open the bigimage.gif file. Use the same syntax for links to external animations and sounds. The only difference is the file extension (.MOV) of the linked file. For example,

```
<A HREF="AdamsRib.mov">link anchor</A>
```

in which ADAMSRIB.MOV specifies a link to a QuickTime movie. Some common file types and their extensions are:

Table 6-4. File Types and Their Extensions

File Type	Extension
Plain text	(.txt)
HTML document	(.html)
GIF image	(.gif)
TIFF image	(.tiff)
X bitmap image	(.xbm)
JPEG image	(.jpg or .jpeg)
PostScript file	(.ps)
AIFF sound file	(.aiff)
AU sound file	(.au)
WAV sound file	(.wav)
QuickTime movie	(.mov)
MPEG movie	(.mpeg or .mpg)

Keep in mind your intended audience and its access to software. Most UNIX workstations, for instance, cannot view QuickTime movies.

Tables

Before HTML tags for tables were finalized, authors had to carefully format their tabular information within <PRE> tags, counting spaces, and previewing their output. Tables are very useful for presenting tabular information and are a boon to creative HTML authors who use the table tags to present their regular Web pages. (See Table 6-5.)

Table 6-5. Table Elements

Element	Description
<TABLE> ... </TABLE>	Defines a table in HTML. If the BORDER attribute is present, your browser displays the table with a border.
<CAPTION> ... </CAPTION>	Defines the caption for the title of the table. The default position of the title is centered at the top of the table. The attribute ALIGN= BOTTOM can be used to position the caption below the table. Note: Any kind of markup tag can be used in the caption.
<TR> ... </TR>	Specifies a table row within a table. You may define default attributes for the entire row: ALIGN (LEFT, CENTER, RIGHT) and/or VALIGN (TOP, MIDDLE, BOTTOM).
TH> ... </TH>	Defines a table header cell. By default, the text in this cell is bold and centered. Table header cells may contain other attributes to determine the characteristics of the cell and its contents.
<TD> ... </TD>	Defines a table data cell. By default, the text in this cell is aligned left and centered vertically. Table data cells may contain other attributes to determine the characteristics of the cell and its contents.

Think of your tabular information in light of the coding explained below. A table has heads in which you explain the column and row inclusions, rows for information, and cells for each item. In the following table, the first column contains the header information, each row explains an HTML table tag, and each cell contains a paired tag or an explanation of the tag's function.

TABLE ATTRIBUTES

Table attributes allow you to customize the way your tables look. They let you control the flow of text, and the alignment of columns and elements within a table.

Note: Attributes defined within <TH> ... </TH> or <TD> ... </TD> cells override the default alignment set in <TR> ... </TR>.

Table 6-6. Table Attributes

Attribute	Description
ALIGN	Horizontal alignment of a cell (LEFT, CENTER, RIGHT)
VALIGN	Vertical alignment of a cell (TOP, MIDDLE, BOTTOM)
COLSPAN=n	The number (n) of columns a cell spans
ROWSPAN=n	The number (n) of rows a cell spans
NOWRAP	Turn off word wrapping within a cell.

GENERAL TABLE FORMAT

The format of a table looks like that of Table 6-7.

The <TABLE> and </TABLE> tags must surround the entire table definition. The first item inside the table is the CAPTION, which is optional. Then, you can have any number of rows defined by the <TR> and </TR> tags. Within a row, you can have any number of cells defined by the <TD>...</TD> or <TH>...</TH> tags. Each row of a table is formatted independently of the rows above and below it. This lets you easily display tables like the one above with a single cell, such as Table Attributes, spanning columns of the table.

Table 6-7. Table Format

Tag	Definition
TABLE>	Start of table definition
<CAPTION> caption contents </CAPTION>	Caption definition
<TR>	Start of first row definition
<TH> cell contents </TH>	First cell in row 1 (a head)
<TH> cell contents </TH>	Last cell in row 1 (a head)
</TR>	End of first row definition
<TR>	Start of second row definition
<TD> cell contents </TD>	First cell in row 2
<TD> cell contents </TD>	Last cell in row 2
</TR>	End of second row definition
<TR>	Start of last row definition
<TD> cell contents </TD>	First cell in last row
<TD> cell contents </TD>	Last cell in last row
</TR>	End of last row definition
</TABLE>	End of table definition

TABLES FOR NONTABULAR INFORMATION

Some HTML authors use tables to present nontabular information. For example, because links can be included in table cells, some authors use a table with no borders to create the appearance of a single image from separate images. Browsers that can display tables properly show the various images seamlessly, making the created image seem like an image map (one image with hyperlinked quadrants).

Fill-Out Forms Web forms let readers return information to a Web server for some action. For example, suppose you collect names and e-mail addresses so you can e-mail information to people who request it. For each person who enters his or her name and address, you need some information to be sent and the respondent's specific information added to a database.

This processing of incoming data is usually handled by a script or program written in Perl or another language that manipulates text, files, and information.

Forms are not hard to code. They follow the same constructs as other HTML tags. What can be difficult is the program or script that takes the information submitted in a form and processes it.

TROUBLESHOOTING

In troubleshooting HTML codes, one tip overrides the rest: Avoid overlapping tags.

Consider this example of HTML:

```
<B>This is an example of <DFN>overlapping</B> HTML tags.</DFN>
```

Word overlapping is contained within both the <B> and <DFN> tags. A browser might be confused by this coding and might not display the words the way you intend. The only way to know is to check each popular browser (which is time-consuming and impractical).

In general, avoid overlapping tags. Look at your tags and try pairing them up. Tags (with the obvious exceptions of elements whose end tags may be omitted, such as paragraphs) should be paired without an intervening tag in between. Look again at the example above. You cannot pair the bold tags without another tag in the middle (the first definition tag). Try matching your coding to see if you have any problem areas that should be fixed before your release your files to a server.

Embed Only Anchors and Character Tags	Although HTML protocol allows you to embed links within other HTML tags, such as: ```<H1><A HREF="Destination.html">My heading</A></H1>```

do not embed HTML tags within an anchor:

```
<A HREF="Destination.html">
<H1>My heading</H1>
</A>
```

Most browsers currently handle this second example, although the official HTML specifications do not support this construct, and your file will probably not work with future browsers. Remember that browsers can be forgiving when displaying improperly coded files. That forgiveness may not last to the next version of the software. When in doubt, code your files according to the HTML specifications.

Character tags modify the appearance of the text within other elements:

```
<UL>
<LI><B>A bold list item</B>
<LI><I>An italic list item</I>
</UL>
```

Avoid embedding other types of HTML element tags. For example, you might be tempted to embed a heading within a list to make the font larger:

```
<UL>
<LI><H1>A large heading</H1>
<LI><H2>Something slightly smaller</H2>
</UL>
```

Although some browsers handle this statement quite nicely, formatting such coding is unpredictable because it is undefined. For compatibility with all browsers, avoid these constructs. (The Netscape <FONT> tag, which lets you specify how large individual characters will be displayed in your window, is not currently part of the official HTML specifications.)

What's the difference between embedding a <B> within a <LI> tag instead of embedding a <H1> within a <LI> tag? Within HTML, the semantic meaning of <H1> is that it's the main heading of a document and should be followed by the content of the document. Therefore, it doesn't make sense to find a <H1> within a list. Character formatting tags also are generally not additive. For example, you might expect that:

```
<B><I>some text</I></B>
```

would produce bold italic text. On some browsers, it does; other browsers interpret only the innermost tag.

Validate Your Code

When you put a document on a Web server, be sure to check the formatting and each link (including named anchors). Ideally, have someone else read and comment on your files before you consider a document finished.

You can run your coded files through an HTML validation service that will tell you if your code conforms to accepted HTML standards. If you are not sure your coding conforms to HTML specifications, this can be a useful teaching tool. Fortunately, the service lets you select the level of conformance you want for your files (i.e., strict, level 2, level 3). If you want to use some codes that are not officially part of the HTML specifications, this latitude is helpful.

Dummy Images

When an <IMG SRC> tag points to an image that does not exist, a dummy image is substituted by your browser software. When this happens during your final review of your files, make sure the referenced image does in fact exist, the hyperlink has the correct information in the URL, and the file permission is set appropriately (world-readable).

Update Your Files

If the contents of a file are static (such as a biography of George Washington), no updating is probably needed. But for documents that are time-sensitive or cover a field that changes frequently, remember to update your documents.

Updating is particularly important when the file contains information such as a weekly schedule or a deadline for a program funding announcement. Remove outdated files or note why something that appears dated is still on a server.

Browsers Differ

Web browsers display HTML elements differently. Remember that not all browsers can interpret all codes used in HTML files. Any code a browser does not understand is usually ignored.

You could spend a lot of time making your file look "perfect" using your current browser. If you check that file using another browser, it will likely display (a little or a lot) differently. Hence, these words of advice: Code your files using correct HTML. Leave the interpreting to the browsers, and hope for the best.

Commenting Your Files

You might want to include comments in your HTML files. Comments in HTML are like comments in a computer program — the text you enter is not used by the browser in any formatting and is not directly viewable by the reader, just as computer program comments are not used and are not viewable. The comments are accessible if a reader views the source file, however.

Comments such as the name of the person updating a file, the software and version used in creating a file, or the date a minor edit was made are normal.

To include a comment, enter:

```
<!- your comments here ->
```

You must include the exclamation mark and hyphens as shown.

FRAMES

Frames are a new and popular feature of HTML 3.0 that allow you to present information in a more flexible and useful fashion. Using this architecture, the window is divided into panes or multiple, scrolling regions called frames. This is accomplished through coding inside a frameset file.

Each frame has several features:

1. It can designate a URL that will allow it to load information independent of other frames on the page.

2. It can be given a NAME, which allows other URLs to target it.
3. It can be dynamically resized if the user changes the window's size. Resizing can also be disabled, ensuring a constant frame size.

These features offer exciting possibilities for Web page design. Some examples of how frames might be used within a Web site include:

1. Control bars, copyright notices, and title graphics can be placed in a static, individual frame. As the user navigates the site in "live" frames, the static frame's contents remain fixed, even though adjoining frames redraw.
2. One frame can contain more functional Table of Contents link that, when clicked, displays results in an adjoining frame.
3. The side-by-side design of frames allows queries to be posed and answered on the same page, with one frame holding the query form, and the other presenting the results.

**Frame
Document
Structure**

A frame document has a structure very much like your HTML document, except the BODY container is replaced by a FRAMESET container that describes the sub-HTML documents, or frames, that make up the page.

```
<HTML>

<HEAD>
</HEAD>

<FRAMESET>
</FRAMESET>

</HTML>
```

The BODY tag can also be used within a frame document, but must follow the FRAMESET tags. The BODY tag should fall between the

NOFRAMES containers. This is useful when you need to support browsers that are not FRAMES-compatible (such as older versions of Mosaic).

Frame Syntax	Frame syntax is similar in scope and complexity to that used by tables, and has been designed to be quickly processed by Internet client layout engines. The syntax has several attributes.

```
<FRAMESET>
```

<Frameset> is the main container for a frame. It has two attributes: ROWS and COLS. A frame document has no BODY and no tags that would normally be placed in the BODY can appear before the FRAMESET tag. If they do, the FRAMESET will be ignored. The FRAMESET tag has a matching end tag, and within the FRAMESET you can only have other nested FRAMESET tags, FRAME tags, or the NOFRAMES tag.

```
ROWS="row_height_value_list"
```

The ROWS attribute is defined by a comma separated list of values. These values can be absolute pixel values, percentage values between 1 and 100, or relative scaling values. The number of rows is implicit in the number of elements in the list. Since the total height of all the rows must equal the height of the window, row heights might be normalized to achieve this. A missing ROWS attribute is interpreted as a single row sized to fit arbitrarily.

VALUES

VALUE

A numeric value is assumed to be a fixed size in pixels. However, since the size of the viewer's window can vary, this is a dangerous value to use. If fixed pixel values need to be used, it may become necessary to mix them with one or more relative size values. If you do not do so, the client browser will override your specified pixel value to ensure that the total proportions of the frame are 100 percent of the width and height of the user's window.

VALUE%

This is a simple percentage value between 1 and 100. The client browser will adjust the values to ensure that the total proportions of the frame are 100 percent of the width and height of the user's window.

1. If the total is greater than 100, all percentages are scaled down.
2. If the total is less than 100, and relative-sized frames exist, extra space will be given to them.
3. If there are no relative-sized frames, all percentages will be scaled up to match a total of 100 percent.

VALUE*

The value on this field is optional. A single '*' character is a "relative-sized" frame and is interpreted as a request to give the frame all remaining space. If multiple relative-sized frames exist, the remaining space is divided evenly among them. If there is a value in front of the '*', that frame gets that much more relative space. "2*,*" would give 2/3 of the space to the first frame, and 1/3 to the second.

Here is an example for three rows, the first and the last being smaller than the center row:

```
<FRAMESET ROWS="30%,*,30%">
```

Here is an example for three rows, the first and the last being fixed height, with the remaining space assigned to the middle row:

```
<FRAMESET ROWS="80,*,80">
```

COLS="COLUMN_WIDTH_LIST"

The COLS attribute is also defined by a comma separated list of values. In fact, its values are of the exact same syntax as the list described for the ROWS attribute.

The FRAMESET tag can be nested inside other FRAMESET tags. In this case, the complete subframe is placed in the space that would be used for the corresponding frame if this had been a FRAME tag instead of a nested FRAMESET.

<FRAME>

This tag defines a single frame in a frameset. It has six possible attributes:

1. SRC
2. NAME
3. MARGINWIDTH
4. MARGINHEIGHT
5. SCROLLING
6. NORESIZE

The FRAME tag is not a container and has no matching end tag.

SRC="URL"

The SRC attribute takes as its value the URL of the document to be displayed in this particular frame. Frames without SRC attributes are displayed as a blank space the size the frame would have been.

NAME="WINDOW_NAME"

The NAME attribute is used to assign a name to a frame so it can be targeted by links in other documents. The NAME attribute is optional; by default all windows are unnamed. Names must begin with an alphanumeric character. Named frames can have their window contents targeted with the new TARGET attribute.

MARGINWIDTH="VALUE"

The MARGINWIDTH attribute is used when you want some control of the left and right margins for the frame. If specified, the value for MARGINWIDTH is in pixels. It is important to note that margins can not be less than one (so that frame objects will not touch frame edges) and margins can not be specified that leave no space for the document contents. The MARGINWIDTH attribute is optional. By default, all frames default to the browser setting for an appropriate margin width.

MARGINHEIGHT="VALUE"
Like MARGINWIDTH attribute, the MARGINHEIGHT attribute controls the upper and lower margins of the frame.

SCROLLING="YES|NO|AUTO"
The SCROLLING attribute is describes whether the frame should have a scroll bar or not. The SCROLLING attribute is optional and the default value is "auto".

1. The "yes" parameter results in scroll bars always being visible on that frame.
2. "No" results in scrollbars never being visible.
3. "Auto" instructs the browser to decide whether scrollbars are needed, and place them where necessary.

NORESIZE
By default, all frames are resizable. The NORESIZE attribute is an optional attribute without any value. It is a flag that indicates that the user cannot resize the frame. Users typically resize frames by dragging a frame edge to a new position. Note that if any frame adjacent to an edge is not resizable, that entire edge will be restricted from moving. This affects the resizability of other frames.

<NOFRAMES>
This tag is for content providers who want to create alternative content that is viewable by non-frames-capable clients. A frame-capable Internet client ignores all tags and data between start and end NOFRAMES tags.

Target

This frames feature gives the document writer a control over where the data appears when a user clicks on a link in a document. It is useful as a stand-alone feature with a document space that can be best viewed with multiple top-level windows.

In HTML, when a user clicks on a link, the new document either appears in the window the user clicked in or it can appear in a new window. The targeting windows feature allows the document writer to assign names to **specific** windows, and *target* certain documents to always appear in the window with the matching name.

A target window name is assigned in one of three ways:

1. A document can be sent with the optional HTTP header Window-target: window_name. This forces the document to load in the window named window_name, or if such a window does not exist, one will be created, and then the document will be loaded in it.
2. A document can be accessed via a targeted link. In this case, there is HTML code that assigns a target window_name to a link. The document loaded from that link will behave as if it had a Window-target set described in method 1 above.
3. A window created within a frameset can be named using the NAME attribute to the FRAME tag.

Within HTML, targeting is accomplished by the TARGET attribute. This attribute can be added to many of the existing HTML tags to target the links that tag refers to. The attribute is of the form: TARGET="window_name". Targets have several tags.

TARGET IN AN ANCHOR *<A>* TAG

The anchor tag normally specifies a link to be loaded when the user clicks on the active item.

Adding the TARGET attribute to the anchor tag forces the link to be loaded into the targeted window.

```
<A HREF="url" TARGET="window_name">Targeted Anchor</A>
```

TARGET IN THE *BASE* TAG

The TARGET attribute establishes a default window_name that all links in the document will be targeted to. This default window_name is overridden by specific instances of the TARGET attribute in individual anchor tags. The TARGET in the BASE tag is used when you want the links in a document to be targeted to the same window.

```
<BASE TARGET="window_name">
```

TARGET IN THE AREA TAG

Client-side image maps define an area tag. This tag describes a shaped area in a client-side image map and provides the link that should be followed when the user clicks there. Adding the TARGET attribute to the area tag forces that link to be loaded into the targeted window.

```
<AREA SHAPE="shape" COORDS="x,y,..." HREF="url"
    TARGET="window_name">
```

TARGET IN THE FORM TAG

Adding the TARGET attribute to the form tag will display the result of the form submission into the targeted window.

```
<FORM ACTION="url" TARGET="window_name">
```

ALLOWED TARGET NAMES

The window name specified by a TARGET attribute must begin with an alphanumeric character to be valid. All other window names will be ignored.

An exception to this is target names. These names all begin with the underscore character. Any targeted window name beginning with underscore that is not one of these names, will be ignored.

TARGET="_BLANK"

This target causes the link to always be loaded in a new blank window. This window is not named.

TARGET="_SELF"

This target causes the link to load in the same window the anchor was clicked in. This is useful for overriding a globally assigned base target.

TARGET="_PARENT"

This target makes the link load in the immediate FRAMESET parent of the document. This defaults to acting as "_self" if the document has no parent.

TARGET="_TOP"

This target makes the link load in the full body of the window. It just defaults to acting as "_self" if the document is already at the top. It is useful for breaking out of an arbitrarily deep FRAME nesting.

<BASE TARGET="_SELF">

This target loads the next URL into the same windowpane.

<BASE TARGET="_WINDOW">

This target opens a new window over the existing window but does not eliminate the existing one.

<BASE TARGET="_PARENT">

This target loads a new parent window replacing the existing window.

Heading Frames Example

```
<HTML>
<HEAD>
<TITLE>HR On-Line: Forms On-Line</TITLE>
</HEAD>

<FRAMESET COLS="*,125">
        <FRAME SRC="open.htm" NAME="main1" MARGINHEIGHT=2 MARGIN-
WIDTH=2 SCROLLING=AUTO>
        <FRAME SRC="menu.htm" NAME="right" NORESIZE MARGIN-
HEIGHT=2 MARGINWIDTH=10 SCROLLING=AUTO>
</FRAMESET>
</HTML>
```

In this frameset you have two frames, named main1 and right. By not specifying a ROW attribute, your browser will automatically scale for one row. Your FRAMESET Tag creates two columns: one of a fixed width of 125 pixels for the right frame, and then allows the browser to assign the remaining screen size area to the main1 column or frame. As it turns out, in this example, the right column is for a menu bar, and uses buttons that are a fixed width.

Figure 6.1 shows how this document looks under Netscape.

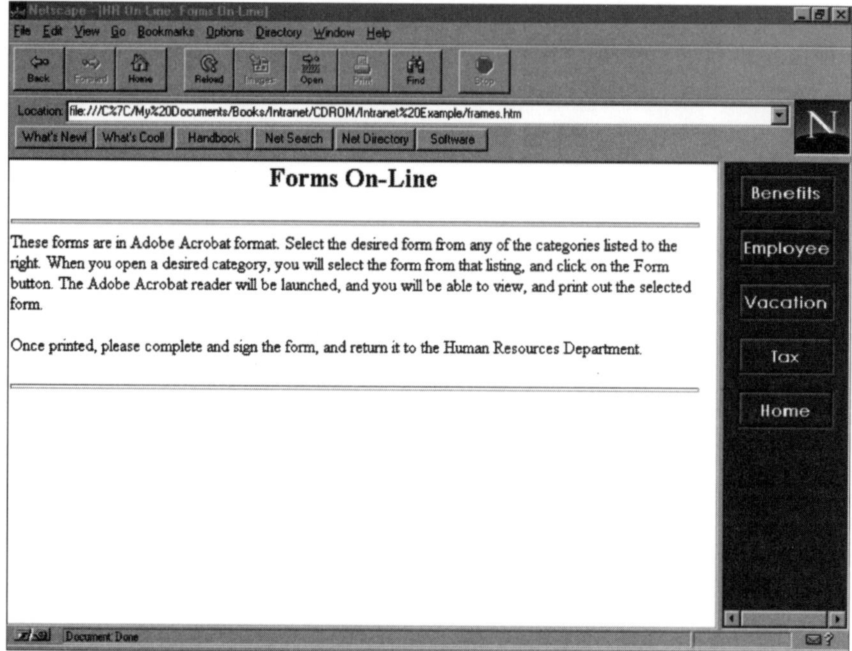

FIGURE *A frame displayed in Netscape.*
6-1

Frames offer vast potential to enhance Web site architecture. With frames, you can present information in a more flexible and useful fashion. However, like everything else you build for the Web, use frames appropriately. Frames can create a fuller user experience or a more frustrating user experience.

Modifying Existing HTML Documents

CONTENTS

One of the most common tasks in HTML programming is making modifications to an existing document. These modifications can be divided by type into several classifications:

- changing an HTML pointer within a document;
- adding an HTML link to an existing document;
- changing an image referred to within an HTML document; and
- creating an HTML link that refers to a section of the same document.

Whatever the change you intend to make, you must first know the correct syntax for the URL your change refers to. If the URL is external, that is, the URL points to a Web page or resource that is not found on your local server, you must supply the full URL to that resource. This is also known as an "absolute path" because you are specifying the full server name, directory, and filename of the resource you are locating.

For example, you may want to point to the Web site home page for Bright Ideas Software (www.bright-ideas.com). Because you are not on that local server, you must specify the full URL:

```
<a href= > tag:
<a href="http://www.bright-ideas.com"></A>
```

If the URL is internal to your Web server, you do not need to specify the entire URL, but can supply the necessary directory and file information. This is referred to as a "relative path" because you have omitted the server name and some directory information. If you want to refer to a page stored on your own Web server, you do not need to specify the complete URL, as your server already knows who the Web page belongs to. All you need to supply is the pathname and filename of the resource you want to access.

For example, your <A HREF= > tag could look like this:

```
<a href="njlnug/lnughp.htm"></A>
```

Because you specified a relative path instead of an absolute path, the <A HREF= > tag looks for the LNUGHP.HTM document in a subdirectory (NJLNUG) of your current HTML directory.

Changing an HTML Pointer Within a Document

Let's make a change to an existing HTML document. For this example, we will use a simple HTML document, shown below:

```
<html>
<head>
<title>Test Page</title>
</head>
<body>
<img src = "spectbar.gif">
<A HREF="http://www.bright-ideas.com"><IMG SRC="home.gif" >
Bright Ideas Software Home Page</A>
<P><center>This page Copyright&#169; 1996 by Bright Ideas
Software, Inc.</center>
</body>
</html>
```

Suppose we want to have this document point to a different HTML document on the Bright Ideas Software server. By changing the <A HREF=> tag to the new URL, we change what the HTML document does, but not how it looks:

```
<html>
<head>
<title>Test Page</title>
</head>
<body>
<img src = "spectbar.gif">
<br>
<A HREF="http://www.bright-ideas.com/test.htm"> <IMG
SRC="home.gif" > Bright Ideas Software Home Page</A>
<P><center>This page Copyright&#169; 1996 by Bright Ideas
Software, Inc.</center>
</body>
</html>
```

All that was changed was the <a href="http://www.bright-ideas.com/test.htm"> entry. We added "/test.htm," which didn't change the appearance of the page, but did change where the page points.

ADDING A **URL** TO AN EXISTING DOCUMENT

We can take the previous example to the next level by adding URLs to an existing HTML document. Adding links to a document is easy, as long as you:

- know the full pathname to the resource you want to link to (this includes images), and
- begin and end your HTML tags correctly.

The main reason HTML documents have errors is because the author did not check these two basic design rules. The result is that your new links don't work and your page format may become distorted. Have you ever visited a Web page and seen a small icon with a tear, instead of the graphic image you were expecting? This is called the broken icon. Browsers substitute a generic image for any graphics the browser can't find or for images that were interrupted during transfer.

Let's add three new links to our HTML document. Our basic document looks like the following:

```
<html>
<head>
<title>Test Page</title>
</head>
<body>
<img src = "spectbar.gif">
<br>
<A HREF="http://www.bright-ideas.com"><IMG SRC="home.gif" >
Bright Ideas Software Home Page</A>
<P><center>This page Copyright&#169; 1996 by Bright Ideas
Software, Inc.</center>
</body>
</html>
```

We want to add links to three new HTML documents located on our Web server in a subdirectory called sales. The three pages are page1, page2, and page3. In addition, we want to represent these links with a button graphic, which is located in a subdirectory called images. Our revised HTML document might look like the following:

```
<html>
<head>
<title>Test Page</title>
</head>
<body>
<img src = "spectbar.gif">
<br>
<A HREF="http://www.bright-ideas.com/sales/page1.htm"><IMG
SRC="button.gif" >Page 1</A><br>
<A HREF="http://www.bright-ideas.com/sales/page2.htm"><IMG
SRC="button.gif" >Page 2</A><br>
<A HREF="http://www.bright-ideas.com/sales/page3.htm"><IMG
SRC="button.gif" >Page 3</A><br>
<A HREF="http://www.bright-ideas.com"><IMG SRC="home.gif" >
Bright Ideas Software Home Page</A>
<P><center>This page Copyright&#169; 1996 by Bright Ideas
Software, Inc.</center>
</body>
</html>
```

This new page would look like the page in Figure 7-1.

Notice that we now have four buttons on the page, along with a caption telling us what each button is for. Clicking on the button or the caption text brings us to the associated URL link.

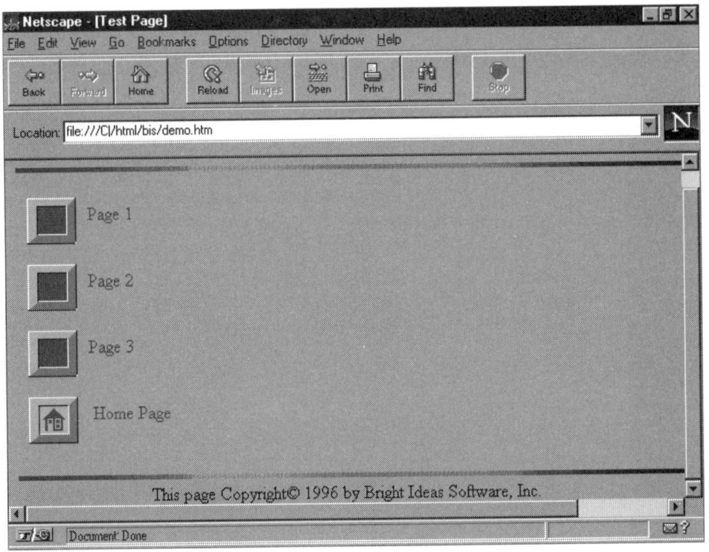

FIGURE *A Sample HTML Page*
7-1

LINKING TO A SECTION WITHIN A DOCUMENT

Let's add a link to a section within an existing HTML document. For this example, we will use a simple HTML document, shown below:

```
<html>
<head>
<title>Test Page</title>
</head>"
<body>
<img src = "spectbar.gif">
<p>
In today's business world, effective networking is the key to
<b>competitive strength</b> and <b>economic advantage</b>. The
ability to link diverse communications and disparate computing
resources can make all the difference in how your business grows
and flourishes. All you need to do is to find the right solution
provider, the right partner, to build a cohesive system to sup-
port your business strategies. Bright Ideas Software is such a
partner.
<p>
Since its inception, Bright Ideas Software has been providing its
clients with the most comprehensive software development and sys-
tems integration solutions in the industry. Whether it's a
Fortune 1000 giant, emerging midsize organization, law firm or
small company, Bright Ideas Software has turned our networking
knowledge into viable corporate business solutions. We help com-
panies become more profitable by making it easy to <i>cooper-
ate</i> and <i>collaborate</i> between locations, departments,
and Workgroups.
<p>
You understand the role your network plays in retaining a compet-
itive edge. <b>So do we!</b> Bright Ideas Software can assist
with existing or on-going projects, connecting every department
and every person involved in accessing or using your vital corpo-
rate information. Our experienced system consultants can even
help you <i>unlock</i> hidden resources, and <i>release</i> the
untapped potential of your network. As your partner in integra-
tion, we will work with you to develop and mold your network to
meet your business requirements.
<p>
<a HREF="http://www.bright-ideas.com"><IMG SRC="home.gif" >
Bright Ideas Software Home Page</A>
<P><center>This page Copyright&#169; 1996 by Bright Ideas
Software, Inc.</center>
</body>
</html>
```

Now, suppose you want to add buttons to this document that point to different sections within the same document. By changing the <A NAME=> tag to each section (with a unique name) and adding the <A HREF=> tag to reference each named section, you get an HTML document that looks like this:

```
<html>
<head>
<title>Test Page</title>
</head>
<body>
<img src = "spectbar.gif">
<center>
<h2>Document Sections</h2>
<a href="#point1"><img src="button1.gif" hspace=10>
<a href="#point2"><img src="button2.gif" hspace=10>
<a href="#point3"><img src="button3.gif" hspace=10>
</center>
<p>

<a name="point1">
<img src = "spectbar.gif">
<h3>Section 1</h3>
In today's business world, effective networking is the key to
<b>competitive strength</b> and <b>economic advantage</b>. The
ability to link diverse communications and disparate computing
resources can make all the difference in how your business grows
and flourishes. All you need to do is to find the right solution
provider, the right partner, to build a cohesive system to sup-
port your business strategies. Bright Ideas Software is such a
partner.

<p>
<a name="point2">
<img src = "spectbar.gif">
<h3>Section 2</h3>
Since its inception, Bright Ideas Software has been providing its
clients with the most comprehensive software development and sys-
tems integration solutions in the industry. Whether it's a
Fortune 1000 giant, emerging midsize organization, law firm or
small company, Bright Ideas Software has turned our networking
knowledge into viable corporate business solutions. We help com-
panies become more profitable by making it easy to <i>cooper-
ate</i> and <i>collaborate</i> between locations, departments,
and Workgroups.

<p>
<a name="point3">
```

```
<img src = "spectbar.gif">
<h3>Section 3</h3>
You understand the role your network plays in retaining a compet-
itive edge. <b>So do we!</b> Bright Ideas Software can assist
with existing or on-going projects, connecting every department
and every person involved in accessing or using your vital corpo-
rate information. Our experienced system consultants can even
help you <i>unlock</i> hidden resources, and <i>release</i> the
untapped potential of your network. As your partner in integra-
tion, we will work with you to develop and mold your network to
meet your business requirements.

<p>
<A HREF="http://www.bright-ideas.com"><IMG SRC="home.gif" >
Bright Ideas Software Home Page</A>
<P><center>This page Copyright&#169; 1996 by Bright Ideas
Software, Inc.</center>
</body>
</html>
```

The new page will look like Figure 7-2.

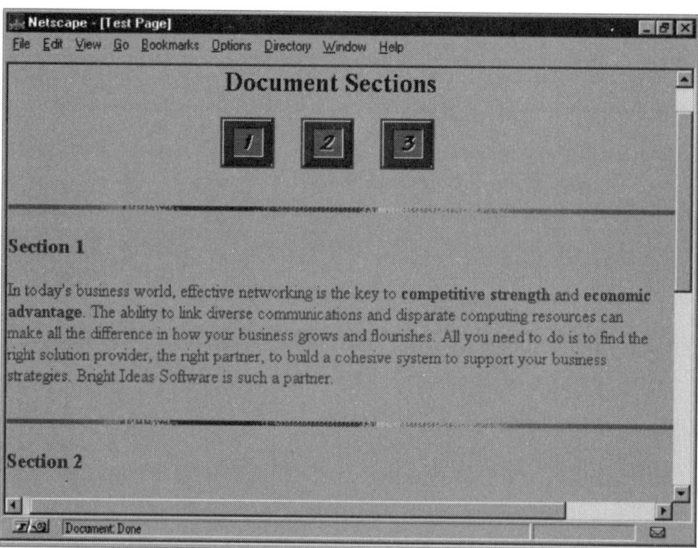

FIGURE *The New Page with Buttons Added*
7-2

Notice that we still use the <A HREF=> tag, but we added the
#name syntax to the resource description. We also added the <A
NAME=> tag at the beginning of each section. These two tags used in

conjuction allow us to navigate to specific sections within a page. We can also use these tags to jump to specific sections on other pages. We simply need to specify the full URL of the resource page and add the *#name* to the end of the full URL.

For example, if we want to jump to section1 of the above DEMO.HTM page from the Bright Ideas Software home page, we might add an HTML line like this:

```
<A HREF="demo.htm#section1></A>
```

From a different server on your intranet, you would need to specify the full URL:

```
<A HREF="www.bright-ideas.com/demo.htm#section1></A>
```

CHANGING AN IMAGE REFERENCE WITHIN AN HTML DOCUMENT

In an earlier example, we saw how to change the <A HREF=> tag to modify where an HTML document points. This changes how the document works, but not how the document looks. We use the <IMG SRC=> tag to tell the browser which graphic image to display. Used with the <A HREF=> tag, the <IMG SRC=> tag lets us associate a graphic image as a button allowing us to place images on our pages and enhance the overall look. The standard Web client supports files in GIF or JPEG formats.

In our previous example, we added three URLs to link our document to three pages. However, we used the same graphic image (button.gif). Now, let's modify the same document to use different image files for these links. The file might look something like this:

```
<html>
<head>
<title>Test Page</title>
</head>
```

```
<body>
<img src = "spectbar.gif">
<br>
<A HREF="http://www.bright-ideas.com/sales/page1.htm"><IMG
    SRC="button1.gif">Page 1</A><p>
<A HREF="http://www.bright-ideas.com/sales/page2.htm"><IMG
    SRC="button2.gif" >Page 2</A><p>
<A HREF="http://www.bright-ideas.com/sales/page3.htm"><IMG
    SRC="button3.gif" >Page 3</A><p>
<A HREF="http://www.bright-ideas.com"><IMG SRC="home.gif" >
    Bright Ideas Software Home Page</A>
<P><center>This page Copyright&#169; 1996 by Bright Ideas
    Software, Inc.</center>
</body>
</html>
```

As you can see in Figure 7-3, a simple change was all that was needed to make the three existing URLs use three unique images. Again, this enhances the appearance of the page.

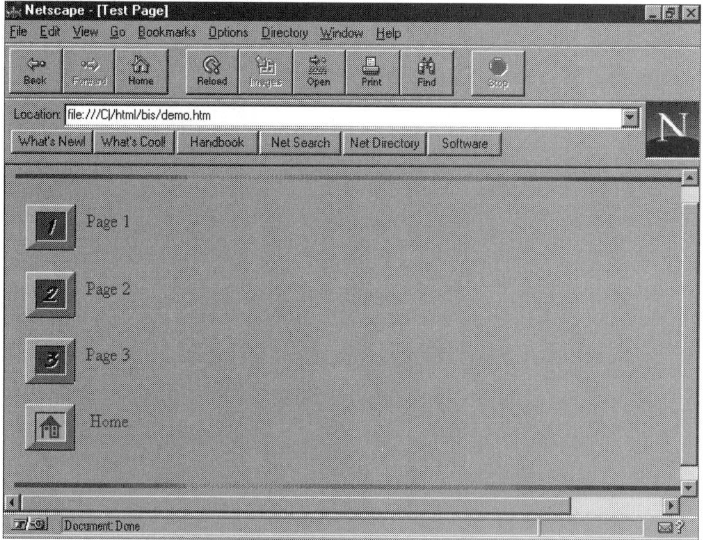

FIGURE *A Page in Which Three URLs Use Three Distinct Images*
7-3

You can also design your graphic images to contain text information. In this case, you can simplify your HTML document by removing the URL captions. Figure 7-4 shows a sample page that uses graphics for the URLs instead of HTML text links.

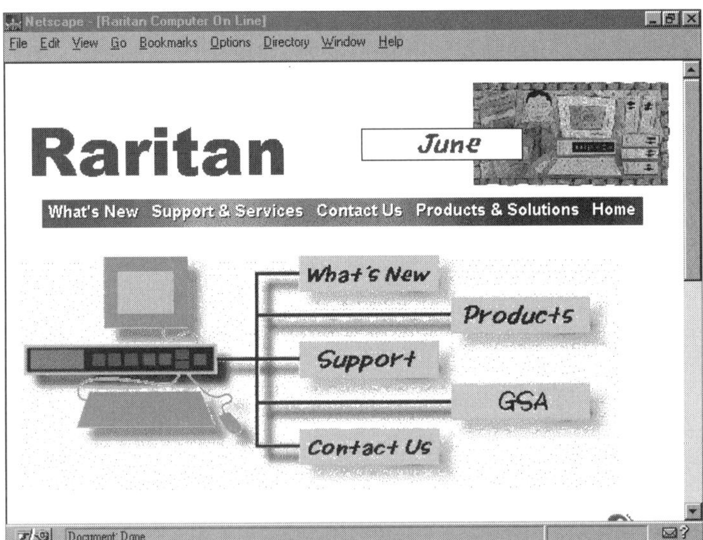

FIGURE 7-4 *A page that Uses Graphics to Represent URLs Instead of HTML Text Links*

Your overall sense of style plays a big part in how your pages look. In the previous examples, all our buttons were vertical. We could have easily oriented the buttons horizontally (as in Figure 7-5) or placed the buttons/links within a table (Figure 7-6 on page 132).

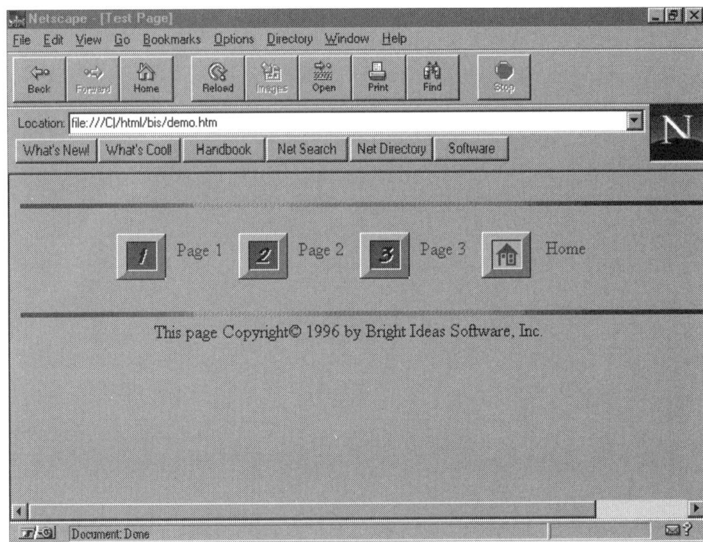

FIGURE 7-5 *Buttons Arranged Horizontally*

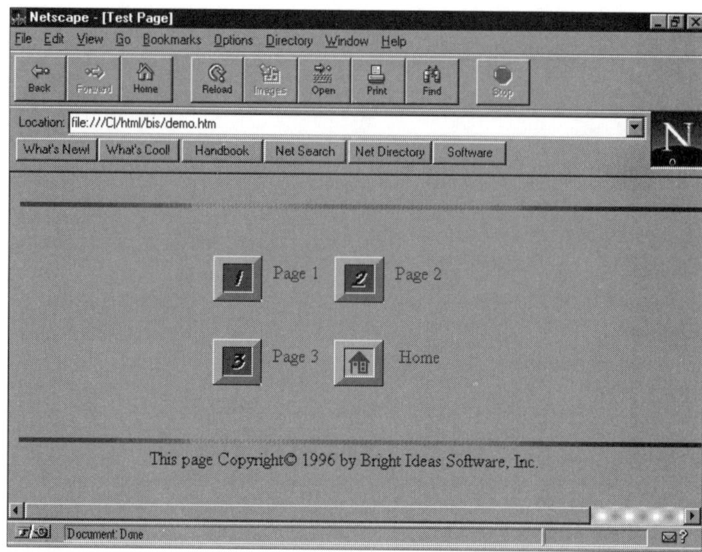

FIGURE *Buttons Arranged in a Table*
7-6

```
<html>
<head>
<title>Test Page</title>
</head>
<body>
<img src = "spectbar.gif">
<br>
<center>
<A HREF="http://www.bright-ideas.com/sales/page1.htm"><IMG SRC=
      "button1.gif" hspace=10 align="middle" border=0 >Page 1</A>
<A HREF="http://www.bright-ideas.com/sales/page2.htm"><IMG SRC=
      "button2.gif" hspace=10 align="middle" border=0 >Page 2</A>
<A HREF="http://www.bright-ideas.com/sales/page3.htm"><IMG SRC=
      "button3.gif" hspace=10 align="middle" border=0 >Page 3</A>
<A HREF="http://www.bright-ideas.com"><IMG SRC="home.gif"
      hspace=10 align="middle" border=0 > Home </A>
</center>
<P>
<img src = "spectbar.gif">
<center>This page Copyright&#169; 1996 by Bright Ideas Software,
Inc.</center>
</body>
</html>

<html>
<head>
<title>Test Page</title>
</head>
<body>
<img src = "spectbar.gif">
```

```
<br>
<CENTER>
<TABLE CELLPADDING=15 WIDTH="50%">
<TR>
<TD>
<A HREF="http://www.bright-ideas.com/sales/page1.htm"><IMG SRC=
    "button1.gif" hspace=10 align="middle" border=0 >Page 1</A>
<A HREF="http://www.bright-ideas.com/sales/page2.htm"><IMG SRC=
    "button2.gif" hspace=10 align="middle" border=0 >Page 2</A>
</TD></TR>
<TR><TD>
<A HREF="http://www.bright-ideas.com/sales/page3.htm"><IMG SRC=
    "button3.gif" hspace=10 align="middle" border=0 >Page 3</A>
<A HREF="http://www.bright-ideas.com"><IMG SRC="home.gif"
    hspace=10 align="middle" border=0 > Home </A>
</TD>
</TR>
</TABLE>
</CENTER>
<P>
<img src = "spectbar.gif">
<center>This page Copyright&#169; 1996 by Bright Ideas Software,
    Inc.</center>
</body>
</html>
```

Try to keep your graphic sizes small and manageable. Even though you have more bandwidth on your intranet than on the Internet, keeping page graphics small improves the overall network performance. Besides, large graphic files flying around your network may hinder your overall network operation.

CAVEATS FOR IMAGES

Here are some tips to keep in mind when you create images for your Web pages:

- Keep the images small in dimension (only a few inches by a few inches) and small in file size (less than 100KB is best; less than 25KB is better).
- Don't use too many images. Use only those images you need to convey necessary information.

- Don't just use images to "pretty" up a page. Images take time to download and detract from the overall effect of your page if they take a long time to display.
- Use the <ALT> tag for every image. Be considerate of users with inferior browsers.
- Upload images in "raw" mode. Make sure you reset the transfer mode for all ".GIF" files to "Raw data," or they will not upload correctly.

Transparent Images

The GIF images you create are "opaque," meaning they completely obscure the background behind them. It is also possible to create "transparent" GIF images (called GIF-89 format) in which one color of the image allows the background to show through.

Transparent images are useful if you do not want a large white rectangular border on the image, such as when you create an equation in an equation editor such as MathType, and then make a GIF image of the equation for your Web page. Figure 7-7 is an example of an image saved as a normal GIF, and then in GIF-89 format.

FIGURE 7-7 *On the left is a normal GIF file; the file on the right is in GIF-89 format, which makes the background color transparent.*

Notice the difference? The easiest way to create transparent images is with a graphics program such as Paint Shop Pro or Transparency. In Paintshop Pro, you set the transparent color for a GIF image from the GIF Transparency Options dialog box. When the image is displayed, the transparent color will be replaced by the display context.

For example, consider the image of a book against a white background, with its transparent color set to white. When the image is displayed against a gray fill, the white will be replaced by the gray, so the book appears against a gray background.

Imagemaps

The Common Gateway Interface (CGI) allows a Web server to interact with programs running on the remote computer. This interface allows the Web server and, thus the client browser to run remote programs and pass data to and from those programs. Examples include performing database searches and numerical calculations, generating new images, and processing HTML forms and imagemap output.

THE NCSA IMAGEMAP PROGRAM

The National Center for Supercomputer Applications (NCSA) version of imagemap is a fairly simple C program. It takes three pieces of input: the x and y coordinates of a mouse-click within an image, and the name of a special file called a "map." From this input, it returns to the WWW server (and, thus, the browser) one of a number of predefined files, usually other HTML files. For a user, this means you will see an image in a Web page. Clicking in different parts of that image will take you to other Web pages. Thus, an imagemap is a graphical set of links to other pages.

Most people like to use imagemaps as a "control panel" for providing access to other pages via snazzy graphics or buttons. Although these graphics look nice, they do nothing more than a simple text link would and often take a lot of time to download and display. Use your imagemaps sparingly.

To use imagemaps, you'll need at least two things:

- The NCSA imagemap program. Your Web server may use a slightly different version of this program. Whatever version or imagemap program works for you, it will usually be in the directory /CGI-BIN/. If you don't have a copy of imagemap, you may have to download the source code, which also means you need to compile the program. Your Web server must allow use of CGI programs.

- An image map editing program such as Mapedit for Windows or WebMap for the Macintosh. You can get WebMap from http://www.city.net/cnx/software/webmap.html.

Mapping an Image

Mapping an image consists of associating different clickable regions of the image with links to other pages. Regions within an image can be based on rectangles, circles, polygons, points, or a default background.

Clicking the mouse in one of these regions takes you to the specified Web page. If you've also specified a default link, clicking the mouse in the background of the image takes you to that page.

The Image MAP File

An image map file, which usually has the extension ".map," is a text file that describes regions within an image and the URLs of pages to link them to. The imagemap program reads this file when it processes the mouse-click and uses the region definitions to find the region (if any) that contains the mouse-click. The program then returns a reference to the URL associated with the region, and the server delivers that page.

Creating an Imagemap

You need a GIF file to lay out your imagemap. You can use any GIF image to create your imagemap. The following image (Figure 7-8) is used for this example, as it can be divided into regions:

FIGURE 7-8 *A GIF Image Used to Create an Imagemap*

Create a MAP File for the Image

Start the program and open the GIF file you want to map. The following example uses the Mapedit program. If you are using a different imagemap creation program, your steps may differ slightly. With Mapedit, you will see the screen shown in Figure 7-9.

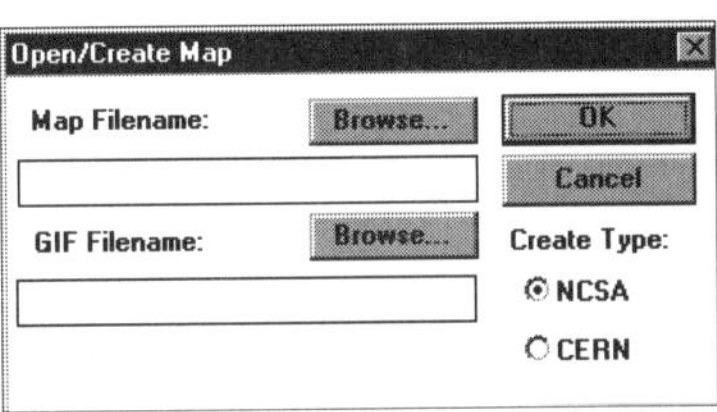

FIGURE 7-9   *A Screen Created with Mapedit*

Fill in the map filename and the GIF filename fields. You can use the *Browse* buttons to locate your GIF files and your MAP file (if you are editing an existing imagemap).

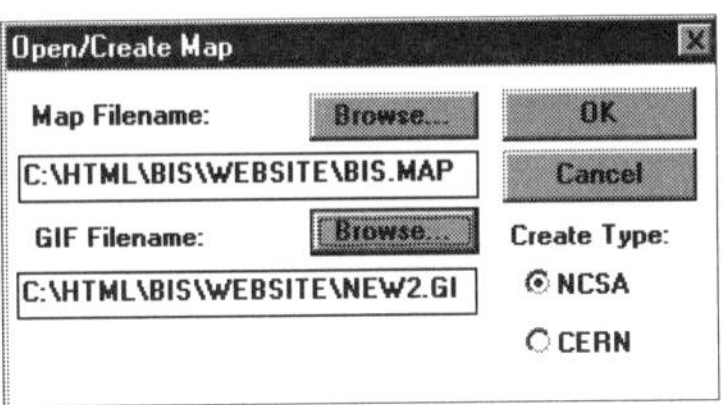

FIGURE 7-10   *Using the Browse Buttons to Locate GIF and MAP Files*

Click on the OK button when you are ready to continue. If you are creating a new MAP file, Mapedit responds with a dialog box stating that the map file does not exist. It then asks you if you would like to create it now. Click on *OK* to continue.

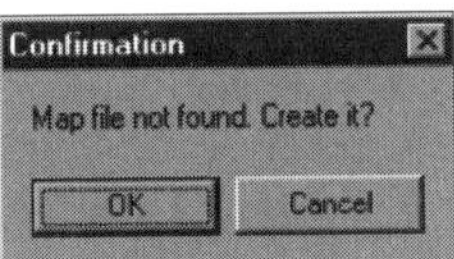

FIGURE 7-11   *Mapedit Dialog Box if the MAP File Does Not Exist*

Mapedit now loads your specified .GIF image into the window. From the tools menu, select the desired "shape" for the region you want to create. In this example, we will be creating rectangular regions over the text on the lower right side of the image.

FIGURE 7-12 *The Mapedit Tools Menu*

Once you have selected the tool, move your mouse to the start of the region. Click the left mouse button once to begin to define the region. Drag the mouse over the region. Notice the tool shape you selected will begin to be outlined as you drag your mouse. When the region shape is right, click the right mouse button. The following screen will be displayed:

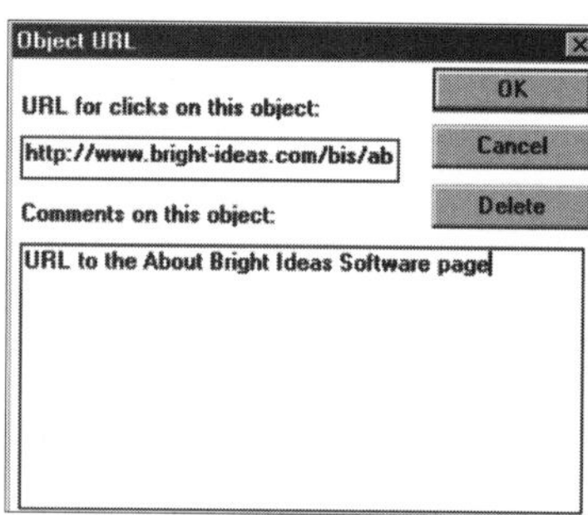

FIGURE 7-13 *Defining the Region's Shape*

Enter the desired URL information for this region. You may also provide an optional description for this region, as well. Click on *OK* when finished. Repeat this procedure for all the regions on your image. When you are finished defining regions on this image, click on the *File* menu and select the *Save* option.

Sample .MAP File

```
default http://www.bright-ideas.com/index.html
rect http://www.bright-ideas.com/bis/about.htm 295,149 387,180
rect http://www.bright-ideas.com/bis/service.htm 269,187 387,218
rect http://www.bright-ideas.com/bis/consult.htm 233,224 387,252
rect http://www.bright-ideas.com/bis/dev.htm 210,257 387,291
```

Create an Imagemap Page

Use the HTML code below as a template to create a starting page for your imagemap links:

```
<html>
<head><title>Imagemap Test Page</title></head>
<body>
<br>
<h1>Imagemap Test </h1>
<h3>Click on a part of the image below:</h3>

<a href="http://your.server.name/cgi-bin/imagemap/your map file
location ">
<img src="your map image location" ismap></a><p>

</body>
</html>
```

Add the imagemap .map link. Note the following lines in the HTML source code for this page:

```
<a href="http://your.server.name/cgi-bin/imagemap/your map file
location ">
<img src="your map image location" ismap></a><p>
```

The link tag <HREF> consists of two parts:

```
http://your.server.name/cgi-bin/imagemap and your map file location
```

The first part tells the server the name of the program to link to (in this case, the NCSA imagemap program in the /CGI-BIN/ directory). The second part of this link is the name of the map file imagemap should use to perform mapping for the image. This part of the <HREF> is passed to the imagemap program by the server.

Now edit this URL to replace "your.server.com" with the name of your Web server. This format is the "new" mapping syntax for the imagemap. You must specify the complete pathname of the map file you want to use. You may also specify the path relative to your PUBLIC_HTML directory.

In addition, you should note the "ismap" keyword in the <IMG> tag for the map1.gif file. This tells the browser to send the coordinates of a mouse-click in the image along with the map filename when it calls the imagemap program. Your browser must, of course, support the ismap keyword.

If your pages don't work, check the following:

- Your server can run the imagemap program, and the program is the latest version.
- Your server allows CGI programs.
- You have correctly uploaded all your pages.
- The permissions are set correctly for all your pages (everyone should have read permission).
- You have created your MAP file, and the region definitions in it are correct.
- You have used the correct link to the imagemap program and have specified the map file according to the "new" format.
- You have used the "ismap" keyword in your image, and your browser supports this keyword.

SUMMARY

In this chapter, you learned how to do some of the Web page maintenance tasks a web master may need to perform on an ongoing basis. This chapter came about from clients of mine, who wanted to be able to maintain Web pages that I had created for them. These tasks, such as adding a URL to an existing page or modifying a page link, are commonplace, but can be confusing to a novice Webmaster. They are tasks that you may inherit when your Webmaster goes on vacation.

8 Common Gateway Interface

CONTENTS

The Common Gateway Interface (CGI) has emerged as the standard for interfacing external applications with information servers, such as HTTP (Web) servers. An HTML document that is retrieved by HTTP is static: It is a text file that doesn't change. On the other hand, a CGI program is executed in real time and can output dynamic information.

Internet (or intranet) access to a corporate database from the Web is a good example. To accomplish this, you need to create a CGI program that executes on the HTTP server to transmit information to the database engine, receive the results, and display them to the client. The database example is a simple idea, but not a simple one to implement.

There is essentially no limit as to what you can interface to from the Web. Keep in mind that whatever your CGI program does, it should not take too long to process. Otherwise, the user will just be staring at their browser waiting for something to happen.

CGI SPECIFICS

Because a CGI program is executable, it is equivalent to letting your clients run a program on your server. This poses a potential security problem, and, thus, there are security precautions you need to implement when using CGI programs. The most common issue is that CGI programs need to reside in a special directory so the Web server knows to execute the program instead of displaying it in the browser. In most configurations, the Webmaster or systems administrator maintains control of this directory. This prohibits the average user from creating CGI programs.

Depending on your Web server, you might have a directory called /CGI-BIN. This is the directory mentioned above where all your CGI programs reside. A CGI program can be written in any language that allows it to be executed on the system, such as:

- AppleScript
- C++

- Fortran
- PERL
- TCL
- UNIX shell
- Visual Basic

The language you use depends on what you have available on your system and what CGI or APIs are supported by your system. If you use a programming language such as C or Fortran, you are familiar with the concept of compiling the program before you can execute it. If you look in the /CGI-SRC directory that came with your server (or its equivalent), you will find the source code for some of the CGI programs. However, if you use one of the scripting languages (PERL, TCL, or a UNIX shell), only the script needs to reside in the /CGI-BIN directory, as there is no associated source code. CGI scripts are easier to debug, modify, and maintain than a typical compiled program.

Fill-Out Forms　　　The most common application of CGI scripting is the creation and processing of fill-out forms, often an HTML document with specific tags your server parses through a CGI gateway.

The CGI gateway is called through a POST or GET command, which is passed from the HTML document. Once the server parses the document to the CGI engine, the various information that was entered into the form is parsed and acted on.

Just as you created other HTML documents, you must include special CGI-specific tags in your Web page to identify it as a fill-out form and so your CGI gateway will understand how to process the information.

THE FILL-OUT FORM TAGS (The <FORM> Tag)

The <FORM> tag specifies a fill-out form within an HTML document. More than one fill-out form can be in a single document, but forms cannot be nested.

```
<FORM ACTION="url"> ... </FORM>
```

The attributes are as follows:

- ><ACTION is the URL of the query server to which the form contents are submitted; if this attribute is absent, the current document URL is used.
- <METHOD> is the HTTP method used to submit the fill-out form to a query server. Which method you use depends on how your particular server works; however, the <POST> method is the most recommended method. The valid choices are:
- <GET> — This is the default method and causes the fill-out form contents to be appended to the URL as if they were a normal query.
- <POST> — This method causes the fill-out form contents to be sent to the server in a data body rather than as part of the URL.

```
<FORM METHOD="POST" ACTION="http://www.myserv.com/cgi-bin/post-query">
```

- <ENCTYPE> specifies the MIME encoding for the fill-out form contents. This attribute applies only if <METHOD> has been set to <POST>. <ENCTYPE> currently has only one value which is *application/x-www-form-urlencoded*.

Inside a <FORM>, you can have anything except another <FORM>. Specifically, <INPUT>, <SELECT>, and <TEXTAREA> tags are used to specify interface elements within the form.

Forms are not automatically visually differentiated from any other portion of an HTML document. You should consider using the <HR> (horizontal rule) tag before and after a form to differentiate it from surrounding text and/or other forms.

The `<INPUT>` Tag

The <INPUT> tag is used to specify a simple input element inside a <FORM>. It is a standalone tag; it does not surround anything and there is no terminating tag. In many ways, it is used in much the same way as the <IMG> tag.

Various types of <INPUT> tags are displayed as widgets (text entry fields, toggle buttons, pushbuttons, etc.).

The attributes of <INPUT> are as follows:
<TYPE> must be one of the following:

- "text" (text entry field; this is the default)
- "password" (text entry field; entered characters are represented as asterisks)
- "checkbox" (a single toggle button; on or off)
- "radio" (a single toggle button; on or off; other toggles with the same name are grouped into "one of many" behavior)
- "submit" (a pushbutton that causes the current form to be packaged up into a query URL and sent to a remote server)

```
<INPUT TYPE="submit" VALUE="Submit Query">
```

- "reset" (a pushbutton that causes the various input elements in the form to be reset to their default values)

```
<INPUT TYPE="reset" VALUE="Reset To Default Values">
```

- <NAME> is the symbolic name, not a displayed name (normal HTML within the form is used for that purpose) for this input field. This must be present for all types except "submit" and "reset." <NAME> is used when putting together the query string to send to the remote server when the filled-out form is submitted.

```
<INPUT NAME="entry1" VALUE="Sample Text">
```

- <VALUE>, for a text or password entry field, can be used to specify the default contents of the field. For a checkbox or radio button, <VALUE> specifies the value of the button when it is checked (unchecked checkboxes are disregarded when submitting queries); the default value for a checkbox or radio button is "on." For types "submit" and "reset," <VALUE> can be used to specify the label for the pushbutton.
- <CHECKED> (no value needed) specifies that this checkbox or radio button is checked by default; this is appropriate only for checkboxes and radio buttons.

```
<INPUT TYPE="checkbox" NAME="box1" VALUE="activated" CHECKED>
```

- <SIZE> is the physical size of the input field in characters; this is appropriate only for text entry fields and password entry fields. If this is not present, the default is 20. Multiline text entry fields can be specified as <SIZE=width, height>; e.g., <SIZE=60,12>.

Note: The SIZE attribute should not be used to specify multiline text entry fields because the <TEXTAREA> tag is available and is better suited for this purpose.

- <MAXLENGTH> is the maximum number of characters that will be accepted as input. The <MAXLENGTH> tag is appropriate only for text entry fields and password entry fields (basically, only for single-line text entry fields). If this is not present, the default is unlimited. The text entry field is assumed to scroll appropriately if <MAXLENGTH> is greater than <SIZE>.

The <SELECT> Tag

Inside <FORM> ... </FORM>, any number of <SELECT> tags are allowed, freely intermixed with other HTML elements (including <INPUT> and <TEXTAREA> elements) and text (but not additional forms). <SELECT> tags are displayed as option menus and scrolled lists.

Unlike <INPUT>, <SELECT> has both opening and closing tags. Inside <SELECT>, only a sequence of <OPTION> tags, each followed by an arbitrary amount of plain text and no HTML markup, is allowed.

```
<SELECT NAME="Fruit of the Month">
<OPTION> Apple
<OPTION> Orange
<OPTION> Peach
<OPTION> Plum
<OPTION> Pineapple
<OPTION> Watermelon
<OPTION> Pear
</SELECT>
```

The attributes of <SELECT> are as follows:

- <NAME> is the symbolic name for this <SELECT> element. This must be present, as it is used when putting together the query string for the submitted form.
- If <SIZE> is 1 or if the <SIZE> attribute is missing, <SELECT> is represented as the default option menu. If <SIZE> is 2 or more, <SELECT> is represented as a scrolled list; the value of <SIZE> then determines how many items are visible.

- <MULTIPLE>, if present (no value), specifies that <SELECT> should allow multiple selections (n of many behavior). <MULTIPLE> forces <SELECT> to be represented as a scrolled list, regardless of the value of <SIZE>.

The <OPTION> Tag

The attributes to <OPTION> are as follows:

- <SELECTED> specifies that this option is selected by default. If <SELECT> allows multiple selections (via the <MULTIPLE> attribute), multiple options can be specified as <SELECTED>.

The <TEXTAREA> Tag

The <TEXTAREA> tag can be used to place a multiline text entry field with optional default contents in a fill-out form. The attributes of <TEXTAREA> are as follows:

- <NAME> is the symbolic name of the text entry field.
- <ROWS> is the number of rows (vertical height in characters) of the text entry field.
- <COLS> is the number of columns (horizontal width in characters) of the text entry field.

<TEXTAREA> fields automatically have scrollbars; any amount of text can be entered in them. The <TEXTAREA> element requires an opening and a closing tag. A <TEXTAREA> tag with no default contents looks like this:

```
<TEXTAREA NAME="foobar" ROWS=5 COLS=20></TEXTAREA>
```

A <TEXTAREA> tag with default contents looks like this:

```
<TEXTAREA NAME="foobar" ROWS=5 COLS=20>
Default contents go here.
</TEXTAREA>
```

The default contents must be straight ASCII text. Newlines are respected. In the above example, there is a newline before and after "Default contents go here."

Form Submission

FOR <METHOD=GET

If your form has <METHOD="GET"> in its <FORM> tag, your CGI program receives the encoded form input in the environment variable QUERY_STRING. When the submit button is pressed, the contents of the form are assembled into a query URL that looks like this:

```
action?name=value&name=value&name=value
```

In this example, "action" is the URL specified by the <ACTION> attribute to the <FORM> tag, or the current document URL if no <ACTION> attribute was specified.

Strange characters in any of the "name" or "value" instances are escaped as usual; this includes "=" and "&."

Note: This means instances of "=" that separate names and values, and instances of "&" that separate name/value pairs, are not escaped. For text and password entry fields, whatever the user entered is the value; if the user didn't enter anything, the value is empty, but the "name=" part of the query string is still present. For checkboxes and radio buttons, the <VALUE> attribute specifies the value of a checkbox or radio button when it is checked. An unchecked checkbox is disregarded completely when assembling the query string. Multiple checkboxes can have the same <NAME> (and different <VALUEs>), if desired. Multiple radio buttons intended to have "one of many" behavior should have the same <NAME> and different <VALUEs>.

FOR <METHOD=POST>

If your form has <METHOD="POST"> in its <FORM> tag, your CGI program receives the encoded form input on STDIN. The server does not send you an EOF on the end of the data. Instead, you should use the environment variable CONTENT_LENGTH to determine how much data you should read from STDIN.

The contents of the form are encoded exactly as with the <GET> method (mentioned earlier), but rather than appending them to the URL specified by the form's <ACTION> attribute as a query, the contents are sent in a data block as part of the <POST> operation. The <ACTION> attribute is the URL to which the data block is <POSTed>.

Decoding the Form Data

When you write a form, each of your input items has a <NAME> tag. When a user places data in these items in the form, that information is encoded into the form data. The value each of the input items is given by the user is called the value.

Form data is a stream of *name=value* pairs separated by the & character. Each *name=value* pair is URL-encoded. That is to say, spaces are changed into pluses and some characters are encoded into hexadecimal.

The basic procedure is to split the data by the ampersands. Then, for each *name=value* pair you get, you should URL-decode the name and then the value, and process them. This is the job of your CGI gateway parser.

PERL SCRIPT FOR FORM PARSER

```
#!/usr/bin/perl — -*- C -*-

# Define Variables
$date = `/usr/bin/date`; chop($date);
$mailprog = 'sendmail';
$recipient = 'yourname@yourhost.com';

# Get the input
read(STDIN, $buffer, $ENV{'CONTENT_LENGTH'});

# Split the name-value pairs
@pairs = split(/&/, $buffer);

foreach $pair (@pairs){
   ($name, $value) = split(/=/, $pair);

   $value =~ tr/+/ /;
   $value =~ s/%([a-fA-F0-9][a-fA-F0-9])/pack("C", hex($1))/eg;
   $name =~ tr/+/ /;
   $name =~ s/%([a-fA-F0-9][a-fA-F0-9])/pack("C", hex($1))/eg;

   $FORM{$name} = $value;
}

if ($FORM{'redirect'}) {
   print "Location: $FORM{'redirect'}\n\n";
}
else {
```

```perl
        # Print Return HTML
        print "Content-type: text/html\n\n";
        print "<html><head><title>Thanks You</title></head>\n";
        print "<body bgcolor=#FFFFFF><h1>Thank You for your
          submission</h1>\n";
        print "Below is what you submitted to us:\n";
}


# Open The Mail
open(MAIL, "|$mailprog $recipient $FORM{'email'} $FORM{'name'}") || die
     "Can't open $mailprog!\n";
print MAIL "To: $FORM{'recipient'}\n";
print MAIL "From: $FORM{'email'} ($FORM{'realname'})\n";
if ($FORM{'subject'}) {
    print MAIL "Subject: $FORM{'subject'}\n\n";
}
else {
    print MAIL "Subject: WWW Form Submission\n\n";
}
print MAIL "Below is the result of your feedback form. It was\n";
print MAIL "submitted by $FORM{'realname'} ($FORM{'email'}) on $date\n";


foreach $pair (@pairs) {
    ($name, $value) = split(/=/, $pair);

    $value =~ tr/+/ /;
    $value =~ s/%([a-fA-F0-9][a-fA-F0-9])/pack("C", hex($1))/eg;
    $name =~ tr/+/ /;
    $name =~ s/%([a-fA-F0-9][a-fA-F0-9])/pack("C", hex($1))/eg;

    $FORM{$name} = $value;
    unless ($name eq 'recipient' || $name eq 'subject' || $name eq
      'email' || $name eq 'realname' || $name eq 'redirect') {
        # Print the MAIL for each name value pair
        if ($value ne "") {
            print MAIL "$name:  $value\n";
            print "<br>\n";
              }

        unless ($FORM{'redirect'}) {
           if ($value ne "") {
               print "$name = $value\n";
           }
         }
      }
}
close (MAIL);

unless ($FORM{'redirect'}) {
print "<p><a href='http://www.yourserver.com/somepage.htm'>";
print "Return to the Home Page</a> <HR size=4>\n";
print "</body></html>";
}
```

In the previous code sample, you need to replace the following variables with information specific to your Web server, mail address, and home page:

$mailprog = 'sendmail';	Replace with the name and location of your e-mail program
$recipient = 'yourname@yourhost.com';	Replace with your full e-mail address, or the name and address of the user you want to receive this form submission
www.yourserver.com/somepage.htm	Replace with the HTML link you want the user to return to

The Form Parser works in the following manner:

1. This section of code reads in the form:

```
# Get the input
read(STDIN, $buffer, $ENV{'CONTENT_LENGTH'});
```

2. This section of code breaks up the data that was just read into name-value pairs:

```
# Split the name-value pairs
@pairs = split(/&/, $buffer);

foreach $pair (@pairs){
   ($name, $value) = split(/=/, $pair);

   $value =~ tr/+/ /;
   $value =~ s/%([a-fA-F0-9][a-fA-F0-9])/pack("C", hex($1))/eg;
   $name =~ tr/+/ /;
   $name =~ s/%([a-fA-F0-9][a-fA-F0-9])/pack("C", hex($1))/eg;

   $FORM{$name} = $value;
}
```

3. This section of code sends the contents of the form to your mail program, and fills in some of the default mail fields:

```
# Open The Mail
open(MAIL, "|$mailprog $recipient $FORM{'email'} $FORM{'name'}")
    || die "Can't open $mailprog!\n";
```

```perl
print MAIL "To: $FORM{'recipient'}\n";
print MAIL "From: $FORM{'email'} ($FORM{'realname'})\n";
if ($FORM{'subject'}) {
   print MAIL "Subject: $FORM{'subject'}\n\n";
```

4. This portion of code displays the information you submitted, and writes it into the body of the mail message:

```perl
foreach $pair (@pairs) {
   ($name, $value) = split(/=/, $pair);

   $value =~ tr/+/ /;
   $value =~ s/%([a-fA-F0-9][a-fA-F0-9])/pack("C", hex($1))/eg;
   $name =~ tr/+/ /;
   $name =~ s/%([a-fA-F0-9][a-fA-F0-9])/pack("C", hex($1))/eg;

   $FORM{$name} = $value;
   unless ($name eq 'recipient' || $name eq 'subject' || $name eq
    'email' || $name eq 'realname' || $name eq 'redirect') {
      # Print the MAIL for each name value pair
      if ($value ne "") {
         print MAIL "$name:   $value\n";
         print "<br>\n";
            }

      unless ($FORM{'redirect'}) {
         if ($value ne "") {
            print "$name = $value\n";
         }
      }
   }
}
close (MAIL);
```

5. Finally, this section displays the HTML to link the user to another hypertext document:

```perl
unless ($FORM{'redirect'}) {
print "<p><a href='http://www.yourserver.com/somepage.htm'>";
print "Return to the Home Page</a> <HR size=4>\n";
print "</body></html>";
}
```

Any line you want to print, must be preceded by a print statement and enclosed in quotes. In addition, any portion of your HTML code you want to generate via the CGI parser, and which is normally enclosed in double-quotes, must be enclosed in single-quotes. You will also notice that you insert an end-of-line character manually, by adding a \n before the end-quotation in the print statement.

CGI is virtually the only mechanism on the Web to obtain and process information from your users. As Internet and intranet technologies develop, you will see more emerging techniques and utilities to make your Web applications more interactive. To this end, two of the best Web-enabled technologies available, which require no CGI programming to develop interactive applications, are Lotus Notes and Domino.

However, if you plan on doing any Perl or CGI programming, you should obtain some good reference books on the subject. Two excellent books include *CGI Programming on the World Wide Web*, by Shishir Gundavaram, published by O'Reilly & Associates and *HTMI & CGI Unleashed*, by John December and Mark Ginsburg from SamsNet. You might also consider picking up a copy of *Learning Perl*, by Randal Schwartz, also published by O'Reilly & Associates.

9 New Toys

CONTENTS

A new class of software has emerged, driven entirely by the prolif-eration of the World Wide Web. This software is almost exclu-sively for the enhancement of basic Web document and server functionality. As you know, HTML documents are static and flat. You can add CGI scripts and programs to improve the interactivity of your Web pages, but CGI has its limitations and problems.

In an effort to accentuate the basic functionality of Web pages, a new breed of applications and programming tools was born. These applica-tions are designed to fill in the gaps left by HTML and CGI. These new software tools allow you to view different file formats, add animation, and even link to legacy systems from within your HTML documents. This chapter explores some of these applications and discusses how to integrate them into your Web pages.

JAVA

Java is a programming language, much like C++, which was developed by Sun Microsystems. According to Sun, Java is "a simple, object-ori-ented, distributed, interpreted, robust, secure, architecture-neutral, portable, high-performance, multithreaded, dynamic, buzzword-compli-ant, general-purpose programming language. Java supports program-ming for the Internet in the form of platform-independent Java applets."

So what does that mean to us? Java is a relatively simple language to learn and implement. Programmers who have experience in C and C++ can rapidly learn and develop Java programs. Java is secure. Even though users are actually running short Java programs on your server, Java inher-ently discourages mischievous hackers from destroying your system.

Java is platform-independent. This means you can run the same applet from any machine: IBM PC, Macintosh, or UNIX. Unlike CGI applica-tions, Java programs are highly interactive. CGI scripts usually require a great deal of user action, a.k.a., the "submit" button. With Java, users sim-ply place the mouse over an image and click or use keys on the keyboard.

Feedback is almost immediate and the user no longer has to deal with a series of page reloads.

Java's platform-independence builds on users being able to access the World Wide Web using different types of machines and Web browsers, but still see the same information in nearly the same format.

Java's greatest asset is its user interaction. A small Java applet inserted into a long, complex Web document can give a user a much-needed graphical illustration or diversion. Depending on how the applet was written, users may be able to change parameters within the Java applet. This is very useful in applications where it is important to immediately see the effect the change creates.

Java can be used to actually show how things work, as opposed to static HTML documents, which only describe what's happening.

Java programs, more commonly referred to as "applets," like any C or C++ program, must be compiled after they are written. Once the applet has been compiled, it can go into any HTTP server in any directory that can serve Web documents. The only special software needed is a Web browser that will interpret Java applets. The server where the applet is stored treats it as any other file. The applet is interpreted on the client side by the user's Web browser.

Sample Java Applets	**JAVA ANIMATOR** The following applet displays a spinning graphic on a Java-enabled browser. This is a good, overall applet to help jazz up a Web page. This applet uses the Java Animator Class and assumes the images to be animated are named T1 .. Tx.

```
<applet code=Animator.class width=200 height=200>
<param name=imagesource value="images/voe">
<param name=startimage value=1>
<param name=endimage value=16>
<param name=pause value=100>
</applet>
```

The Java Animator Class can be obtained from the Sun Microsystems Java Web site (www.sun.com).

The images for this animation consist of 16 separate .GIF files, which produce a flip-book-style animation of a spinning logo on the screen. Notice that line one of our Java HTML code starts with the <APPLET> tag and specifies the Java class being called.

Java code begins and ends with the <APPLET> ... </APPLET> tags. Within the framework of these tags, your Java applet will have parameter tags that, depending on the applet, allow you to specify different values that affect the performance and operation of the applet.

For the Animator Class, the parameters control the location of the image files, the start image, the ending image, and the delay or pause between images. The applet class parameter even allows control over the image display area.

You can reuse this Java application within your Web pages. Simply replace the GIF images with your own. Remember that this applet assumes the GIF files will be named T1 through the last image (Tx).

JavaScript

JavaScript is a new scripting language developed by Netscape. According to Netscape:

"JavaScript is a compact, object-based scripting language for developing client and server Internet applications. Netscape Navigator 2.0 interprets JavaScript statements embedded directly in an HTML page, and LiveWire enables you to create server-based applications similar to Common Gateway Interface (CGI) programs.

"In a client application for Navigator, JavaScript statements embedded in an HTML page can recognize and respond to user events such as mouse clicks, form input, and page navigation.

"For example, you can write a JavaScript function to verify that users enter valid information into a form requesting a telephone number or zip code. Without any network transmission, an HTML page with embedded JavaScript can interpret the entered text and alert the user with a message dialog if the input is invalid. Or you can use JavaScript to perform an action (such as play an audio file, execute an applet, or communicate with a plug-in) in response to the user opening or exiting a page."

Although JavaScript can be used to drive many events that occur when a user interacts with an HTML page, it is most useful in place of or in combination with more traditional CGI and forms environments.

JavaScript code is often placed within the HTML code of the page on which it will appear. Unlike Java applets, JavaScript is not compiled. Because the interpretation and actual running of the program occur on the client side, you do not need any special server consideration or settings to serve JavaScript. The only special software needed is a Web browser that will interpret JavaScript.

JavaScript Applet

The following JavaScript applet displays a scrolling message along the bottom of the Netscape Navigator 2.0 (or higher) status bar.

```
 1. <html>
 2. <head>
 3. <title>JAVA APPLET #1: Scrolling Messages on the Status
    bar</title>
 4. <SCRIPT LANGUAGE="JavaScript">
 5. function scrollit_r2l(seed)
 6. {
 7. var m1 = "  ";
 8. var m2 = "  ";
 9. var m3 = "  ";
10. var m4 = "  ";
11. var m5 = "  ";
12. var msg=m1+m2+m3+m4+m5;
13. var out = "  ";
14. var c = 1;
15. if (seed > 100) {
16. seed--;
17. var cmd="scrollit_r2l(" + seed + ")";
18. timerTwo=window.setTimeout(cmd,100);
19. }
20. else if (seed <= 100 && seed > 0) {
21. for (c=0 ; c < seed ; c++) {
22. out+=" ";
23. }
24. out+=msg;
25. seed--;
26. var cmd="scrollit_r2l(" + seed + ")";
27. window.status=out;
28. timerTwo=window.setTimeout(cmd,100);
29. }
30. else if (seed <= 0) {
```

```
31.  if (-seed < msg.length) {
32.  out+=msg.substring(-seed,msg.length);
33.  seed-;
34.  var cmd="scrollit_r21(" + seed + ")";
35.  window.status=out;
36.  timerTwo=window.setTimeout(cmd,100);
37.  }
38.  else {
39.  window.status=" ";
40.  timerTwo=window.setTimeout("scrollit_r21(100)",75);
41.  }
42.  }
43.  }
44.  // - End of JavaScript code --------- ->
45.  </SCRIPT>
46.  </head>
47.  <body onLoad="timerONE=window.setTimeout
     ('scrollit_r21(100)',500);">
48.  </html>
```

Note: The line numbering is included for reference only. If you are going to enter this Java applet, do not include the line numbers.

How to Use This Applet

Line 47 is a critical line. This is part of the body section of your HTML document and must include these parameters and variables, or the applet will not function. You can also include standard body extensions, such as background color, background graphics, text, and link colors.

Lines 7 thru 11 hold the text message you want to have scrolled across the status bar. You may add more lines of text, but you must use a unique variable name for each line, and you must remember to include this variable name on line 12.

A sample of how text might look within this applet is as follows:

```
1.  var m1 = "Hello, and Welcome to Company XYZ's Intranet!";
2.  var m2 = "The Cafeteria will close today at 2:00, for
    repairs.";
3.  var m3 = "Congratulations to Manufacturing for shattering
    last month's production record!";
4.  var m4 = " ";
5.  var m5 = "Today we announce our latest product to the world...";
```

In the previous example, line 4 was used as a spacer to provide a "pause" between messages on the screen. You can use as many of these lines as you need. You are limited to 256 characters per line (total, not just within the parentheses).

Applications

Here are some examples of the types of information that can be put on your company's intranet:

1. Message of the Day
2. Corporate Mission Statement
3. New Product Announcements
4. Sales Promotions
5. Employee Announcements: "Today is Jim's Birthday!"

Why Use JavaScript?

There are some substantial differences between Java and JavaScript. The techniques used in Java and JavaScript differ — JavaScript is a scripting language, and Java is a programming language. JavaScript does not have Java's static typing and strong type checking, although it supports most of Java's expression syntax and basic control flow constructs.

Java is an object-oriented programming (OOP) language similar to C++, which is capable of creating traditional standalone applications that can be embedded within a Web page. When a Java application is embedded within a Web page, it is know as an "applet". These applets are compiled into byte code on the server and then run within the client's browser. The process of writing and compiling an applet can be difficult without previous programming experience. Table 9-1 shows the similarities and differences between JavaScript and Java.

Java programs consist exclusively of classes and their methods. Java's requirements for declaring classes, writing methods, and ensuring type safety make programming more complex than JavaScript authoring. Java's inheritance and strong typing also tend to require tightly coupled object hierarchies.

In contrast, JavaScript descends in spirit from a line of smaller, dynamically typed languages such as HyperTalk and dBASE. These scripting languages offer programming tools to a much wider audience because of their easier syntax, specialized built-in functionality, and minimal requirements for object creation. This makes JavaScript the more likely candidate for novice programmers.

Table 9-1. A Comparison of JavaScript and Java

JavaScript	Java
Interpreted (not compiled) by client.	Compiled on server before execution on client.
Object-based. Code uses built-in, extensible objects, but no classes or inheritance.	Object-oriented. Applets consist of object classes with inheritance.
Code integrated with, and embedded in, HTML.	Applets distinct from HTML (accessed from HTML pages).
Variable data types not declared (loose typing).	Variable data types must be declared (strong typing).
Dynamic binding. Object references checked at run time.	Static binding. Object references must exist at compile time.
Secure. Cannot write to hard disk.	Secure. Cannot write to hard disk.

This capability also makes JavaScript more portable because the code is linked directly into the HTML document. When you download an HTML document, you get the entire JavaScript source code, not a pre-compiled applet. Because JavaScript is not compiled, you can make changes to the script and see the results considerably faster than with Java. With Java, you must re-compile your applet every time you make a change.

Because JavaScript is embedded in the HTML document, sharing new JavaScript applications is easy. When you save the document source code from within your Web browser, you now have a copy of the JavaScript source code. You can include this functionality into your HTML documents. In addition, you can borrow from this source code and modify the JavaScript application to suit your needs. This makes it possible for developers to learn by example and to eventually write bigger and better JavaScript programs.

GIF89A

If you are just looking to spruce up a Web page and you don't want to add sound to your video, try the GIF89a specification instead of Video for Windows or Quicktime. GIF89a is a graphics file that can contain multiple frames. The specification includes frame rate, support for transparency and overlays, pushbutton actions, and more.

Understanding GIF89a	The GIF image format uses a built-in LZW compression algorithm, which is patented and currently owned by Unisys Corp. As of 1995, Unisys decided that commercial vendors, whose products use GIF LZW compression, must license its use from Unisys. Users, online services, and nonprofit organizations do not pay this royalty. Since its inception, GIF has been a royalty-free format. Only as of 1995 did Unisys decide to collect royalties. To avoid this royalty, vendors have developed an alternative to GIF called GIF87a that supports transparency and interlacing called PNG ("ping"), the Portable Network Graphic.

The predecessor of GIF89a, GIF87a, was released in 1987. GI87a allowed the following features:

- LZW-compressed images;
- multiple images encoded within a single file;
- positioning of the images on a logical screen area; and
- interlacing.

This means that nine years ago, it was possible to do simple animation with GIFs by encoding multiple images, what we will refer to as "frames," in a single file. GIF89a is an extension of the GIF87a specification, which does the following:

- adds the number of 100ths of a second to wait before displaying the next frame;
- waits for user input;
- specifies transparent color;
- includes unprintable comments;
- displays lines of text;
- indicates how the frame should be removed after it has been displayed; and
- supports application-specific extensions encoded inside the file.

Netscape Navigator is the only browser than comes close to full GIF89a compliance. The display lines of text and wait for user input options are not currently supported in Netscape Navigator 2.0, and the image removal function doesn't support removal by the previous image. Most browsers support single-image GIF87a and recognize the transparency flag of GIF89a and nothing else.

GIF89a is still a 256-color maximum format. GIF allows for any number of colors between 2 and 256. The fewer colors used, the less data needed and the smaller the graphic files will be. If your GIF uses only four colors, you can reduce the palette to only two bits (4-color) and decrease the file size by at least 75 percent.

Structure of a GIF89a Animation File	GIF89a animation files have the following format: GIF89A HEADER LOGICAL SCREEN DESCRIPTOR GLOBAL PALETTE LOOP : Netscape 2.0 Loop COMMENT "Created By..." CONTROL for IMAGE #1 IMAGE #1 CONTROL for IMAGE #2 IMAGE #2 CONTROL for IMAGE #3 IMAGE #3 TRAILER
Benefits of GIF89a Animations	1. All the benefits of GIF: transparency, compression, interlacing, 2, 4, 8, 16, 32, 64, 128, and 256-color palettes for optimum size and compression. 2. The animation is supported by the basic Netscape 2.0 product. No plug-ins or additional software are needed.

3. Animations were tested on Windows 3.1x, Windows 95, Macintosh, UNIX, Sun, Linux, and Irix.

4. The Web designer does not need access to the Internet Service Provider's Web server, server-side includes (SSI), or CGI/PERL scripting.

5. The animation is repeatable and reusable. You can place the same image on a page multiple times. It performs a single download for all and loops all from the cache.

6. The animation loads only once, so your modem doesn't keep downloading constantly. It is faster than server-reliant methods.

7. The animations are surprisingly compact. The static image of a construction sign is 4,471 bytes, while the animated version is only 7,080 bytes.

8. Anyone can use it on his or her Web page.

Limitations of GIF89a Animations	

Limitations of GIF89a Animations

1. GIF89a animations have all the limitations of GIFs: a maximum of 256 colors; photographs are better compressed by JPEG.

2. The animations play only in Netscape 2.0 or better, but does work with many platforms (Windows, Macintosh, UNIX, etc.).

3. Animations play once or continuously. Refresh will not play the image again, but the reload command or resizing the windows will. If the viewer returns back to the page from elsewhere, the image will play, even if cached. Later revisions of Navigator may support finite iterations of the animations.

4. It cannot be used as a background GIF. Only the first frame will display.

5. Netscape does not fully support GIF89a.

   - It ignores user input.
   - It does not handle the previous image for image-removal controls.
   - Plain text is not displayed.
   - A bug in Windows version prevents timed displays of less than 1/3 of a second between images.

6. The animation can be slowed down or interrupted by other images being downloaded and other playing animations.
7. Animation can be borrowed as easily as any GIF.
8. Nonsupporting browsers display the first image or the last image.

The GIF89a Specification

CompuServe released the technical specification for GIF89a in July 1989. The technical specification is an exact breakdown of the byte-for-byte structure and rules for interpreting and building this format. If you are interested in a more technical explanation of the format, you can read the specifications as published by CompuServe.

GIF89a Sample

Figure 9-1 is a GIF89a sample animation. The file was created with the GIF Construction Set from Alchemy Mindworks, Inc. One nice feature of GIF89a animation is that virtually anyone can create cool animations with little effort. The sample image is included on the CD-ROM.

If you open the image in the GIF Construction Set, you will see all the various elements we discussed in the previous chapter. However, if you open the file in a standard graphics program, such as Paint Shop Pro, you will see only the first image in the loop.

To use this image in a Web page, simply specify the <IMG SRC=> tag as you would in any HTML document:

```
<html>
<body>
<img src="bulbtst.gif">
</body>
</html>
```

The result of this HTML document is a display of a light bulb flipping back and forth. It's not really that useful (unless you are designing a page for the Jumping-Bulb Company). However, this example illustrates the ease of using GIF89a animation.

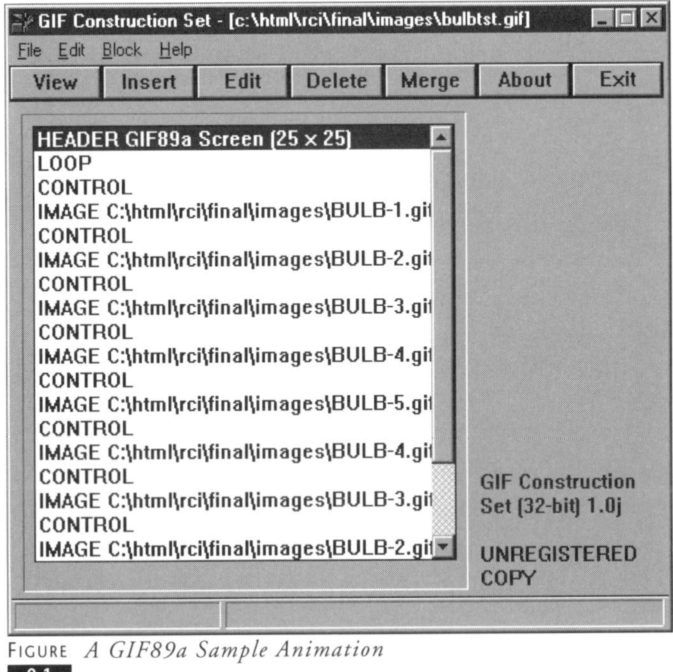

FIGURE 9-1 *A GIF89a Sample Animation*

INTRANET VIDEO

Quick Video Server (QVS), from InfoValue, is Windows NT-based video server software that can seamlessly deliver interactive, real-time, high-quality video over networks.

QVS offers the quickest way to turn ordinary PCs into powerful video servers. With QVS on the network, users simply click to see the video they want — there is no waiting for the video file to be downloaded. QVS automatically takes care of storage, management, real-time sharing, and immediate delivery of high-quality video files.

QVS is a client/server product that jump-starts PC users into the world of network video computing. QVS allows any workgroup application to incorporate network real-time video. With QVS, any amount of valuable video content can be stored on inexpensive PC-based video servers, and users at desktop PCs can simply point and click to see the video they want. Playback quality is guaranteed. In addition, playback is interactive, capable of supporting VCR-like features such as pause, stop, play, fast forward, and fast rewind. Users can simultaneously play the same or different files at their preferred time and pace.

The QVS software is cost-effective. A complete software package for five concurrent video streams costs $999. QVS supports all international and industry-standard video formats including MPEG-1, MPEG-2, Indeo, QuickTime, Cinepak, and Motion-JPEG, as well as other video formats.

Highlights	QVS consists of QServer and QClient. The QClient runs on most desktop environments, including Windows and Windows 95, requiring no hardware or network changes. QVS supports Microsoft's Media Control Interface, so no new proprietary APIs are required for developing new applications. QVS works very well with industry-standard LANs (Ethernet, token-ring, Fast Ethernet, FDDI, and ATM) and TCP/IP WANs. QVS can be integrated with other servers on your intranet, including Novell NetWare, Lotus Notes, and World Wide Web servers.

As far as hardware is concerned, InfoValue's QVS is performance-optimized and highly scaleable. A standard Intel Pentium-grade PC server can serve up to 60 concurrent MPEG-1 streams. A Pentium 60MHz machine or faster is recommended. The real-time throughput is scaleable via processor upgrade (Alpha processor or multiple and collaborating servers).

Quick Video Server Applications	Network video is the ultimate in network-centric multimedia computing. QVS is specifically designed to enable cost-effective, on-demand video sharing. Listed are some possible applications of incorporating network video using the Quick Video Server.

TRAINING AND EDUCATION

Training and education are crucial for corporations and institutions looking to stay competitive. And one of the best ways to present material is through a multimedia-enhanced curriculum. QVS can transform conventional instructor-centered, one way lecturing into a student-centered, self-paced interactive learning experience.

VIDEO PRODUCTION AND ARCHIVING

Storage and management of large collections of video data is critical to many organizations, such as news and advertising agencies. QVS immediately solves the problems inherent in using videotape. Once video data is converted to compressed digital video files, users have almost instantaneous access to a library of high-quality video.

MULTIMEDIA GROUPWARE

Networked business collaboration tools such as Lotus Notes and the World Wide Web have become an integral part of many organizations. For the first time, it is possible to incorporate high-quality, real-time video quickly, easily, and at a low cost to your existing groupware systems. QVS is capable of simultaneously delivering video data to up to 60 client PCs.

VIDEO KIOSKS

Kiosks are specially configured PCs used for information retrieval in public locations such as shopping malls, convention centers, airports, and museums. QVS can greatly enhance the function of these standalone kiosks. The kiosk user can be treated to a continually updated, interactive, video-enhanced presentation.

ONLINE VIDEO HELP

Many current help systems use only text and graphics, which can make them cumbersome. Interactive video makes it possible for the user to quickly and accurately pinpoint and answer questions. It also adds significantly to the appeal and appearance of the system.

PLUG-INS

A plug-in is a new functionality-enhancing feature that provides inline support for a huge range of Live Objects. With Live Objects, developers can deliver rich multimedia content through Internet sites, allowing users to seamlessly view that content without launching any external helper applications. Browsers, such as Netscape Navigator 2.0, offer plug-in capability for a number of popular software programs.

Using the appropriate plug-ins, users can read Acrobat Reader .PDF documents, explore Director presentations, and watch Quicktime movies within the Netscape 2.0 window. This feature promises to reduce the "window juggling" associated with running multiple software applications.

In Netscape Navigator, plug-ins are placed in the Plug-ins folder, which can be found in the main Netscape 2.0 folder. The Acrobat Reader, WebFX, and Shockwave plug-ins allow for the application to

Table 9-2 Plug-ins for Netscape Navigator 2.0

Classification	Name	Platform
VRML VRML plug-ins turn flat Web documents into spacious 3-D environments	Live3D	Windows 3.1 Windows 95 Windows NT
PDF document reader Makes it possible for users to download pages of PDF documents one at a time. The PDF document appears embedded within the Web page.	Amber	Windows Windows 95 Macintosh
Macromedia Director Allows Macromedia Director presentations to be displayed within a Web document	Shockwave	Windows Windows 95 Macintosh
Quicktime allows Apple QuickTime movies to be viewed within a Netscape 2.0 browser window	Viewmovie	Macintosh
text-to-speech adds voice narration to the presentation options of Web pages	Talker	Macintosh

appear within the browser window. The functionality of plug-ins is as varied as the software programs the plug-ins support.

Shockwave	Shockwave is a key component of Macromedia's solution for creative professionals who develop digital media for the World Wide Web. It enables creative professionals, already familiar with Macromedia software (such as Authorware, Director, and FreeHand), to use their existing authoring tools, skills, and content immediately.

Shockwave consists of Shockwave plug-ins for Macromedia's Authorware, Director, and FreeHand authoring tools for Netscape Navigator 2.0 and other popular Web browsers, as well as the Afterburner utilities or Xtras that compress and optimize content for delivery on the Web.

Since its introduction, more than a million people have downloaded and used Shockwave to view thousands of "shocked" Web sites. Macromedia introduced Shockwave on December 5, 1995, when it unveiled Shockwave for Director 4. Almost overnight, it revolutionized the Internet by bringing interactive multimedia to the World Wide Web. On April 15, 1996, Macromedia introduced new Shockwave software with expanded capabilities to display additional forms of interactive multimedia, learning, and digital arts to the World Wide Web.

Macromedia's authoring tools are popular for creating and distributing digital media. Shockwave provides extensions to those tools so the expertise and existing body of work owned by those creative professionals can be moved immediately to the World Wide Web. The "shocked" content that authors can bring to the Web completely changes the look of Web pages compared to static HTML. Web pages now include interactive multimedia, vector graphics, sound, interactive information, and more as Macromedia's tools develop.

Shockwave solutions are available for Macromedia's three most widely used authoring tools (Director, Authorware, and FreeHand), and will be available for all of Macromedia's authoring products before long. Likewise, Shockwave will be ubiquitous in that it will be available for common computer platforms and for the most widely used Web browser architectures. Shockwave plug-ins packaged as Active Objects for use with Microsoft Internet Explorer will be available in the near future.

To encourage development and use of shocked content on the Web, Macromedia makes the Shockwave player plug-ins and Afterburner authoring software freely available to download at http://www.macromedia.com/.

With Shockwave software, anyone using the Netscape Navigator 2.0 browser can view interactive multimedia on the Web, including animation, sound, and high-resolution scalable and zoomable digital art. Surfing the in-house intranet will now become dynamic, informative, entertaining, and fun.

Customers who use one of Macromedia's authoring tools (Director, FreeHand, or Authorware 3.5 for Windows or Macintosh) can create a shocked piece for the Internet or intranet. Users simply create the piece, compress it using Macromedia's compression software (Afterburner) to optimize the piece for Web delivery, and upload it to their Web page.

Shockwave software is made up of two distinct parts: the Shockwave plug-ins and the Afterburner applications. Shockwave plug-ins are a set of viewers for Macromedia datatypes that are packaged as plug-ins to the two major Web browser architectures and that play back Macromedia titles on the network. The Afterburner application is a Macromedia Xtra, or separate utility program, that compresses and optimizes standard Macromedia files for use on the Web. Separate plug-ins and Afterburners are available for Director, FreeHand, and Authorware, and for different platforms of Netscape Navigator 2.0, including 16-bit and 32-bit on Microsoft Windows, and 680xx and PowerPC on the Apple Macintosh.

Shockwave software is optimized for online multimedia and interactive graphics. Developers have produced:

- Online advertising (Director)
- Games (Director and Authorware)
- Presentations for communicating marketing and product messages (Director and Authorware)
- Computer-based training and educational courseware, including quizzes (Authorware)

- Interactive reference works and publications (Authorware)
- Kiosks for both communication and user input (Director and Authorware)
- Surveys and questionnaires (Authorware)
- Maps and site plans (FreeHand)
- Online technical illustrations and product catalogs (FreeHand)
- Presentation of illustrations, logos, artwork, and other graphic images (FreeHand)
- "Highlight" animations such as "flying logos" that add interest to Web pages (Director)

Adobe Acrobat

Adobe Acrobat is a software utility that lets you create electronic documents from a wide range of authoring tools. Because Acrobat is platform-independent, you can share your Acrobat-translated documents across different computer platforms. To create an Acrobat document, simply "print" files in the Adobe Portable Document Format (PDF) directly from your application. Once a document is in an Acrobat-readable format, you can distribute your documents over a wide range of electronic media, including the World Wide Web, e-mail, Lotus Notes, corporate networks, CD-ROMs, and print-on-demand systems.

The Acrobat Reader is available for Macintosh, Windows, DOS, or UNIX clients, and can be distributed free. Thus, you can send a PDF file and a copy of the Acrobat Reader to just about anyone, and he or she can view or print the document with the hardware and software they already have. This cross-platform capability makes more documents available to more people. And, because PDF files can be easily integrated with other PDF and HTML files on the Web, you can build helpful links to guide viewers quickly through your documentation, across your home page, and around the Web.

PDF files look exactly like the original document. Controlling the appearance of your documents on the Web is a challenge. With PDF, however, you can achieve the highest quality and maintain the greatest control, thereby preserving the integrity of your design, including scalable typefaces

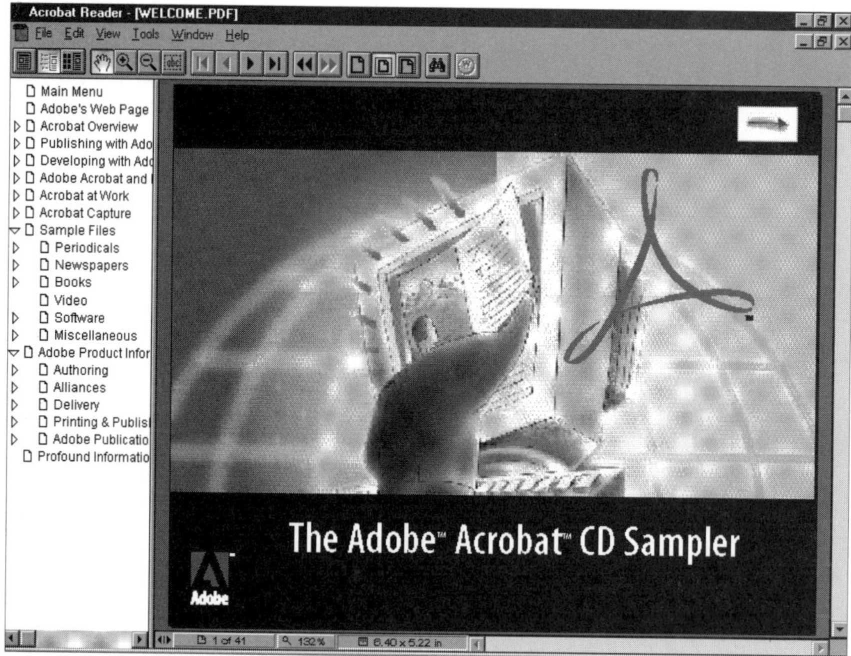

FIGURE *Adobe Acrobat Startup Page*
9-2

and graphics. Although PDF files contain the complete formatting of your original document, they are compact, allowing you to conveniently share even the most complex information. Best of all, PDF files maintain their formatting even when printed, no matter what printer you use.

Creating PDF files (from your favorite desktop publishing application) is as easy as it is from word-processing and spreadsheet applications. Simply print the document to PDF. There's no need to rewrite your document, and you can create files for online viewing or printing using software you already know. That means you'll save time and money by publishing the information just once and delivering it as many times as you'd like over any electronic medium.

If you are posting PDF files on your Web site, use the Get Acrobat button and the PDF file icons. The Get Acrobat button directs visitors to instructions for downloading the free Adobe Acrobat Reader. The PDF file icons provided by Adobe can be used to represent the PDF files that you post on your intranet site. Once you've enabled your intranet clients to download the Acrobat Reader by clicking the Get Acrobat button, or by installing the Acrobat Reader on their workstations, they can view any PDF file on your Web site.

You can download the Get Acrobat button and the PDF file icons for use on your intranet site by following these easy steps:

1. Connect to Adobe's Web site at www.adobe.com.
2. To use these icons, you must license them from Adobe Systems Inc. Complete the Adobe Acrobat Trademark License Agreement for PDF and Get Acrobat Icons by downloading the PDF file, then printing and sending it to Adobe Systems Inc., 1585 Charleston Road, Mountain View, CA 94039.

Note: The Get Acrobat button and PDF file icons may not be modified in any manner, including text, size, or color.

3. Download the images to your local drive by following your browser's directions for downloading an image.
4. Use the PDF file icons to represent the PDF files that you post.
5. All Acrobat Readers can be redistributed without needing any further permission from Adobe.

You may need to configure your server if you want to distribute PDF documents. In general, your server must know about the PDF MIME type (application/PDF), how to identify PDF documents on your server (.PDF extension), and, perhaps, how to treat a PDF data stream of binary data.

HOW TO MODIFY NETSCAPE NAVIGATOR TO RECOGNIZE PDF FILES

After Acrobat Reader or Acrobat Exchange software has been installed, you will need to modify your set of Helper applications in Netscape Navigator.

1. From the Options menu, select General Preferences. (See Figure 9-3 on page 184.)
2. Choose Helpers from the tabs at the top. (See Figure 9-4.)
3. Click on the Create New Type button. (See Figure 9-5.)

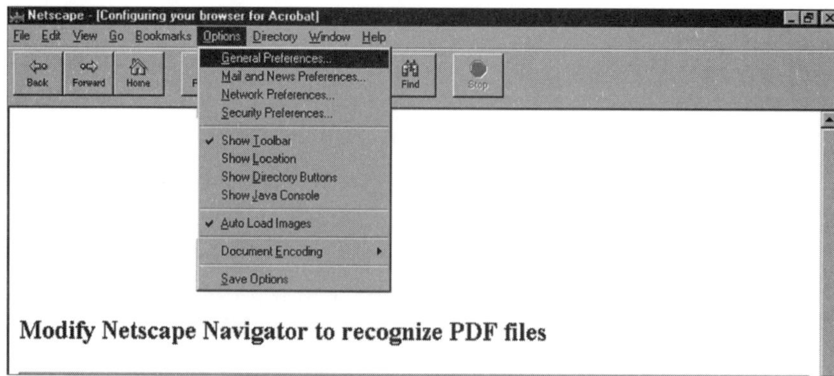

FIGURE 9-3 *Netscape Navigator Option Menu.* Copyright 1996 Netscape Communications Corp. All Rights Reserved. This page may not be reprinted or copied without the express written permission of Netscape.

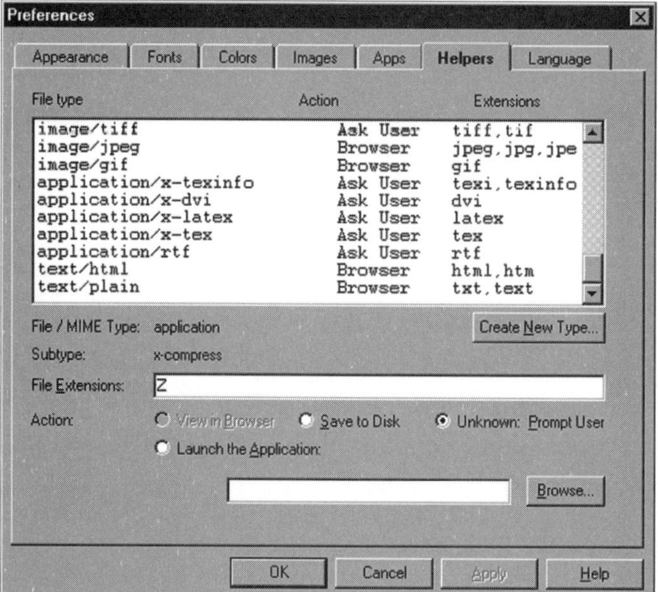

FIGURE 9-4 *Netscape Navigator General Preferences Menu.* Copyright 1996 Netscape Communications Corp. All Rights Reserved. This page may not be reprinted or copied without the express written permission of Netscape.

FIGURE 9-5 *Creating a new Helper type.* Copyright 1996 Netscape Communications Corp. All Rights Reserved. This page may not be reprinted or copied without the express written permission of Netscape.

4. Enter `application` into the MIME type field and enter `PDF` in the MIME subtype field. Click on the OK button.

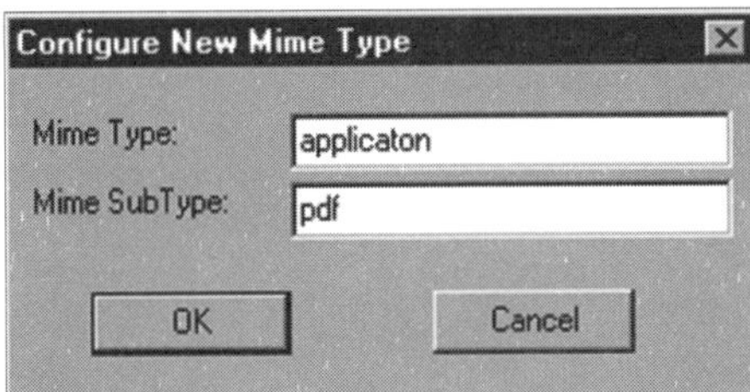

FIGURE 9-6 *Filling out the Helper Application specifications.* Copyright 1996 Netscape Communications Corp. All Rights Reserved. This page may not be reprinted or copied without the express written permission of Netscape.

5. Enter `PDF` in the File Extensions field.

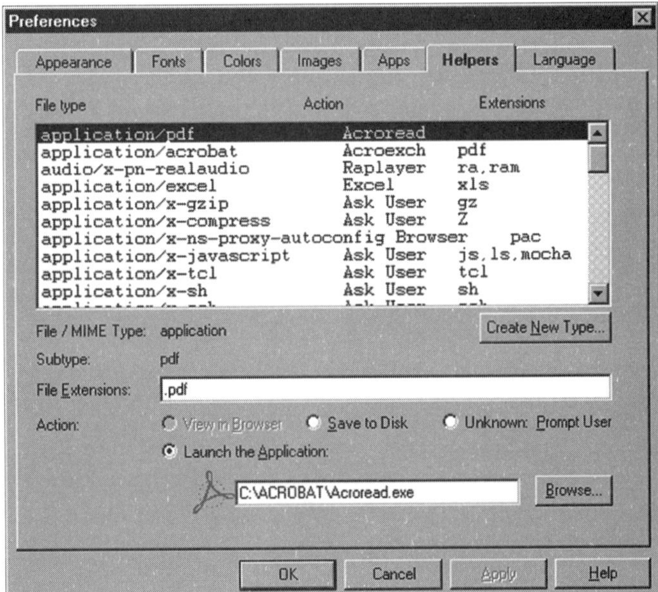

FIGURE 9-7 *Enter the file extension in the File Extension Field.* Copyright 1996 Netscape Communications Corp. All Rights Reserved. This page may not be reprinted or copied without the express written permission of Netscape.

6. Click on the Browse button. Use the file browser to navigate until you find and select your copy of the Acrobat Reader or Acrobat Exchange application, and click on the Open button. (See Figure 9-8.)

7. Select the Launch the Application radio button from the Action choices.

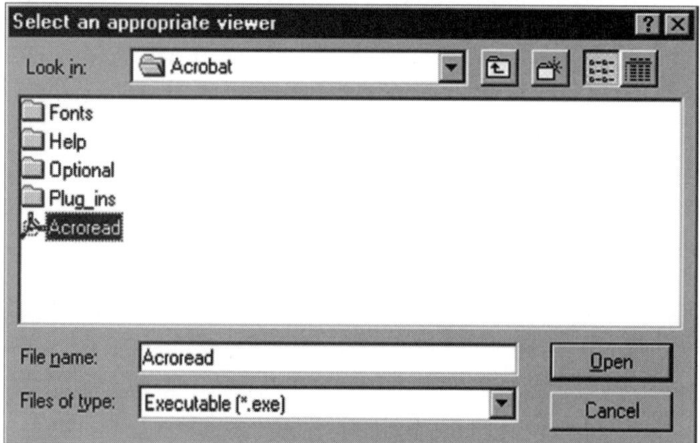

FIGURE 9-8 *Using the File Browser feature to locate your Helper Application.* Copyright 1996 Netscape Communications Corp. All Rights Reserved. This page may not be reprinted or copied without the express written permission of Netscape.

8. Click on the OK button at the bottom of the Preferences dialog.

9. You are finished. When you click on a link that is a PDF file, Netscape Navigator will download that file to your default TEMP folder and automatically launch your Acrobat Reader software to open and view the file.

EMISSARY HOST PUBLISHING SYSTEM

Attachmate is the developer of the Emissary Host Publishing System, a comprehensive, easy-to-use intranet client/server development solution. With the Emissary Host Publishing System, you can access host and client/server applications from a Web browser without a major re-engineering effort.

You can use Emissary Host Publishing System to develop applications for a corporate intranet without needing to train developers on the intricacies of host communications conversions or Web-specific programming. With the Emissary Host Publishing System you can use OCX-enabled development tools such as Visual Basic to build client/server applications that integrate host information. Emissary dynamically converts these applications into HTML pages. It also converts existing client/server applications, providing a migration path to a corporate intranet.

Emissary Host Publishing System runs on a Windows NT Server and includes the following components:

- Attachmate's Emissary Host Publishing Server, a high-performance Systems Network Architecture-based (SNA) communications engine, which provides a gateway to the host computer.
- Attachmate's HLLAPI server. This 3270-type information access software resides on the Windows NT Server and supports up to 250 simultaneous users.
- Attachmate's middleware. These tools can integrate data on host screens and databases into client/server applications.
- The Emissary Host Translator, an OCX utility, that dynamically converts Visual BASIC programs into HTML pages.

With the Emissary Host Publishing System, host computers already programmed to handle tasks such as querying a database, retrieving documents, placing orders, or requesting services can be accessed by Web browsers. This lets you leverage your investment in host technology. The middleware component links these host functions to client/server applications without communications programming.

What this means to your users is that they can transparently interact with client/server applications using their browser in much the same way they would interact with a Visual Basic form in Windows. Using Web client software, such as Netscape Navigator, they can even submit information for processing by a host application or for storage in a host database. The Web pages will capture and dispense information, taking no storage space on the server and no administration time.

Emissary Host Publishing System allows developers unfamiliar with host communications programming or HTML to build intranet applications that integrate host data. Anyone who knows how to use graphical client/server development tools can produce host-enabled, client/server applications for intranets or the Internet in a few easy steps:

1. Identify the screens or data on the host you want to access from the Web.
2. Build a client/server application using Visual Basic. If the application already exists, check and modify any Visual Basic features that might not be supported in HTML.
3. Link the host data to the client/server application using the middleware components.
4. Dynamically translate the application to HTML pages using the Emissary Host Translator.
5. Associate the client/server application's URL with the HTML page on the Web server.

Emissary Host Publishing System works with all UNIX and Windows NT Web servers. It provides source code for CGI scripts that call the host-enabled client/server application for UNIX servers and ISAPI scripts for the Microsoft Windows NT Server. That means any Web server can dovetail into any host application, preserving your investment in technology.

The Emissary Host Publishing System provides integrated component management. Installation, configuration, administration, and monitoring details such as the number of open sessions and connection status are available on one server.

Host Access Components	Emissary includes a number of components, for accessing host computers.

THE SNA COMMUNICATIONS ENGINE

Emissary Host Publishing Server has a robust 32-bit communications engine running one of the fastest SNA protocol stacks in the industry. The engine easily scales to handle IBM 3270 application and host database access for hundreds of connected users.

THE HLLAPI SERVER

Attachmate's HLLAPI server offers IBM mainframe information access unlike any other software available today. It provides interactive access to existing IBM 3270 applications without re-engineering host code. Up to 250 simultaneous users can extract data and enter information from the host using the HLLAPI server.

EMISSARY HOST TRANSLATOR

Emissary Host Translator works behind the scenes to dynamically convert Visual BASIC forms to HTML pages. It works as an ActiveX control that, when invoked, automatically moves a fully functional client/server application to the Web. The translator works with Visual Basic, and in the future, will work any other graphical development tools with support for ActiveX custom controls.

EMISSARY DEVELOPER SERIES

Attachmate's middleware components, known collectively as the Emissary Developer Series, make adding host access to your intranet-enabled client/server applications easy. You can quickly integrate data on host screens or databases into your application using the included middleware communications tools. Host information will then be at the fingertips of anyone who has a browser. No communications code or HTML programming is required.

QUICKAPP SERVER, VERSION 3.0

QuickApp Server is a powerful middleware communications tool that integrates information housed in host screens into applications built with leading client/server tools. QuickApp Server navigation technology empowers the developer to incorporate data from many host screens into a Web browser — without writing communications code. For the user, QuickApp Server obviates the need to log on to each host and navigate through IBM SNA mainframe screens to accomplish a business task.

QuickApp Server brings host security, transaction volume, and client/server productivity technologies to the intranet.

QuickDB Server, version 3.0

Through Open Database Connectivity (ODBC) access, QuickDB Server gives developers the ability to query databases. In the IBM environment, QuickDB Server brings data from all DRDA-compliant databases to the intranet using only the SNA communications engine included in the system. It currently supports IBM DB2.

INTRANET GENIE 1.1

Intranet Genie is a complete intranet solution, providing a modular, well-integrated solution based on open systems. Intranet Genie's client applications and components are designed for Windows 95 and Windows NT, with a version for Windows 3.x coming soon. Intranet Genie's server components are designed for Windows NT. Intranet Genie runs on existing TCP/IP networks, including TCP/IP networking resources that are bundled into Windows 95 and Windows NT. Intranet Genie also runs on Novell networks.

Intranet Genie specifically targets companies with limited in-house technical expertise and limited budgets. Through the use of installation and application wizards, Intranet Genie enables virtually anyone to set up an intranet and have it operational in a matter of hours. Once installed, the program is easy to use and well-integrated, saving time for novices as well as experts. Intranet Genie does not require extensive technical expertise to install, implement, manage, or maintain. Intranet Genie allows intranet administrators to simply drag and drop files off the LAN or a hard drive to the Web server. Intranet Genie provides administrators with helper applications (Wizards) that intuitively guide them in setting up interactive workflow applications for the organization. Training costs are significantly reduced through ease of use and a standard interface.

Frontier Technologies provides a single point of contact for technical support of the corporate intranet, eliminating the hassle of coordinating with a myriad of vendors for support. Intranet Genie also provides remote administration and built-in Web page builders that empower corporate departments and users, thus reducing reliance on the IS department.

Security	Intranet Genie provides a unique multilevel security architecture that offers SSL V2 and V3 client/server authentication, client/server encryption, and secure multimedia e-mail (S/MIME). Internal communications are automatically verified by both sender and recipient, ensuring optimal security and protection of sensitive company information. Secure Internet transactions may be conducted with other commercial entities or with the federal government. Remote employees may safely and securely access the corporate intranet. If desired, secure access to portions of the corporate intranet may be accessed by valued customers, resellers, vendors, press contacts, and others. These powerful security tools protect sensitive company information throughout the intranet and/or the Internet.
Content Creation	Intranet Genie includes a built-in Web page builder along with an image map editor. These WYSIWYG tools are as easy to use as a word processor, empowering everyone within an organization with the capability to create and administer content. Administration and access rights may be assigned as needed to create multilevel security of information within the organization.
Electronic Document Distribution and Management	Documents and other information may be quickly and efficiently distributed electronically and then stored, accessed, and managed in a centralized or decentralized fashion, depending on the organization's needs.

Intranet Information Organization	Intranet Genie offers an Intranet Organizer, which allows users to conduct searches by keyword on the Web server or on other shared resources on the network. Indexed by the Verity search engine, the documents may be in HTML format or other formats supported by the Document Indexer. The information can be "bookmarked" in user-defined categories. Off-line searching of information retrieved from the Internet is also made possible.
Search and Retrieval	Intranet Genie offers a unique convergence of searching capabilities. Documents and other information may be found through keyword searches, whether the information is physically located on the server, on client PCs, or on the Internet. Various types of documents and resources may be located, including e-mail messages, word-processing documents, graphics, spreadsheets, Web pages, etc. Users may conduct meta searches of multiple search engines available on the Internet. A company may also set up Intranet Genie's Internet searching capabilities such that Internet searches are conducted at timed intervals and Internet information is then made available off-line to corporate intranet users.
Productivity and Workflow Applications	Intranet Genie includes ready-to-go, useful back-end applications to aid an organization's productivity and workflow. Among the applications are an interactive telephone directory, service request form, and resource scheduler. Expense and sales report templates are also included. Additional client-side productivity applications include "Smart" S/MIME E-mail, NNTP Newsreader, Remote Web Server Administration Toolset, WebDesigner, and Internet Browser.
Conversion of Legacy Documents	Frontier Technologies bundles NetTransit's easy-to-use legacy document conversion tools into Intranet Genie. This allows you to convert existing word-processing documents into HTML without having to write one line of HTML code.

Intranet Genie will appeal to companies of all sizes that have the common need for a ready-to-use intranet. Intranet Genie will especially appeal to companies that are more concerned with implementing and using a productive intranet as quickly as possible, rather than a piecemeal solution. It is possible to purchase Intranet Genie's components and modules separately; however, the overall goal of Intranet Genie is to provide a complete, integrated solution. This will benefit companies that were previously unable to implement an intranet due to time or budget constraints, as well as those organizations without extensive in-house technical expertise. In general, medium to small companies and corporate departments will benefit from Intranet Genie's integrated, one-stop solution.

Cold Fusion

Cold Fusion is a Web Application Development (WAD) platform for Windows NT and Windows 95. Cold Fusion can be used to create a wide variety of applications that integrate relational databases with the Web on intranets and the Internet. Applications range from dynamic Web sites to enterprise-wide groupware.

Cold Fusion enables dynamic, data-driven Web sites that use pages generated on-the-fly from information stored in databases and provided by users. Page content can be instantly customized based on user requests. Dynamic sites allow users to enter and retrieve information and offer ease of maintenance and administration.

More complicated applications include online customer feedback, order entry, event registration, bulletin board style conferencing, technical support, interactive training, and a wide variety of information publishing applications. Advanced applications include internal client/server systems and Web-based groupware. These applications can be used on the Internet or as part of an intranet.

Developing applications with Cold Fusion does not require coding in a traditional programming language such as Perl, C/C++, Visual

Basic, Java, or Delphi. Instead, developers build applications by combining standard HTML with high-level database commands stored in templates. This method of Web application development is simpler, faster, and more flexible than first generation, code-intensive techniques. With Cold Fusion, developers can leverage the power of the Web and relational databases to create dynamic Web sites and full-scale Web applications.

Listed below are major Cold Fusion features and functions. In addition to these features, take a look at the Cold Fusion Fuel Packs such as the Web Application Wizards, data-driven Java Graphs, and ISAPI for added functionality.

Basic Functions	<ul><li>Inserts and updates records in database tables with HTML forms</li><li>Submits database queries that can then be used to dynamically generate Web pages</li><li>Intermixes the results of queries with HTML tags and text for complete control over how data is displayed and formatted</li><li>Presents the results of queries in formatted tables</li><li>Sends SMTP-based e-mail messages that use address and message content from database queries</li><li>Tracks users and customizes their view of Web pages by using information about their browser, location, or other preferences</li></ul>
Advanced Data Input and Reporting Features	<ul><li>Validates form field entries as integer, floating point, date, or numeric range</li><li>Requires entry into form fields</li><li>Accesses CGI variables to track records with date and time, client IP address, browser type, e-mail address, and other information</li><li>Controls output formatting for dates, times, numbers, and currency values</li></ul>

- Replaces CR/LF sequences automatically with <P> tags to correctly format output from memo fields

Advanced Development Features	

- Makes conditional statements ("if...else" branching) to dynamically customize output returned to users, and makes decisions about queries submitted to the database
- Includes templates within other templates to reuse complex code, formats, or functions
- Embeds Sequenced Query Language (SQL) statements in templates to specify queries. SQL statements may be dynamically customized using data from form submissions, URL query strings, and CGI environment variables, as well as the results returned from other queries.
- Places variables within SQL statements to specify queries and choose databases
- Allows developers to choose what SQL statements are sent within any given SQL query
- Executes multiple SQL queries and sends SQL queries to multiple databases for each client request
- Calls stored procedures (with parameters) in databases that support them
- Delivers data-driven Java applets and dynamically generated JavaScript
- Administers (locally and remotely) options and preferences with an easy-to-use GUI
- Declares variables within templates and creates "cookies" (variables that are stored in the browser)
- Generates comprehensive error reporting, debugging data and logging information to enable rapid and easy application development
- Sets content type for documents to support database-driven VRML and other standards
- Draws on comprehensive online support available directly on the Web, including software, technical articles, a user conference, and a searchable knowledge base.

REALAUDIO SERVER 2.0

RealAudio Server 2.0 is a software solution that allows your Web site to deliver live and on-demand audio over the Internet or your company network. With RealAudio Server 2.0, your audience will hear audio instantly over connections as slow as 14.4Kbps, with no more annoying download delays. RealAudio Server can also serve audio streams over an intranet LAN connection.

RealAudio Server 2.0 Features	• Integrates live and on-demand audio into your Web site or company network • Delivers audio to your audience in real time, without download delays • Provides full random access to audio, just like with a CD player • Provides monitoring of performance and traffic • RealAudio Intranet solutions allow your company to deliver services such as training, education, and company announcements
Technical Specifications	To make the best use of RealAudio, you must have a Web site and a registered domain. The RealAudio Server is compatible with any Web server that supports configurable MIME types, including: • Netscape Netsite • O'Reilly Website NT • Macintosh HTTPD • NCSA HTTPD (v1.3 or v1.4) • Emwac HTTPS 0.96 • CERN HTTPD (v3.0) • Webstar for Macintosh

Network Connection Requirements	Depending on the level of audio compression, a single stream of RealAudio requires 10 to 22KB per second of audio bandwidth. The speed and capacity of your network connection should be configured to accommodate the demand you anticipate.

Table 9-3. Stream Capacity of Available Connecting

Connection	Stream Capacity (10kbps/stream)
56KBps Frame Relay	4 streams
ISDN BRI Service	5-10 streams
T1 Connection	100 streams
T3 Connection	3,000-4,000 streams

Table 9-4. Hardware Requirements

Manufacturer	Min. Hardware Configuration	Operating System
Sun Microsystems	Sparc, 24MB RAM	Solaris 2.x, SunOS 4.1x
IBM/PC Compatibles	486/66 or better, 16MB of RAM	Windows NT, BSDI 2.0 or later, LINUX 1.x, FreeBSD
Silicon Graphics	Indy, 24MB RAM	IRIX 5.3 or later
Macintosh	Power Macintosh, 16MB	System 7.5 (With Open Transport)
Digital	Alpha, 24M	Digital UNIX v3.2, Windows NT
Hewlett-Packard	PA-RISC, 24M	HP/UX 10.01
IBM	PowerPC, 24M	AIX 4.0

Table 9-5. Memory and Storage Requirements

Server Storage	RealAudio Server requires approximately 2MB of hard disk space
Audio Storage	Depending on the level of audio compression, RealAudio files require hard disk space equal to approximately 1.1-2.4KB per second of audio.
Sound Requirements	RealAudio encodes most common monoaural PC formats. RealAudio 2.0 comes with two audio encoding algorithms. The RealAudio 14.4 algorithm provides AM sound quality, while the 28.8 algorithm offers FM sound quality.

Table 9-6. Audio File Storage Requirements

Program Length	RealAudio14.4Kbps	RealAudio28.8Kbps
1 hour	3.6MB	8MB
5 hours	18MB	40MB

REALAUDIO ENCODER 2.0

RealAudio Encoder 2.0 enables users to create RealAudio content by compressing digital audio files in common formats and converting them to RealAudio format.

RealAudio files created with the Encoder can be delivered over the Internet with the RealAudio Server. The RealAudio Player can play RealAudio files delivered by the Server over connections of 14.4Kbps or better and can play RealAudio files that have been saved locally.

RealAudio Encoder 2.0 supports better sound, including music-quality audio compression for delivery over 28.8Kbps, or better connections and improved sound quality for the RealAudio 14.4 algorithm. RealAudio Encoder 2.0 also features an improved graphical user interface.

RealAudio Encoder 2.0 is available for the following platforms:

- Microsoft Windows 95
- Microsoft Windows NT
- Microsoft Windows 3.1
- Macintosh OS
- UNIX

Windows System Requirements

RealAudio Encoder is designed to work in the Windows 95 and Windows NT environments. The following table explains which hardware is required for specific encoder uses. Note that different hardware is required for encoding from a file and encoding a live audio stream.

Table 9-7. RealAudio Hardware Requirements

Requirement	File Encoding	Live Encoding
CPU	486/66 DX	Pentium/586, 75Mhz
RAM	8MB	8MB required, 16MB recommended
Hard Disk Space (software)	1MB	1MB
Hard Disk Space (files)	1KB per second for 14.4 files	18KB per second for 28.8 files
Sound Card	16-bit sound card capable of recording an 8khz signal	16-bit sound card capable of recording an 8khz signal

Table 9-8. RealAudio Encoder Input File Formats Supported

Type	Sampling Rate	Resolution
.wav Audio	8khz, 11khz, 22khz, or 44khz	8- or 16-bit, monophonic
.au Audio	8khz, 22khz, 44khz	monophonic
.pcm Raw Data	8khz, 11khz, 22khz, 44khz	16-bit, monophonic

RealAudio Encoder does not support stereo files or compressed variants of the formats described above. If you encounter problems encoding a file, verify that it is not in a compressed format or stereophonic. If it is, use a sound editing utility to convert it to a supported format.

The sampling rate of .wav and most .au files is determined automatically. For .pcm files and .au files without "headers" identifying their properties, the Encoder displays a dialog box for choosing the sampling rate and format information.

Macintosh System Requirements

To use the Macintosh Encoder, the minimum system requirements are as follows:

1. Apple System 7.1 or later
2. Macintosh with a floating point co-processor

For best results, recommended systems are:

1. A PowerMac
2. Quadra 700 or better

Real Audio Personal Server	You don't have to be a large company or have a lot of money to provide real-time audio to Internet users. With the RealAudio Personal Server, you can provide audio streams right from your desktop or personal Web page.

The RealAudio Personal Server supports two external streams and one local stream. This means you and two other people can listen to sound-clips concurrently, in real time, without download delays.

The Personal Server runs on the following platforms:

- Windows 95
- Windows NT
- Macintosh OS 7.5.x

The Personal Server includes instant access to the RealAudio Encoder for encoding audio files in RealAudio format. A graphical user interface allows you to monitor who's listening and what they're listening to.

10 The Sample Intranet

CONTENTS

The intranet, as with the Internet, is about evolution, not revolution. Projects, such as this sample intranet, evolve over time. In fact, intranet projects seem to explode at an exponential rate once various departments within the organization get wind of what the intranet is capable of delivering.

This chapter takes a phased approach to the development of an intranet within a small to midsize organization. The goal of this chapter is not to take you through building the complete intranet, but to show how the intranet evolves from simple to slightly more advanced applications and uses. With this in mind, this section will take you through the completion of phase 1 and into the beginning of phase 2 of the intranet project. Again, these are the early stages of intranet development, and as the intranet grows and flourishes, it will expand well beyond phases 2 and 3.

As the intranet grows and matures, you will need to address issues concerning integration with back-end host data and corporate databases. These issues require considerably more time to develop, architect, and debug than the simple applications presented here. The current intranet committee may even need to outsource the expertise required to design and install these types of applications.

Phase 1 of the sample intranet sticks to the basic HTML and JavaScripting skills most MIS departments should be able to handle without too much trouble. The entire phase 1 intranet site can be found on the companion CD-ROM in the back of this book. With your Web browser, open the "Sample intranet" Folder, and open the intranet HTML document. You will need a frames-compatible browser, as well as a browser that can run JavaScript. Use Netscape Navigator 2.01 or Microsoft Internet Explorer 3.0 (or higher).

This section shows you how an intranet is built, from the ground up. It provides examples of various intranet services and how they are designed, added, and tested. It makes the following assumptions:

- management has approved the project;
- departments have supplied information for intranet applications;
- the intranet committee has approved all applications;
- Netscape Navigator is the universal client all employees will use;
- Microsoft Windows NT is the operating system.

Note: The selection of Windows NT Server as the intranet server operating system is used as an example only. The intranet could be built on Macintosh, UNIX, or NetWare servers, as well;

- the Windows NT servers have been built and tested;
- the intranet topology and access method are 10BASE-T Ethernet;
- TCP/IP is the default network protocol (at least it has been installed on the client workstations); and
- there is a mix of Macintosh and Windows 95 workstations on the intranet.

This section will show you how to implement Phases 1 and 2. Because building an intranet is an evolving process, use your imagination on the remaining phases.

IMPLEMENTATION SCHEDULE

Like any other project, you'll need to put together an implementation schedule so tasks are completed on time and in the proper order. The planned implementation schedule for our various intranet phases are as follows:

Phase 1   To begin when MIS turns over the intranet servers to the Webmaster; to be completed when the intranet goes "live"

Phase 2   To be implemented in the quarter following Phase 1

Phase 3   To be implemented in the quarter following Phase 2

During the planning sessions for the intranet project, the intranet committee constructs a formal and detailed project management milestone plan. (See Table 10-1.) One of the first initiatives is to align the tasks associated with the intranet project with the users' expected results. The intranet committee works with the various departments to perform an information-collection effort focused on securing a complete understanding of the explicit and implicit requirements, as well as current and future plans.

Table 10-1. A Sample Project Management Milestone Plan

Intranet Application	Implementation Phase
Human Resources Online	Phase 1
Suggestion Box	Phase 1
Company Newsletter	Phase 1
"About Our Department"	Phase 1
Corporate Events Calendar	Phase 1
Update and Modify Phase 1 Applications	Phase 2
The Virtual Company Store	Phase 2
"About Our Company" Kiosk	Phase 2
Update and Modify Phase 2 Applications	Phase 3
Sales and Marketing Presentation Repository	Phase 3
Computer Resources Help Desk FAQ	Phase 3
Annual Reports	Phase 3
Department-Specific Applications	Phase 3

Based on an analysis of this information, the intranet committee develops key milestones and identifies their relationships to each of the technical activities and responsibilities. All project tasks are documented and tracked in relation to the key milestones. As the project develops and matures, the milestones will be adjusted.

An individual is appointed as the intranet committee project manager who ensures that the intranet committee members and Webmasters adhere to their commitments as noted in the milestone plan.

The intranet committee employs automated project management software to develop the milestone plan. After the milestone plan has been finalized, any revisions to it are approved only by the intranet committee and are communicated to the appropriate department(s).

Milestone Initiation

Work toward each milestone begins with a project kickoff meeting. This meeting is normally attended by the intranet committee project manager, assigned technical consultant(s), and all project team subcontractors who have task responsibilities for achieving the milestones. The meeting agenda includes:

- reviewing the project plan, highlighting the particular milestone;
- addressing questions from the client's team;
- performing pre-project activities in conjunction with the milestones;
- understanding the critical path for the task; and
- defining the interrelationships of tasks that may affect multiple milestones.

END-USER FEEDBACK

With each phase of the intranet project, the intranet committee solicits feedback from the company employees on the following items:

1. Are the applications useful?
2. Is the intranet easy to use?
3. Is the information provided useful?
4. What do you like most about the intranet?
5. What information or feature of the intranet do you use the most?
6. What don't you like about the intranet?
7. What applications would you like to see?
8. What changes would you like to see made to existing intranet applications?

You can obtain this information via a fill-out form on the company intranet and by randomly interviewing company employees. In our example, upper management has requested that the intranet committee meet once a week for the first quarter of the intranet roll-out, and biweekly from then on. During these meetings, they collectively review employee and departmental feedback on the intranet, and discuss new applications to be added or required, and desired modifications to existing applications. During these meetings, the Webmaster has an opportunity to present new intranet technologies and report on intranet usage statistics.

The intranet Webmaster in our example is a collection of people. Each member of the MIS department will take on one or two of the tasks of the Webmaster. The director of IS will have overall architectural responsibility for the intranet project.

HARDWARE/SOFTWARE

The Webmaster, after determining the list of intranet applications available on the intranet, prepares a list of minimum hardware and software required. Based on the desired intranet applications, the hardware and software required for the intranet project is:

1. A dedicated server (Pentium 100MHz or better, 32MB RAM, a 2GB hard disk, an SVGA monitor, and a 10BASE-T Ethernet adapter);
2. Windows NT Server v3.51 or 4.0;
3. An uninterruptible power supply (UPS);
4. Web server software; and
5. HTML authoring software.

Prior to approval, the IS director submits a working budget to management, estimating the hardware, software, training, and overtime costs necessary to get the intranet project off the ground. This budget is based on the initial list of intranet applications to be implemented and includes plans for intranet growth and expansion.

Although the initial hardware and software list calls for a single Web server, the director of IS bumps up the requirements to three dedicated servers. Planning for growth, this new configuration allows services to be distributed across multiple machines and provides an additional layer of fault tolerance. If one server crashes, its services can be reinstalled or restored from backup to one of the remaining intranet servers.

In addition, the IS director adds software for other intranet services, such as a search engine and the Domain Name Service (DNS). Subsequently, intranet phase III will allow other departments to bring up their departmental intranet pages. When this occurs, it will be easier to refer to these servers via their domain name than to remember an IP address. The Domain Name Service takes care of this function. The search engine software will be used to index the intranet site and to allow users to search through information on the intranet, such as the phase 3 Sales and Marketing Presentations Repository.

The new hardware and software list now reads:

1. Dedicated server 1:
   a Pentium 100MHz or better, 64MB RAM,
   a 2GB hard disk, an SVGA monitor, and a 10BASE-T Ethernet adapter
   Windows NT Server v3.51
   an uninterruptible power supply (UPS)
   Web server software

2. Dedicated server 2:
   a Pentium 100MHz or better, 64MB RAM,
   a 2GB hard disk, an SVGA monitor, and a 10BASE-T Ethernet adapter
   Windows NT Server v3.51
   an uninterruptible power supply (UPS)
   Web server software

3. Dedicated server 3:
   a Pentium 100MHz or better, 64MB RAM,
   a 2GB hard disk, an SVGA monitor, and a 10BASE-T Ethernet adapter
   Windows NT Server v4.0
   an uninterruptible power supply (UPS)
   Web server software

4. HTML authoring software

5. DNS software

6. Search engine software

7. HTML conversion utilities
8. Adobe Acrobat
9. CGI programming books
10. HTML books
11. Java/JavaScript programming books

Notice that the IS director has added books to the end of the list. It is important to maintain a current technical library, and this project should be no exception.

CAST OF CHARACTERS

In approving the intranet project, management issues the following memo and makes the following requirements:

The management believes that a corporate intranet can be of great benefit to everyone in this organization. However, it can only be as successful as you, the employees, make it. Therefore, for management to allow this project to be initiated, we require that:

Volunteers from each department sign up to be on the intranet Committee. We ask that at least one, but no more than two individuals from each department be present at each intranet Committee meeting. If more people from your department are interested, they can rotate attendance at each meeting.

Each department will hold meetings to decide which applications and departmental information they want to contribute to the intranet. This information is to be given to the departmental representatives on the intranet Committee.

For the initial meeting of the intranet Committee, the following departments were represented:

Department	# of Representatives
IS	4
Sales	2
Marketing	2
Human Resources	2
Facilities	1
Executive Secretary	1

A representative from Human Resources is elected intranet project manager. Representatives from IS and Marketing are assigned the task of creating the necessary user and support documentation for the intranet project. IS presents the intranet physical plant project schedule and distributes a flowchart template for the various departments to use when designing their static Web documents. IS also posts a schedule for HTML document training. One of management's final requirements is that an executive secretary be present at all intranet committee meetings to take minutes. All minutes from the meeting are distributed to the intranet committee members and to upper management.

PHASE 1 APPLICATIONS

Now that the Web servers are in operational order, the phase 1 intranet applications can be installed. During the initial meetings, the intranet committee decided to implement these Phase 1 intranet applications:

Intranet Application	Implementation Phase
Human Resources Online	Phase 1
Suggestion Box	Phase 1
Company Newsletter	Phase 1
"About Our Department"	Phase 1
Corporate Events Calendar	Phase 1

While the IS Department was busy ordering and configuring Web servers, the various phase 1 intranet applications were being designed. Each application was designed for flow, content, and function. Intranet application development is no different from other forms of application development. You need to have a function to perform, you need to define the audience for each function, you must have content to present, and you must know how to present this content to your users.

Each application is defined in these terms. In addition, before anyone writes *any* HTML, JavaScript, or CGI code, a flowchart should be constructed for each application. For each application, an individual or group of individuals becomes the content provider. The content provider provides the initial application data, as well as timely updates. When information or content in an application changes, the content provider can easily update the application. The goal is to keep information provided on the intranet current and fresh.

GETTING STARTED

In our sample intranet, you've placed the order for the dedicated file servers. Your reseller is having a promotion and the servers come with Microsoft Windows NT Server v4.0 loaded and with 10BASE-T network adapters installed. You've compiled a task list for the Webmasters to complete, so these Windows NT servers will be functional intranet servers.

The task list for preparing these servers is:

1. Name each server.
2. Create user IDs for IS staff on each server.
3. Configure TCP/IP on each machine.
4. Install the Web server software on the two servers.

For phase 1 of the intranet project, the Domain Name Service (DNS) server will not be implemented. Thus, access to the intranet servers will be via IP address. You will use an internal class C IP addressing scheme and will eventually apply to the InterNIC (Network Solutions) for a valid range of IP addresses (in the event the company intranet may someday connect to the Internet). For the Web server software, you selected O'Reilly WebSite and Microsoft Internet Explorer.

MAKING THE SERVER CHANGES

To install and configure the Web server software, the Windows NT servers need to be configured with unique names and correct IP addresses. Both of these functions are accomplished through the Windows NT Control Panel. Open the Control Panel and double-click on the Network icon. The following window, similar to that shown in Figure 10-1, will open on your Windows NT Server.

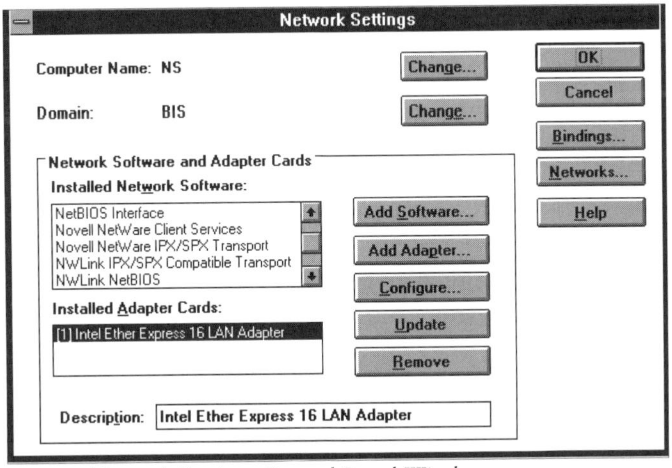

FIGURE *Network Settings Control Panel Window*
10-1

Click on the Change button next to the Computer Name. You will get a dialog box similar to that shown in Figure 10-2.

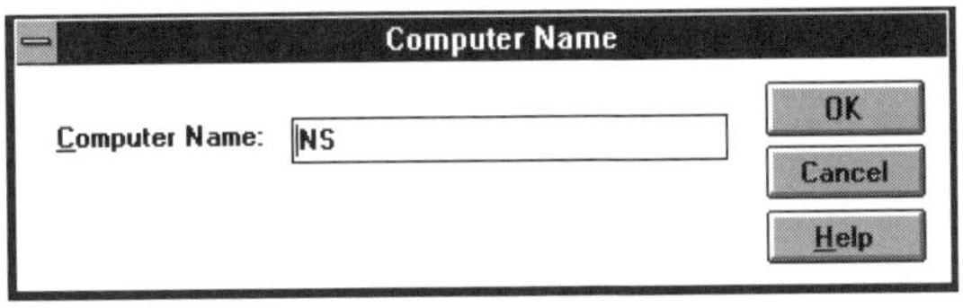

FIGURE *Computer Name*
10-2

Enter the name for this NT server and click on *OK* when finished, or click on *Cancel* to exit this screen and return to the Network Settings Control Panel window.

From the Network Settings Control Panel window, scroll down the list of Installed Network Software (shown in Figure 10-1) until you locate the TCP/IP stack. If this software has not been installed on your computer, you must install it now before you can proceed with installation of the Web server software.

To install the TCP/IP software, click on the Add Software button. You will see the dialog box shown in Figure 10-3.

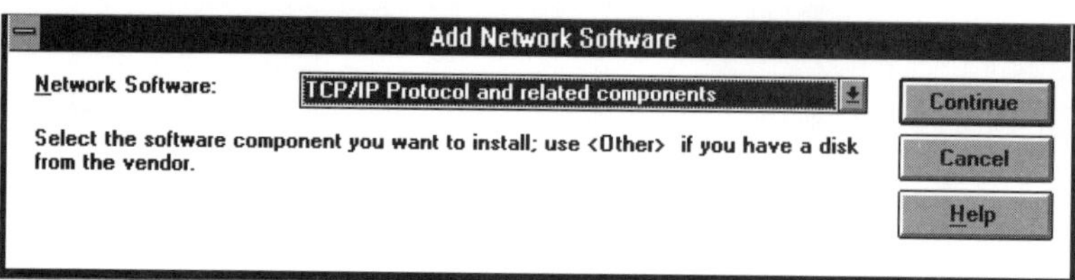

FIGURE *Add Network Software Dialog Box*
10-3

Select *TCP/IP Protocol and related components* from the list of available software, and click on the Continue button. You will see the following dialog box (Figure 10-4).

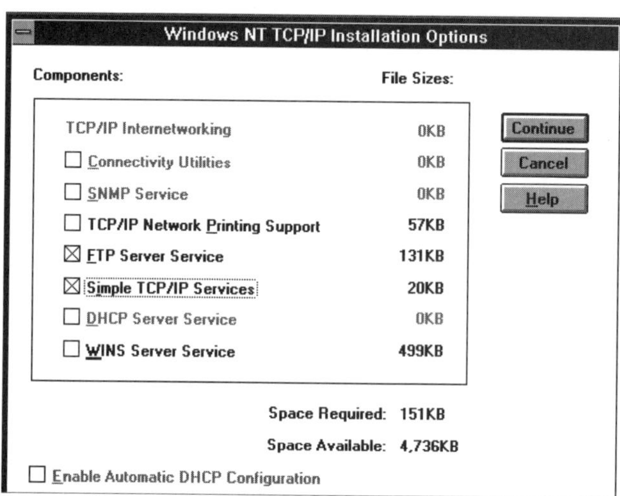

FIGURE *Windows NT TCP/IP Installation Options*
10-4

Select the TCP/IP features you want to install and click on the Continue button. At a minimum, you should check *Simple TCP/IP Services.* The software will be installed on your Windows NT server. If you are installing from diskette, you will be prompted for each disk as needed. If you are installing from CD-ROM, all you need to do is watch. When the software has been installed, you need to restart your Windows NT Server.

Once the software has been installed, you need to configure TCP/IP for your network adapter. Return to the Network Settings Control Panel shown in Figure 10-5.

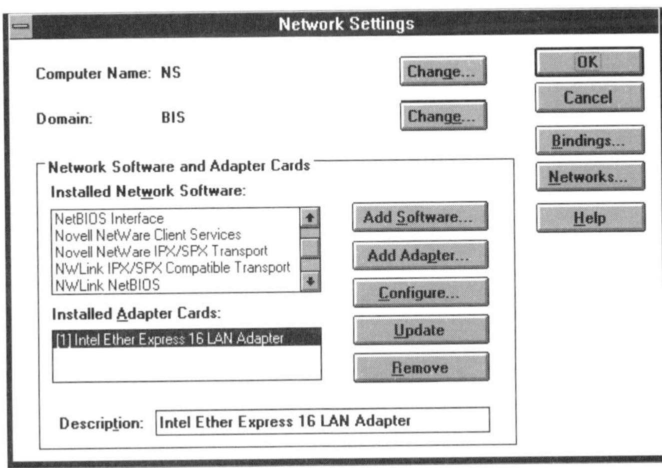

FIGURE *Network Settings Control Panel*
10-5

Scroll through the Installed Network Software window until you find the TCP/IP service. Click on the Configure button. A dialog box similar to that shown in Figure 10-6 will be displayed.

You need to complete at least three of the fields displayed in this window. If you do not know the appropriate information, do not fill it in. First, select the Adapter you want to configure. Next, specify the valid IP Address and the network Subnet Mask. Leave all other fields blank, unless you have an explicit value for those fields.

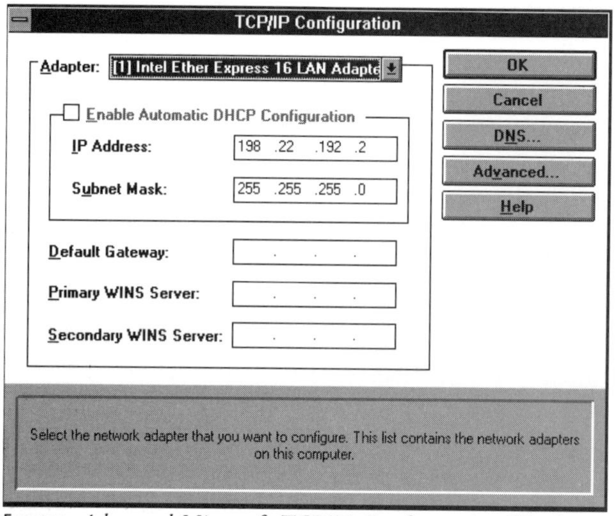

FIGURE **10-6** *Advanced Microsoft TCP/IP Configuration Window*

The IP address needs to be unique for every network device on your intranet, just as the Windows NT Server name needs to be unique for every Windows NT Server. For this intranet, a Class C network address (198.22.192.2) is selected. The address range is 198.22.192.1 - 256, with a subnet mask of 255.255.255.0. All intranet servers will have IP addresses in the range of 198.22.192.1 - 20, and IP clients will have IP addresses in the range of 198.22.192.21 - 254.

PING

Once the servers have been configured, you should test them on the network. Because the primary protocol is TCP/IP, one of the better tests you can run is to PING the servers from network clients. The PING utility is available from a number of sources. To use PING, enter PING followed by the IP address of the device you want to test. For example:

```
ping 198.22.192.2
Pinging 198.22.192.2 with 32 bytes of data:
Reply from 198.22.192.2: bytes=32 time=3ms TTL=32
```

```
Reply from 198.22.192.2: bytes=32 time=2ms TTL=32
Reply from 198.22.192.2: bytes=32 time=2ms TTL=32
Reply from 198.22.192.2: bytes=32 time=1ms TTL=32
```

The PING utility, if it finds the host in question, will replay as shown in the previous example. If the PING utility cannot find the IP host, it will return with a result similar to the following:

```
ping 198.22.192.20
Pinging 198.22.192.20 with 32 bytes of data:
Request timed out.
Request timed out.
Request timed out.
Request timed out.
```

Once you have a successful PING from each intranet server, install the intranet services. For our intranet example, we can now install the Web server software on the two Windows NT servers. On our intranet, the intranet committee has chosen O'Reilly's WebSite for the Web server software. (See Figure 10-7.)

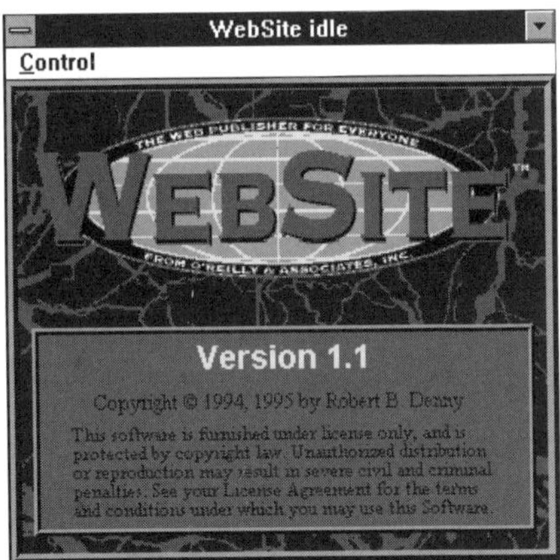

FIGURE *O'Reilly & Associates WebSite*
10-7

O'REILLY & ASSOCIATES WEBSITE

The latest version of O'Reilly's WebSite runs under Windows 95 or Windows NT Server and is supplied on a CD-ROM. This release of

WebSite contains a revised setup package, which conforms to the new components of WebSite Windows 95 style and includes extra features and protection.

WebSite Requirements

- A PC running Windows 95 (M7 release or later) or Windows NT Workstation or Server (preferred).
- A disk volume that supports long file names. Under Windows NT, this is not a problem. If you're running Windows 95, WebSite will be installed with long filenames enabled (disabling them is an installation option). You should have at least a few megabytes of free space on the disk.
- A TCP/IP hookup, preferably with DNS available. The server machine should be registered with DNS.

Table 10-2. WebSite Features

WebSite Software Components	Description
Server	A 32-bit HTTP server for Windows NT Server 3.5 and Windows 95. It runs as an application or as an NT service and is usually minimized on your desktop.
Server Admin	A graphical tool for configuring your WebSite server. The tabs along the top of the window take you to different configurable parameters.
WebView	A graphical tool for visualizing and editing your Web site. You can view the properties and edit documents in your HTML documents in particular.
MapEdit	A graphical tool for editing information about mouse-sensitive regions in mapped images embedded in HTML documents.
WebFind	A virtual document used by browsers of your Web site to find documents through free-form text searches.
WebIndex	A graphical tool for creating the index used in WebFind searches. This program creates an index before WebFind is used and updates the index whenever you significantly change your Web site.

- The file VBRUN300.DLL should be installed in your Windows SYSTEM directory. Without it, several demonstration items will not work. This file is the Visual Basic runtime library and is freely distributed on FTP sites, CompuServe, and BBSes.
- If you are running Windows NT, you should install the POSIX environment that comes with the Windows NT Resource kit. You might as well install the whole Resource Kit. The 3.1 kit runs OK for the most part on Windows NT 3.5. Put the POSIX directory into the SYSTEM directory's path.
- You may want to add associations in the File Manager for .SH to the POSIX shell, and if you have Windows NT Perl, add one for .PL to the Perl interpreter. Any other shell(s) you want to use need associations, too.

WebSite supports many of the common server-side includes (SSI) plus a unique set of page-counter server-side include functions. The page-counter features are very efficient and require no configuration of any kind. The SSI processor uses advanced memory-mapped processing and an assembly language tag-finder, so it efficiently finds and substitutes text. The internal imagemapper can read from NCSA-format imagemap files as well as from registry-based maps. Any file with the extension .map will be detected as an imagemap.

A new item, "Pause," has been added to the server's control and context menus, which allows you to pause the server when it is running as a desktop application. A paused server responds to incoming requests with a "503 Service Temporarily Unavailable" message. If the server is running as an application, a dialog box appears that allows you to customize the message sent. The server's icon title shows "Pausing (n)" when the server is first paused, if it was active before pausing. This allows you to see when the number of connections drops to zero. At that time, the title changes to "Paused." This feature works whether you pause the server from the Services Control Panel (running as a service) or from the server's own menu(s) (running as an application).

You can control the maximum number of simultaneous connections the server accepts. This provides a way to guarantee a level of service and is particularly useful if you have a low-speed communications line. The server responds to over-limit incoming requests with the "503 Service Temporarily Unavailable" HTTP message instead of appearing dead. The server supports the connection keep-alive feature implemented by Microsoft's Internet Explorer v2.0 and Netscape Navigator 2.0, permitting the browser to reuse the same connection to fetch inline GIF images. Each connection remains open for the duration of the receive timeout you set on the General page of the server's property sheet, or until the browser closes it.

The Windows CGI interface supports decoding of the multipart form data. This is used with the new forms-based uploading feature of Netscape Navigator 2.0. Standard CGI supports writing directly to the socket via the Win32 standard output file handle. This permits you to develop Netscape-style server-push applications. All CGI interfaces use short-form pathnames, so 16-bit CGI programs can operate where the server is under a directory whose name exceeds 8.3 or has blanks.

The tabs are displayed in two rows, which conform to the Windows 95 user interface guidelines. A new tab, Identity, has been added to the latest version of WebSite. See Figure 10-8.

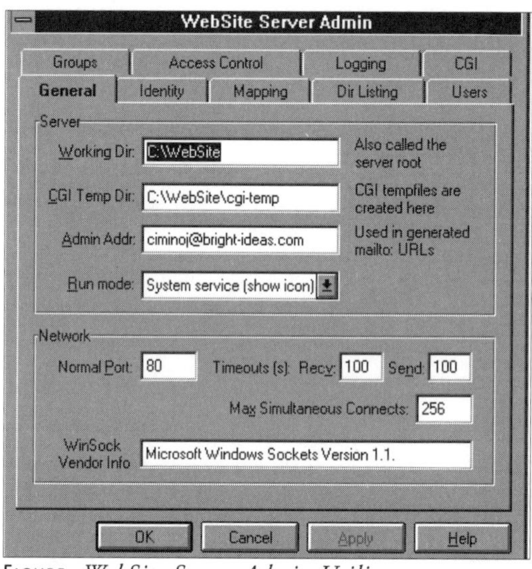

FIGURE 10-8 *WebSite Server Admin Utility*

This Identity tab is used to enable multihoming and for assigning host names and URL prefixes to each of a server's identities (IP addresses).

The user interface detects which IP addresses are in use on your system and puts them into a dropdown list (see Figure 10-9). The first time the Multiple Identities option is enabled and whenever your set of IP addresses changes, the user interface will alert you to verify that the settings for all IP addresses are appropriate. The Identity tab has a button that activates a new Identity Wizard that can greatly simplify multi-identity setup.

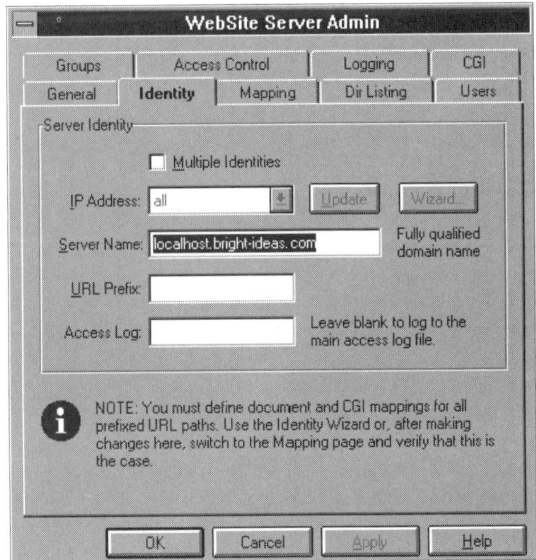

FIGURE *WebSite Identity Configuration Screen*
10-9

WebSite comes with excellent written documentation. The online documentation is good and will probably be sufficient to get your server up and running. The O'Reilly WebSite server leverages the server platform's security model, which is why Windows NT Server is an ideal platform of choice.

Another excellent Web server software package is Microsoft's Internet Information Server Explorer.

MICROSOFT INTERNET INFORMATION SERVER

The Microsoft Internet Information Server was obtained as a free download from the Microsoft Web site. It runs only under Windows NT Server or Workstation version 3.51 or higher. Microsoft Internet Information Server requires the Service Pack 3 upgrade if you want to run it on Windows NT Server v3.5.

The Microsoft Internet Information Server comes with a simple management utility, the Microsoft Internet Service Manager. You can use Internet Service Manager to enhance the configuration and performance of your server. Internet Service Manager helps you configure and monitor all Internet services running on any Windows NT Server-based computer in your network. (See Figure 10-10.)

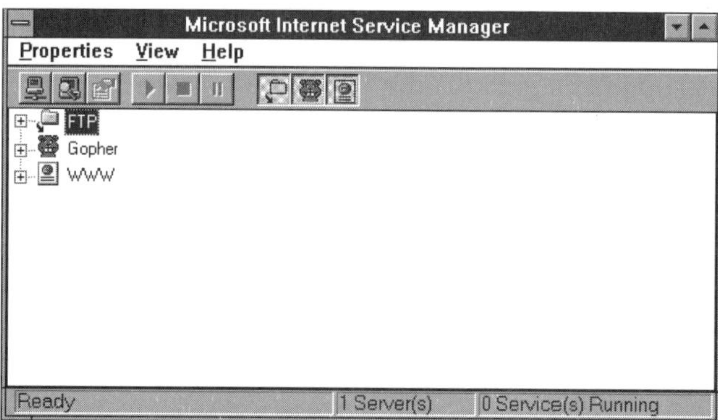

FIGURE *Microsoft Internet Service Manager.*
10-10 Screen shot reprinted with permission from Microsoft Corporation.

There are three views available in the Internet Service Manager. They are:

1. Reports,
2. Servers, and
3. Services.

The default is Report view, which alphabetically lists the selected computers, showing each installed service as a separate line item. This view is probably most useful for small sites with only a couple of computers running Internet Information Server.

The Server's view displays services running on network servers by computer name. The Server's view is most useful for sites running multiple computers, and gives you quick access to the status of the services installed on a specific computer.

The third view is the Services view, which lists the services on every selected computer grouped by service name. This is the view you would use if you have sites with widely distributed servers.

Microsoft Internet Service Manager has a discovery mechanism that finds computers running Microsoft Internet services on your network. To discover the Microsoft Internet Information Server computers on your network, choose *Find All Servers* in the Properties menu. The Internet Service Manager can also be used to start, stop, or pause an Internet Information Server service.

Configuring and managing Internet services is accomplished through the use of the Internet Service Manager property sheets. Double-click on a computer or service name to display its property sheets. Simply click on the tab at the top of each property sheet to display the properties for that category. The Services applet is also used to start, stop, and pause the WWW, Gopher, and FTP services. You can use the Startup button to configure how the service starts when the computer starts.

If your server provides files that are in multiple formats, your server must have a Multipurpose Internet Mail Extension (MIME) mapping for each file type. Most MIME types are set up in Internet Information Server. Web browsers may not be able to retrieve the file if MIME mapping on the server is not set up for your specific file type. The Microsoft Internet Information Server has more than 100 common MIME mappings installed by default.

The Microsoft Internet Information Server can run applications or scripts that remote users launch from within HTML documents. Using programming languages such as C or Perl, you can create applications or scripts that communicate with the user in dynamic HTML pages. Interactive applications or scripts can be written in almost any 32-bit programming language, such as C or Perl, or as Windows NT batch files (.BAT or .CMD). When you write your applications or script, you can use one of two supported interfaces: the Microsoft Internet Server Application Programming Interface (ISAPI) or the Common Gateway Interface (CGI). Documentation for ISAPI is available from Microsoft via subscription to the Microsoft Developer Network (MSDN). Applications that use ISAPI are compiled as dynamic-link libraries (DLLs) that are loaded by the WWW service at startup. Because the programs are resident in memory, ISAPI programs are significantly faster than applications written to the CGI specification.

The Microsoft Internet Information Server integrates Windows NT authentication (username and password) security and NT file system (NTFS) security. Additional security is implemented in the Internet Information Server by using IP address security and directory access settings. The source IP address of every packet received is checked against the settings in the Advanced property sheet. If the Internet Information Server is configured to allow access by all computers except those listed as exceptions to that rule, access will be denied to any computer with an IP address included in that list. IP address security is probably most useful on the Internet to exclude everyone except known users. IP address security can also be used to exclude individuals or entire networks that you do not want to grant access to.

By default, all requests use anonymous access through the IUSR_COMPUTERNAME user account created during Internet Information Server setup. This account is a user account, and it grants the right to log on locally. Username authentication is probably most useful if you want to control access to your server by individual user or group.

When you assign home and virtual directories for use by Internet Information Server services, you also specify the type of access users have for the files in that directory. The WWW service allows you to assign these permissions to a directory: Read, Execute, Require Secure SSL Channel, and NTFS.

Each of the Internet services can publish from multiple directories. Each directory can be located on a local drive or across the network by specifying the directory with a Universal Naming Convention (UNC) name, username, and password for access permission. Virtual directories on network drives must be on computers in the same Windows NT domain as the Internet Information Server. An Internet service can have one home directory and any number of other publishing directories. These other publishing directories are referred to as "virtual directories."

When a virtual directory is defined in Internet Service Manager, an alias is associated with the virtual directory. The alias is the subdirectory name that will be used by clients to access information in the virtual directory. If alias names for virtual directories are not specified by the administrator, an alias name will be generated automatically by Internet Service Manager. To create more than five virtual servers, you must change a Windows NT Registry entry.

When you install Microsoft Internet Information Server, the default method of logging in is to log in to a file. You must install ODBC version 2.5 if you prefer to collect logs in a database. You should then use the sample HTML pages installed with Internet Information Server to set up a log to a database. For best results, log in to a Microsoft SQL Server version 6.0 database. Do not install any ODBC drivers if you do not want to log in to a database, or use the Internet Database Connector on a Web server.

Installation of the Microsoft Internet Information Server is easy. The software will occupy about 3.5MB of server disk space, which includes a copy of Microsoft Internet Explorer and some very good HTML sample documents. Setup takes a matter of minutes for the basic Internet Information Server configuration; however, you should be well versed in Windows NT Server administration if you wish to set up more advanced security, or if you want to configure virtual servers. Online documentation is very good, and you can download reams of information and documentation from Microsoft's Web site.

THE FRONT END

The intranet committee made some rudimentary decisions about the overall structure and flow of the company's intranet. One of those decisions was about the intranet front end. This was an area of much contention, but it was generally agreed to that the opening screen for the intranet needed to have impact, yet should be simple to navigate. There were several options they could choose from:

- a simple, button-driven interface;
- a server-side imagemap;
- a client-side imagemap;
- a Shockwave application; and
- a Java/JavaScript applet.

The client-side imagemap was quickly dismissed when someone from IS said he was not sure if every browser installed was capable of supporting client-side imagemaps. In addition, the committee could not decide on the graphic to use for the imagemap. Perhaps this would be something that would change in phase 2 or 3.

Shockwave was an interesting suggestion, but the company did not have a copy of Macromedia Director, and nobody within the organization knew Lingo, the programming language needed to construct hypertext applications within Macromedia Director. Using Shockwave would require an outside consultant or someone from within the orgainzation who could learn this application. Shockwave was tabled for a later date.

Java and JavaScript were definite contenders. The intranet site had already seen some JavaScript applications, so it would be a simple matter to design the front end and write the JavaScript to support it. One of the IS members of the intranet Committee had just obtained some software, called Applet Ace. This is a free Java applet program from Macromedia that allows users to create buttons, banners, imagemaps, and bullets as animated Java applets.

The final issue was time. The intranet committee wanted to launch the corporate intranet as soon as possible, and most of the ideas for the front end would take longer than desired. It was decided that for phase 1 of the corporate intranet, a simple, button-driven front end would be used. Figure 10-11 shows the phase 1 intranet front end.

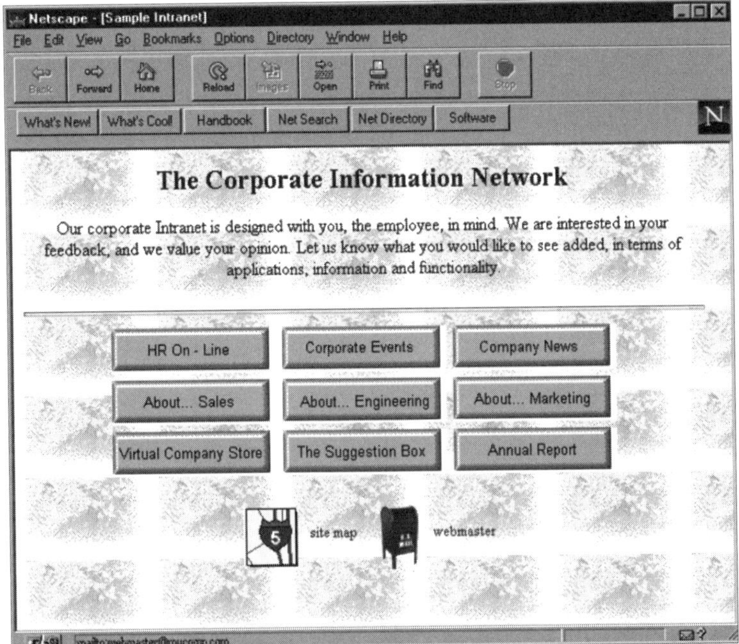

FIGURE 10-11 *Phase 1 Intranet Front End*

The following source code is the HTML code for the intranet front end. The source code can be found on the companion CD-ROM in the back of this book.

Note: As with all the examples in this book, the actual data as been omitted so you may more easily reuse or modify these templates for your own intranet applications.

In this example, some of the actual pages do not exist (such as sales.htm, market.htm, engineer.htm, or annual.pdf).

```html
<html>
<title>Sample intranet</title>
<body bgcolor="#FFFFFF" background="cloud.gif ">
<center><h2>The Corporate Information Network</h2><p>
Our corporate intranet is designed with you, the employee, in
mind. We are interested in your feedback, and we value your opin-
ion. Let us know what you would like to see added, in terms of
applications, information, and functionality.</center><p>
<hr size=3"><center>
<table cell padding="15%">
```

```
<tr>
<td valign="top"><a href="hrOnline.htm"><img src="btton1.gif"
border=0></a></td>
<td valign="top"><a href="calendar.htm "><img src="btton2.gif"
border=0></a></td>
<td valign="top"><a href="news.htm"><img src="btton3.gif" bor-
der=0></a></td>
</tr>
<tr>
<td valign="top"><a href="sales.htm"><img src="btton4.gif" bor-
der=0></a></td>
<td valign="top"><a href="engin.htm"><img src="btton5.gif" bor-
der=0></a></td>
<td valign="top"><a href="market.htm"><img src="btton6.gif" bor-
der=0></a></td>
</tr>
<tr>
<td valign="top"><a href="virtual.htm"><img src="btton7.gif" bor-
der=0></a></td>
<td valign="top"><a href="suggest.htm"><img src="btton8.gif" bor-
der=0></a></td>
<td valign="top"><a href="annual.pdf"><img src="btton9.gif" bor-
der=0></a></td>
</tr>
</table>
<p>
<a href="sitemap.htm"><img src="map.gif" border=0 hspace=10
align="middle" ><font size="-1">site map</font></a>
<a href="mailto:Webmaster@mycomp.com"><img src="mail.gif"border=0
hspace=10 align="middle" ><font size="-1">Webmaster</font></a>
</center>
</body>
</html>
```

THE SITE MAP

As you can see on the intranet front end, there is an icon for an intranet site map. The site map is an overall view of the intranet drawn as a complete flowchart of the pages and links contained within the site.

Once the flow of the site has been established, the site map allows easy navigation to a specific subject or area within the intranet. As new items are added to the intranet, this map needs to be updated to reflect these changes.

Because the intranet committee could not agree on an imagemap for the front end, an imagemap was ruled out for the phase 1 site map. The site map would be created as a hypertext document using the HTML <UL> list tag. This will allow subtopics to appear indented.

The following source code is the HTML code that was written for the intranet site map. The source code is on the companion CD-ROM.

Note: As with all the examples in this book, the actual data has been omitted so that you can more easily reuse or modify the templates for your own intranet applications.

```html
<html>
<title>Site Map</title>
<body bgcolor="#FFFFFF">
<center><h3>Site Map</h3></center>
<hr size=3><br>
<ul>
<li><a href="intranet.htm">Home Page</a><br>
<ul>
<li><a href="hrOnline.htm">HR Online</a><br>
<ul>
<li><a href="eom.htm">Employee of the Month</a><br>
<li><a href="hrfaq.htm">HR Frequently Asked Questions</a><br>
<li><a href="fol.htm">Forms Online</a><br>
<ul>
<li><a href="forms1.htm">Benefit Forms</a><br>
<li><a href="forms2.htm">Employee Forms</a><br>
<li><a href="forms3.htm">Vacation Forms</a><br>
<li><a href="forms4.htm">Tax Forms</a><br>
</ul>
<li><a href="suggest.htm">HR Suggestion Box</a><br>
<li><a href="jobs.htm">Jobs Postings</a><br>
</ul>
<li><a href="calendar.htm">Corporate Events Calendar</a><br>
<li><a href="news.htm">Company Newsletter</a><br>
<li><a href="sales.htm">About... Sales</a><br>
<li><a href="engineer.htm">About ... Engineering</a><br>
<li><a href="market.htm">About... Marketing</a><br>
<li><a href="virtual.htm">Virtual Company Store</a><br>
<li><a href="suggest.htm">Suggestion Box</a><br>
<li><a href="annual.pdf">1995 Annual Report</a><br>
</ul>
</ul>
</body>
</html>
```

Figure 10-12 shows the sitemap the user will see.

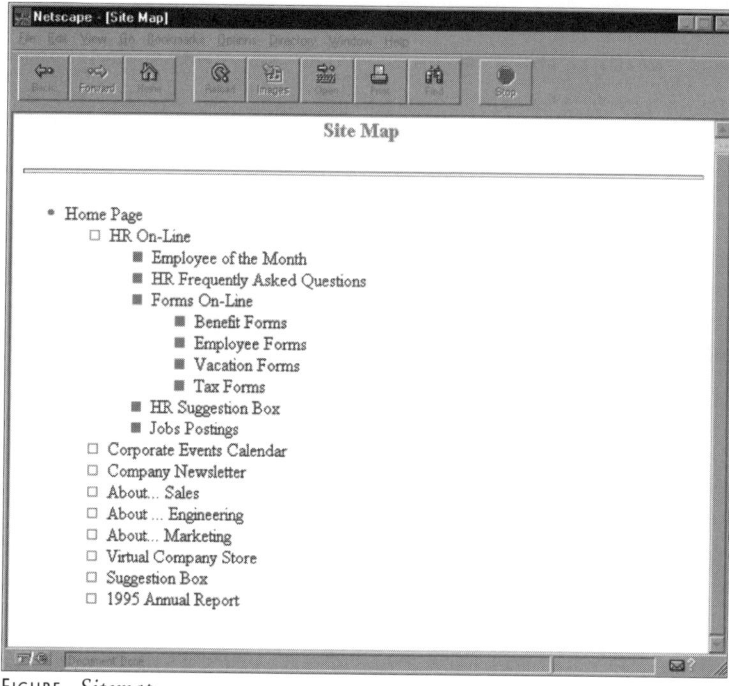

FIGURE *Sitemap*
10-12

HUMAN RESOURCES ONLINE

One of the first intranet applications proposed to the intranet committee was the HR Online application. The target audience of the HR Online application is obvious: the entire organization. The Human Resources department is constantly answering questions about benefits, company policies, and the like. In many cases, the same questions are being asked over and over. The Human Resources department feels the intranet is an ideal forum to post these frequently asked questions and their answers. In addition, HR wants to have a section to post new job openings, as well as an area to showcase the Employee of the Month. (See Figure 10-13.)

One other application HR wants on the intranet was a directory of common forms. Because almost all HR forms require an employee signa-

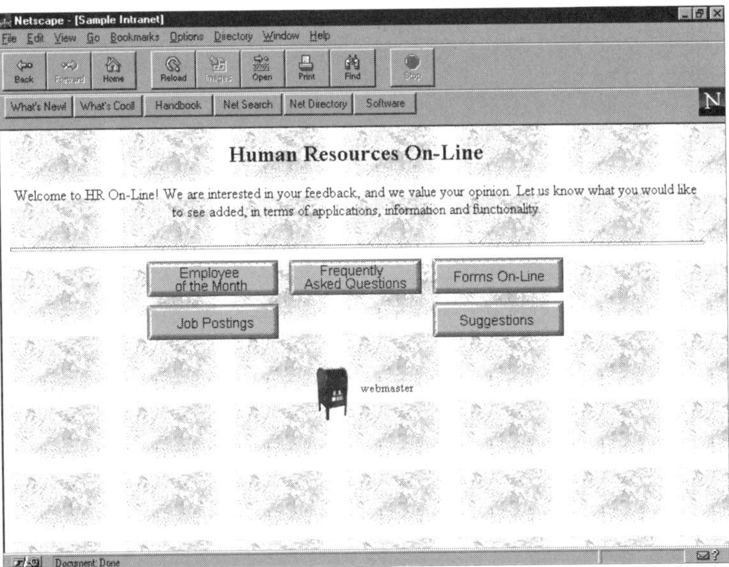

FIGURE **10-13** *Human Resources Online*

ture, using forms within the intranet is not an option. However, by using Adobe Acrobat and installing the Adobe Acrobat Reader plug-in on the client browser, the forms can be obtained easily, and the employee can simply print them and fill them in.

HR Online will continue to grow and develop. The Human Resources department feels these applications would be a good starting point. Employee feedback would be key in expanding the functionality of the HR Online intranet application. Because of this, the Suggestion Box intranet application would also be modified and included within HR Online, specifically for the HR Online intranet functions.

HR Online Structure

The HTML flowchart in Figure 10-14 details the flow of the various phase 1 intranet applications to be provided by the Human Resources department. Each application is elementary in design, but is envisioned to grow in size, complexity, and functionality as user feedback is received and acted on.

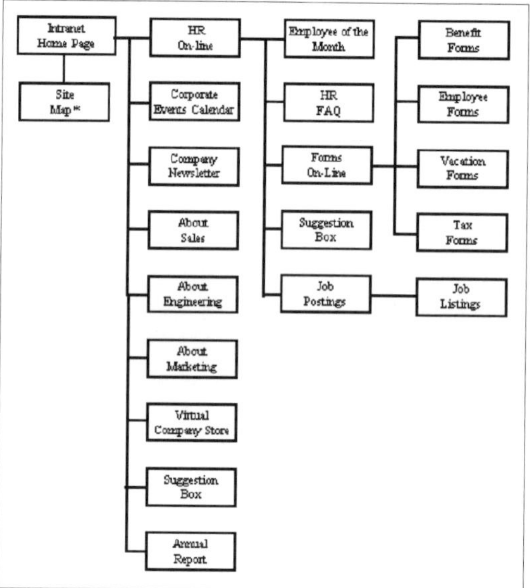

FIGURE 10-14 *HTML Flowchart*

EMPLOYEE OF THE MONTH

The following source code is the JavaScript application written for the Employee of the Month HR Online page. The source code can be found on the companion CD-ROM.

Note: As with all the examples in this book, the actual data as been omitted so you may more easily reuse or modify these templates for your own intranet applications.

```
<HTML>
<HEAD>
<SCRIPT>
// JavaScript Employee of the Month
function select_item(name, value)
{
        this.name = name;
        this.value = value;
 }
function get_selection(select_object)
 {
        contents = new select_item();
        for(var i=0;i<select_object.options.length;i++)
            if(select_object.options[i].selected == true)
    {
                contents.name = select_object.options[i].text;
                contents.value = select_object.options[i].value;
            }
```

```
            return contents;
}
function display_image(formfield)
{
selection = get_selection(formfield.imagename);
myWindow = window.open("", "Preview",
"toolbar=0,location=0,directories=0,status=0,menubar=0,scroll-
bars=0,resizable=0,copyhistory=0,
width=200,height=255");
myWindow.document.open();
myWindow.document.write("<HTML><HEAD>");
myWindow.document.write("<TITLE>Preview</TITLE>");
myWindow.document.write("</HEAD><BODY BGCOLOR=FFFFFF
TEXT=000000>");
myWindow.document.write("<FORM><CENTER><B><FONT SIZE=+1>" +
            selection.name + "</FONT></B><HR>");
myWindow.document.write("<IMG HSPACE=0 VSPACE=0 HEIGHT=150
WIDTH=100 " + "SRC= 'file:///C|/MYDOCU~1/BOOKS/INTRANET/CDROM/"+
selection.value + "'>");
//            modify the path for the directory or URL that the
images can be loaded
myWindow.document.write("<HR><FORM><INPUT TYPE='button'
VALUE='Close' " + "onClick='window.close()'></FORM>");
myWindow.document.write("</CENTER>");
myWindow.document.write("</BODY></HTML>");
myWindow.document.close();
    }
</SCRIPT>
<TITLE>HR Online Employee of the Month</TITLE>
</HEAD>
<BODY BGCOLOR=FFFFFF TEXT=000000>
<CENTER>
<FONT SIZE=+2>Employee of the Month </FONT><BR>
</CENTER>
<FORM NAME="previewForm">
The following is the listing of our company's "Employee of the
Month" for this year. Please make your selection from the follow-
ing list, then select the <B>View</B> button to see who was
selected as that month's "Employee of the Month".<p>
To see additional images, just move the preview window to the
side and select another month from the list.<br>
You do not need to close the preview window.<p>
<CENTER>
<select NAME="imagename">
<option value="donna.gif">January
<option value="intro.gif">February
<option value="jim2.gif">March
</select>
<input type=button value="View"
onClick="display_image(this.form)">
</CENTER>
</FORM>
<HR>
</BODY>
</HTML>
```

When the Employee of the Month application is run, it produces an initial screen as shown in Figure 10-15.

When a user selects a month and presses the View button, a second window opens, displaying the photograph of that month's employee. (See Figure 10-16.) The images were scanned in as .GIF images on the graphics department's flatbed scanner.

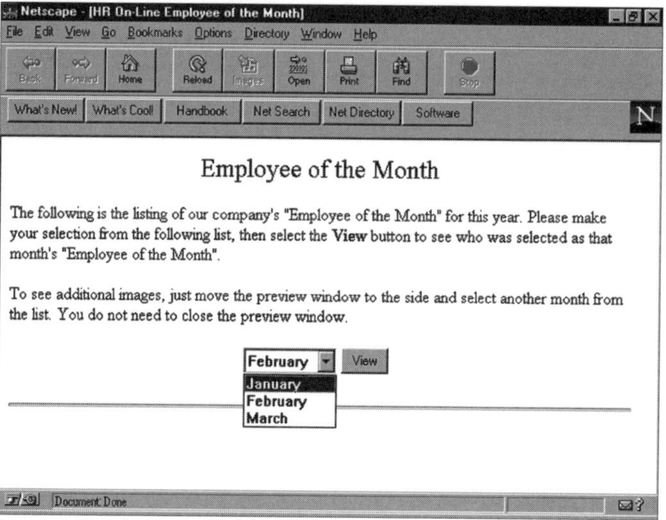

FIGURE *Employee of the Month Application*
10-15

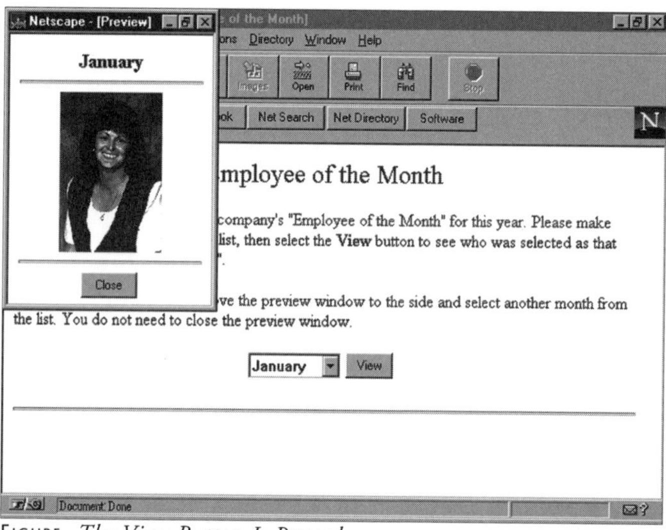

FIGURE *The View Button Is Pressed...*
10-16

The HR Online FAQ Page

The Human Resources Frequently Asked Questions page for HR Online is a simple HTML document. The format of this page has all the questions at the top of the document and all the answers below. Hypertext links jump users between questions and the answers. Designing the document in this manner makes it very easy to add questions, as well as update answers.

The source code for this page, in skeletal form, is presented below. This code is also supplied on the companion CD-ROM. The document is presented in this format to make it easy to modify for any application. Because of the length and repetitive nature of this code, we have removed a large portion of the answers section, but you will get the idea.

```
<html>
<head>
<title>HR Online FAQ</title>
</head>
<body background="bkgrnd.gif">
<a name="top"><center>
<h2>Human Resources Online<br>Frequently Asked Questions
    </h2></center>
<p>
Welcome to the HR Online FAQ Page. This page has been designed to
provide you answers to common HR and company-related questions.
This page will be updated frequently, so keep checking back with
us from time to time.<p>
This page is organized by questions. When you click on a ques-
tion, you will be brought directly to the associated answer. From
there, you can return to the FAQ listing, return to the HR Online
page, or go back to the intranet Home Page.
<p>
<hr><center>
<h2>Frequently Asked Questions</h2></center>
<ul>
<li> <a name="Question1"> <a href="#answer1"> Question 1 </a><p>
<li> <a name="Question2"> <a href="#answer2"> Question 2 </a><p>
<li> <a name="Question3"> <a href="#answer3"> Question 3 </a><p>
<li> <a name="Question4"> <a href="#answer4"> Question 4 </a><p>
<li> <a name="Question5"> <a href="#answer5"> Question 5 </a><p>
<li> <a name="Question6"> <a href="#answer6"> Question 6 </a><p>
<li> <a name="Question7"> <a href="#answer7"> Question 7</a><p>
<li> <a name="Question8"> <a href="#answer8"> Question 8 </a><p>
<li> <a name="Question9"> <a href="#answer9"> Question 9 </a><p>
<li> <a name="Question10"> <a href="#answer10"> Question 10
    </a><p>
<li> <a name="Question11"> <a href="#answer11"> Question 11
    </a><p>
<li> <a name="Question12"> <a href="#answer12"> Question 12
    </a><p>
<li> <a name="Question13"> <a href="#answer13"> Question 13
    </a><p>
```

```html
<li><a name="Question14">  <a href="#answer14"> Question
   14</a><p>
<li><a name="Question15">  <a href="#answer15"> Question
   15</a><p>
<li><a name="Question16">  <a href="#answer16"> Question 16
   </a><p>
<li> <a name="Question17"> <a href="#answer17"> Question 17
   </a><p>
<li><a name="Question18">  <a href="#answer18"> Question 18
   </a><p>
<li> <a name="Question 19"> <a href="#answer19"> Question 19
   </a><p>
<li><a name="Question 20">  <a href="#answer20"> Question 20
   </a><p>
</ul><p>
<hr size=3>
<a name="answer1">
<h2>Answer #1</h2>
<p>
The company offers a blah blah blah blah blah blah blah blah blah
blah blah blah blah blah blah blah blah blah blah blah blah blah
blah blah blah blah blah blah blah blah blah blah blah blah blah
blah blah blah blah blah blah blah blah blah blah blah blah blah
blah blah blah blah blah blah blah blah blah blah blah blah.
<p>
.

.

.
<hr size=3>
<a name="answer20">
<h2>Answer #20</h2>
<p>
The company offers a blah blah blah blah blah blah blah blah blah
blah blah blah blah blah blah blah blah blah blah blah blah blah
blah blah blah blah blah blah blah blah blah blah blah blah blah
blah blah blah blah blah blah blah blah blah blah blah blah blah
blah blah blah blah blah blah blah blah blah blah blah blah.
<p>
<a href="#Question20"><img src="top.gif" border=0" align=middle
   hspace=6>Back to the Top</a>
<a href="hrOnline.htm"><img src="back.gif" border=0" align=middle
   hspace=6>Return to intranet Home Page</a>
<a href="intranet.htm"><img src="home1.gif" border=0" align=
   middle  hspace=6>Return to intranet Home Page</a>
<HR size=3>
<P><center> Copyright &#169 1996 by Bright Ideas Software,
   Inc.</center>
</body>
</html>
```

When this application runs, the user sees the following screen. (See Figure 10-17.)

When a user selects a question from the list, he or she navigates to the appropriate answer shown in Figure 10-18.

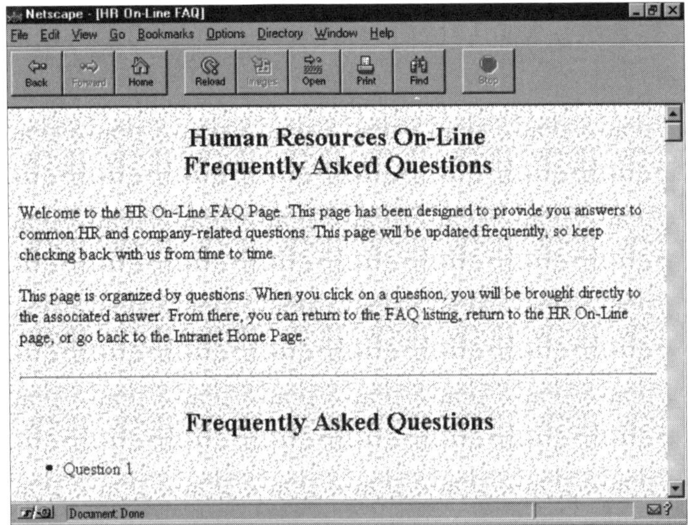

FIGURE **10-17** *The HR Online FAQ Page*

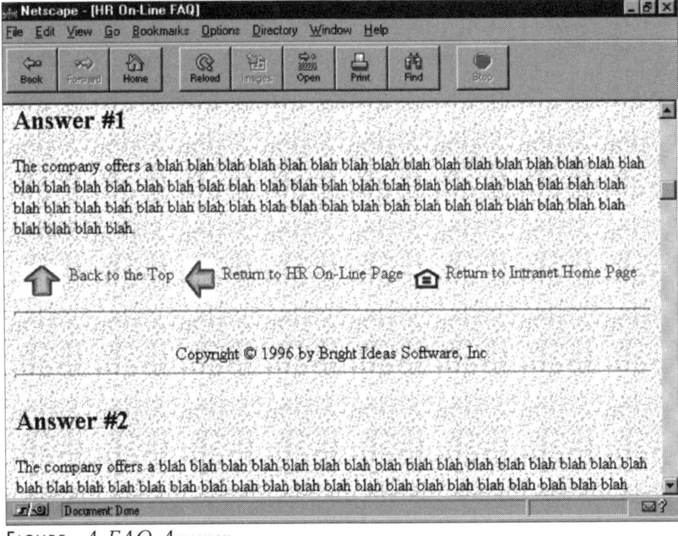

FIGURE **10-18** *A FAQ Answer*

Forms Online

The Forms Online application eases the distribution of common Human Resource forms. In most cases, forms used by the company require a signature; therefore, electronic forms, traditionally used on the internet, would not be acceptable. For the Forms Online section of the Human Resource page, Adobe Acrobat was selected as the method for creating and distributing HR forms over the company intranet. All forms available in this section must be generated in Adobe PDF. PDF stands for "Portable Document Format," a cross-platform standard developed by Adobe Systems for publishing on the World Wide Web, marketed under the name "Adobe Acrobat."

Acrobat lets you create electronic documents from a wide range of authoring tools, retaining all the original formatting, fonts, and layout. If you need a more in-depth explanation of Acrobat and PDF, you can go to the Adobe Acrobat Overview page at the Adobe's Web site (www.adobe.com).

To view .PDF documents, you need to install the Acrobat Reader on your system. The Acrobat Reader is free and can be downloaded from the Adobe Web site. It also comes packaged with many software products, so before you try to download the Acrobat Reader, you may want to examine your recent software purchases to see if the Adobe Acrobat reader is contained on them. You may already have it.

The Acrobat Reader is available for just about any computer platform, and all are available from the Adobe Web site. You can also find the Adobe Acrobat Reader for Windows and Macintosh on the companion CD-ROM.

Documents written in .PDF format can be printed with full PostScript quality, viewed as a standalone slide show, and searched by keyword. They also take up very little space on your hard drive. There are also plug-ins to Netscape Navigator that allow .PDF documents to be viewed within the browser window, rather than as standalone applications.

FORMS ONLINE STRUCTURE

When designing the Forms Online page, the HR department had two design concepts. The first concept was to have buttons represent the different form types available and to use frames. When users clicked on a form type, they would see a page containing buttons for those forms. The second concept was to use JavaScript to create selectable lists of the various form types. As in the first concept, when users clicked on a form type, they would see a page containing buttons for those forms.

The HTML code for both pages is simple, so we will provide examples of both page concepts. For the first Forms Online page, the main HTML document establishes the frames, the second HTML document presents the various buttons within the menu frame, and each subsequent HTML document presents a list of forms for each menu item. For simplicity, we illustrate only one of each HTML document. The entire source for this example can be found on the companion CD-ROM. Figure 10-19 shows the configuration of the Forms Online page.

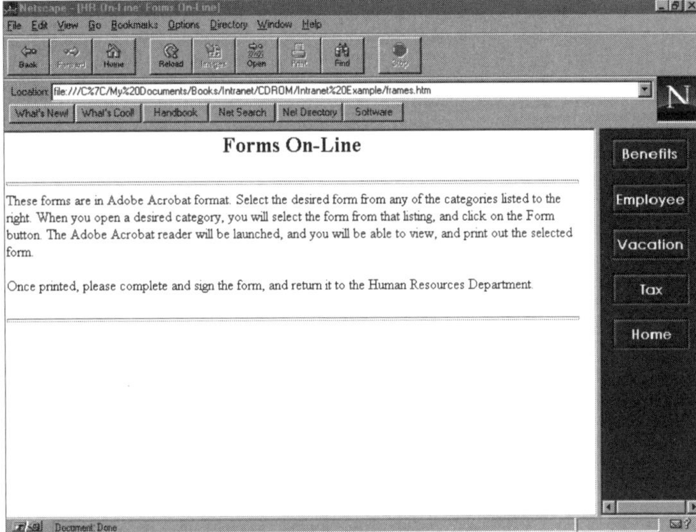

FIGURE   *The Configuration of the Forms Online Page*
10-19

MAIN FORMS ONLINE HTML DOCUMENT (EXAMPLE #1)

```
<HTML>
<HEAD>
<TITLE>HR Online: Forms Online</TITLE>
</HEAD>
<FRAMESET COLS="*,125">
                <FRAME SRC="open.htm" NAME="main1" MARGINHEIGHT=2
MARGINWIDTH=2 SCROLLING=AUTO>
                <FRAME SRC="menu.htm" NAME="right" NORESIZE MAR-
GINHEIGHT=2 MARGINWIDTH=10 SCROLLING=AUTO>
</FRAMESET>
</HTML>
Menu Selector (Example #1):
<HTML>
```

```
<HEAD>
<TITLE>HR Online Forms Menu</TITLE>
</HEAD>
<BODY BGCOLOR="#02356e">
<BASE TARGET="main1">
<P><center>
<A HREF="form1.htm"><IMG SRC="button1.gif" " ALIGN=TOP WIDTH="95"
    HEIGHT="42" BORDER="0" VSPACE="4"></A><BR CLEAR=LEFT>
<A HREF="form2.htm"><IMG SRC="button2.gif" " ALIGN=TOP WIDTH="95"
    HEIGHT="42" BORDER="0" VSPACE="4"></A><BR CLEAR=LEFT>
<A HREF="form3.htm"><IMG SRC="button3.gif" " ALIGN=TOP WIDTH="95"
    HEIGHT="42" BORDER="0" VSPACE="4"></A><BR CLEAR=LEFT>
<A HREF="form4.htm"><IMG SRC="button4.gif" " ALIGN=TOP WIDTH="95"
    HEIGHT="42" BORDER="0" VSPACE="4"></A><BR CLEAR=LEFT>
<A HREF="hrOnline.htm"><IMG SRC="button5.gif" " ALIGN=TOP WIDTH=
    "95" HEIGHT="42" BORDER="0" VSPACE="4"></A><BR CLEAR=LEFT>
</center>
</BODY>
</HTML>
```

INDIVIDUAL FORMS PAGE HTML TEMPLATE (EXAMPLE #1)

```
<HTML>
<HEAD>
<TITLE>HR Online Forms Menu</TITLE>
</HEAD>
<BODY BGCOLOR="#d3d3d3">
<BASE TARGET="main1"><center><p>
<h2>Employee Tax-Related Forms</h2></center><p>
These forms are in Adobe Acrobat format. When you click on any of
these forms, the Adobe Acrobat reader will be launched, and you
will be able to view and print out this form. Once printed,
please complete the form, and return it to the Human Resources
Department.
<hr size="3">
<P> <center>
<A HREF="form1.pdf"><IMG SRC="form1.gif" " ALIGN=TOP WIDTH="93"
    HEIGHT="42" BORDER="0" VSPACE="4" HSPACE="10" ></A>
<A HREF="form2.pdf"><IMG SRC="form2.gif" " ALIGN=TOP WIDTH="93"
    HEIGHT="42" BORDER="0" VSPACE="4" HSPACE="10" ></A>
<A HREF="form3.pdf"><IMG SRC="form3.gif" " ALIGN=TOP WIDTH="93"
    HEIGHT="42" BORDER="0" VSPACE="4" HSPACE="10" ></A>
<A HREF="form4.pdf"><IMG SRC="form4.gif" " ALIGN=TOP WIDTH="93"
    HEIGHT="42" BORDER="0" VSPACE="4" HSPACE="10"  ></A><br>
<A HREF="form5.pdf"><IMG SRC="form5.gif" " ALIGN=TOP WIDTH="93"
    HEIGHT="42" BORDER="0" VSPACE="4" HSPACE="10" ></A>
<A HREF="form6.pdf"><IMG SRC="form6.gif" " ALIGN=TOP WIDTH="93"
    HEIGHT="42" BORDER="0" VSPACE="4" HSPACE="10" ></A>
<A HREF="form7.pdf"><IMG SRC="form7.gif" " ALIGN=TOP WIDTH="93"
    HEIGHT="42" BORDER="0" VSPACE="4" HSPACE="10" ></A>
<A HREF="form8.pdf"><IMG SRC="form8.gif" " ALIGN=TOP WIDTH="93"
    HEIGHT="42" BORDER="0" VSPACE="4" HSPACE="10" ></A>
</center>
</BODY>
</HTML>
```

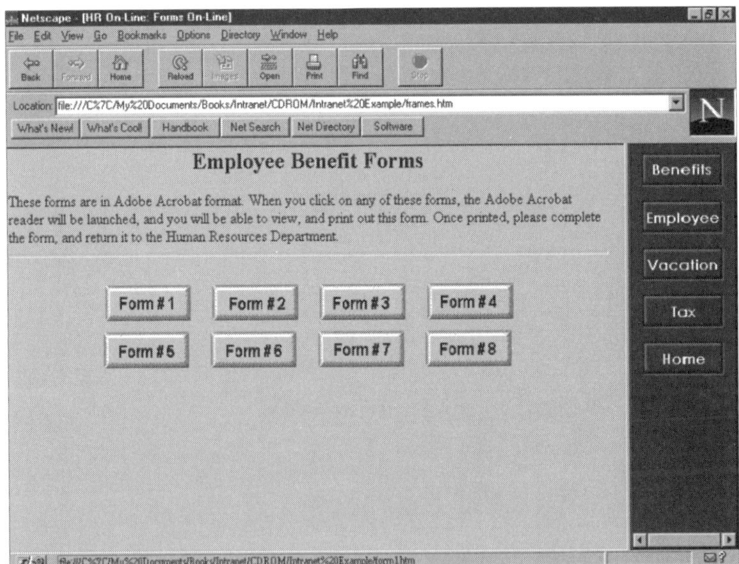

FIGURE *The Forms Requestor Screen*
10-20

FORMS ONLINE (EXAMPLE # 2)

The second configuration option for the Forms Online page uses JavaScript to construct a listing of forms and form categories. The following source code is the template used for this layout. The complete source code can be found on the companion CD-ROM.

```
<html>
<title>HR Online: Form's Online</title>
<script language="JavaScript">
<!- Hide the script from old browsers -
function linkto(form) {
        var myindex=form.dest.selectedIndex
        window.open(form.dest.options[myindex].value,"main","");
}
//->
</SCRIPT>
<center>
<h3>Forms On-Line</h3></center>
<hr size=3>
<p>
These forms are in Adobe Acrobat format. Select the desired form
from any of the categories shown here. When you highlight a
desired form, and click on the <b>Open Form</b> button, the Adobe
Acrobat reader will be launched, and you will be able to view and
print out this form. <p>Once printed, please complete and sign
the form, and return it to the Human Resources Department.
```

```
<p>
<hr size=3>
<center>
<table cell padding="15%">
<tr><td>
<FORM NAME="form1">
  <SELECT NAME="dest" SIZE=1>
    <OPTION SELECTED VALUE="">————— Benefit Forms —————
    <OPTION VALUE="form1.pdf">Form 1
    <OPTION VALUE="form2.pdf">Form 2
    <OPTION VALUE="form3.pdf">Form 3
    <OPTION VALUE="form4.pdf">Form 4
    <OPTION VALUE="form5.pdf">Form 5
    <OPTION VALUE="form6.pdf">Form 6
    <OPTION VALUE="form7.pdf">Form 7
    <OPTION VALUE="form8.pdf">Form 8
  </SELECT>
<P> <center>
<INPUT TYPE="BUTTON" VALUE="Open Form"
onClick="linkto(this.form)"></center>
</FORM></td>
<td>
<FORM NAME="form2">
  <SELECT NAME="dest" SIZE=1>
    <OPTION SELECTED VALUE="">———— Employee Forms ————
    <OPTION VALUE="form1.pdf">Form 1
    <OPTION VALUE="form2.pdf">Form 2
    <OPTION VALUE="form3.pdf">Form 3
    <OPTION VALUE="form4.pdf">Form 4
    <OPTION VALUE="form5.pdf">Form 5
    <OPTION VALUE="form6.pdf">Form 6
    <OPTION VALUE="form7.pdf">Form 7
    <OPTION VALUE="form8.pdf">Form 8
  </SELECT>
<P><center>
<INPUT TYPE="BUTTON" VALUE="Open Form"
onClick="linkto(this.form)"> </center>
</FORM></td></tr>
<tr><td>
<FORM NAME="form3">
  <SELECT NAME="dest" SIZE=1>
    <OPTION SELECTED VALUE="">———— Vacation Forms ————
    <OPTION VALUE="form1.pdf">Form 1
    <OPTION VALUE="form2.pdf">Form 2
    <OPTION VALUE="form3.pdf">Form 3
    <OPTION VALUE="form4.pdf">Form 4
    <OPTION VALUE="form5.pdf">Form 5
    <OPTION VALUE="form6.pdf">Form 6
    <OPTION VALUE="form7.pdf">Form 7
    <OPTION VALUE="form8.pdf">Form 8
  </SELECT>
<P><center>
```

```
<INPUT TYPE="BUTTON" VALUE="Open Form"
onClick="linkto(this.form)"> </center>
</FORM></td>
<td>
<FORM NAME="form4">
  <SELECT NAME="dest" SIZE=1>
    <OPTION SELECTED VALUE="">————— Tax Forms —————
    <OPTION VALUE="form1.pdf">Form 1
    <OPTION VALUE="form2.pdf">Form 2
    <OPTION VALUE="form3.pdf">Form 3
    <OPTION VALUE="form4.pdf">Form 4
    <OPTION VALUE="form5.pdf">Form 5
    <OPTION VALUE="form6.pdf">Form 6
    <OPTION VALUE="form7.pdf">Form 7
    <OPTION VALUE="form8.pdf">Form 8
  </SELECT>
<P><center>
<INPUT TYPE="BUTTON" VALUE="Open Form"
onClick="linkto(this.form)"> </center>
</FORM></td></tr></table></center>
</HTML>
```

When this JavaScript forms requestor application runs, the output appears on the user screen shown in Fiqure 10-21. When a user selects a form category, the output appears on the screen, as shown in Figure 10-22.

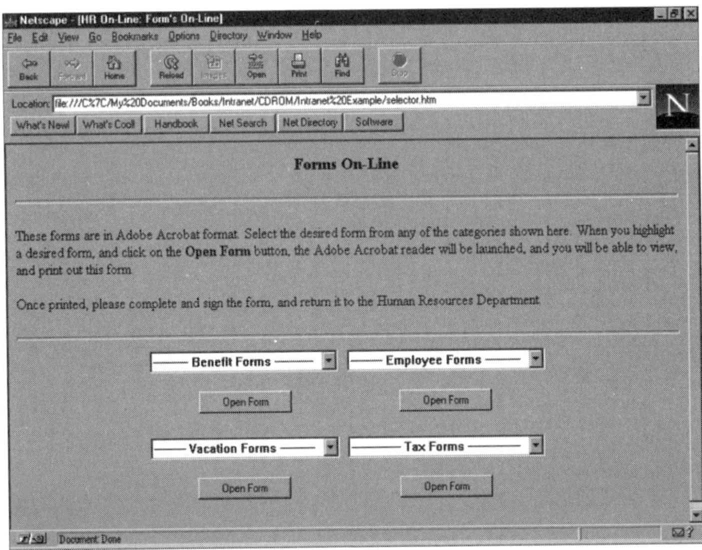

FIGURE **10-21** *The JavaScript Forms Requestor Screen*

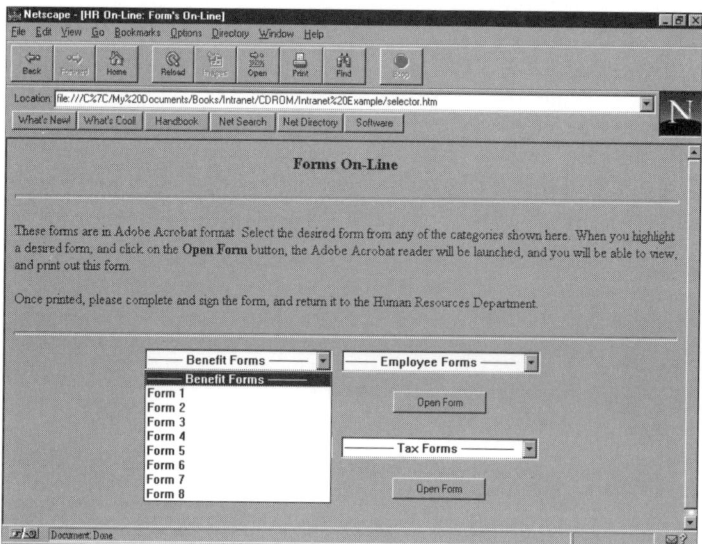

FIGURE *A Forms Listing*
10-22

Job Postings Page

The Human Resources department is constantly receiving notification from departments for new job openings. The policy of the company is to promote from within, so the HR department posts these job openings on the company bulletin board in the cafeteria. With the advent of the company intranet, the HR department wants to move the new job postings to the HR Online section of the intranet for employees with networked computers.

In keeping with the old method of posting the new listings on the company bulletin board, the HR department wants to retain the same look of a bulletin board. With this in mind, the design of the Job Postings application consists of two HTML documents. The first HTML document is used for the front end, from which the user selects from the available job postings; the second HTML document provides the requested job information and requirements.

For the front-end document, graphic design elements create a "pin-up note" look for each new job posting. Each image is used as a "button," which links to the appropriate section of the job description HTML document. The images are created for each job, with the text reflecting the job type or description. The HTML <BODY> tag creates a background on the page that resembles a corkboard.

The job description document, the second part of this application, is a static HTML document. The <NAME> tags are used within the document to differentiate job descriptions. Because the HR department identifies new jobs by a job number, the <NAME> tag reflects the specific job number. This makes it easier for the HR department to add or remove jobs from this page.

The following source code is the template used for this application. The complete source code can be found on the companion CD-ROM.

```
<html>
<title>HR Online:Job Postings</title>
<body background="cork.gif" >
<center>
<p>
<a href="jobs.htm#101">  <img src="note1a.gif" width="25%" bor-
der="0" vspace=0 hspace="10"> </a>
<a href="jobs.htm#102">   <img src="note2a.gif" width="25%" bor-
der="0" vspace=0 hspace="10"> </a>
<a href="jobs.htm#103">  <img src="note3a.gif" width="25%" bor-
der="0" vspace=0 hspace="10"> </a>
<p>
<a href="jobs.htm#104">  <img src="note4a.gif" width="25%" bor-
der="0" vspace=0 hspace="10"> </a>
<a href="jobs.htm#105">  <img src="note5a.gif" width="25%" bor-
der="0" vspace=0 hspace="10"> </a>
<a href="jobs.htm#106">  <img src="note6a.gif" width="25%" bor-
der="0" vspace=0 hspace="10"> </a>
</center>
 <br>
</body>
</html>
```

The following source code is the template used for the second part of the job posting application.

```
<html>
<title>HR Online: Jobs</title>
<body bgcolor="#FFFFFF" >
<a name="101">
<img src="spectbar.gif" width="100%" ><br>
<font size=5.0><b>Job 101: Project Engineer  <br></font> </b>
<font size=3>The following job position is blah blah blah blah
blah blah blah blah blah blah blah blah blah blah blah blah blah
blah blah blah blah blah blah blah blah blah blah blah blah blah
blah blah blah blah blah blah blah blah blah blah blah blah blah
blah blah blah blah blah blah blah blah blah blah blah blah blah
blah blah blah blah blah blah blah blah blah blah blah blah blah
```

```html
blah blah blah blah blah blah blah blah blah blah blah
<br><p></b></font>
<p>
<a href="post.htm"><img src="back.gif" align=middle border="0">
<font size=+1> Back to Jobs Posting  </a></font> <br>
<a href="hrol.htm"> <img src="back.gif" align=middle border="0">
<font size=+1> Back to HR On-Line </a></font> <br>
<a href="hrol.htm"> <img src="home.gif" align=middle border="0">
<font size=+1> Home </a></font> <br>
<p>
<a name="102">
<img src="spectbar.gif" width="100%" ><br>
<font size=5.0><b>Job 102: Sales Associate  <br></font> </b>
<font size=3>The following job position is blah blah blah blah
blah blah blah blah blah blah blah blah blah blah blah blah blah
blah blah blah blah blah blah blah blah blah blah blah blah blah
blah blah blah blah blah blah blah blah blah blah blah blah blah
blah blah blah blah blah blah blah blah blah blah blah blah blah
blah blah blah blah blah blah blah blah blah blah blah blah blah
blah blah blah blah blah blah blah blah blah blah blah
<br><p></b></font>
<p>
<a href="post.htm"><img src="back.gif" align=middle border="0">
<font size=+1> Back to Jobs Posting  </a></font> <br>
<a href="hrol.htm"> <img src="back.gif" align=middle border="0">
<font size=+1> Back to HR On-Line </a></font> <br>
<a href="hrol.htm"> <img src="home.gif" align=middle border="0">
<font size=+1> Home </a></font> <br>
<p>
<a name="103">
<img src="spectbar.gif" width="100%" ><br>
<font size=5.0><b>Job 103: Receptionist  <br></font> </b>
<font size=3>The following job position is blah blah blah blah
blah blah blah blah blah blah blah blah blah blah blah blah blah
blah blah blah blah blah blah blah blah blah blah blah blah blah
blah blah blah blah blah blah blah blah blah blah blah blah blah
blah blah blah blah blah blah blah blah blah blah blah blah blah
blah blah blah blah blah blah blah blah blah blah blah blah blah
blah blah blah blah blah blah blah blah blah blah blah
<br><p></b></font>
<p>
<a href="post.htm"><img src="back.gif" align=middle border="0">
<font size=+1> Back to Jobs Posting  </a></font> <br>
<a href="hrol.htm"> <img src="back.gif" align=middle border="0">
<font size=+1> Back to HR On-Line </a></font> <br>
<a href="hrol.htm"> <img src="home.gif" align=middle border="0">
<font size=+1> Home </a></font> <br>
<p>
<a name="104">
<img src="spectbar.gif" width="100%" ><br>
<font size=5.0><b>Job 104: Sales Manager  <br></font> </b>
<font size=3>The following job position is blah blah blah blah
blah blah blah blah blah blah blah blah blah blah blah blah blah
```

```html
blah blah blah blah blah blah blah blah blah blah blah blah blah
blah blah blah blah blah blah blah blah blah blah blah blah blah
blah blah blah blah blah blah blah blah blah blah blah blah blah
blah blah blah blah blah blah blah blah blah blah blah blah blah
blah blah blah blah blah blah blah blah blah blah blah
<br><p></b></font>
<p>
<a href="post.htm"><img src="back.gif" align=middle border="0">
<font size=+1> Back to Jobs Posting  </a></font> <br>
<a href="hrol.htm"> <img src="back.gif" align=middle border="0">
<font size=+1> Back to HR On-Line </a></font> <br>
<a href="hrol.htm"> <img src="home.gif" align=middle border="0">
<font size=+1> Home </a></font> <br>
<p>
<a name="105">
<img src="spectbar.gif" width="100%" ><br>
<font size=5.0><b>Job 105: Warehouseman<br></font> </b>
<font size=3>The following job position is blah blah blah blah
blah blah blah blah blah blah blah blah blah blah blah blah blah
blah blah blah blah blah blah blah blah blah blah blah blah blah
blah blah blah blah blah blah blah blah blah blah blah blah blah
blah blah blah blah blah blah blah blah blah blah blah blah blah
blah blah blah blah blah blah blah blah blah blah blah blah blah
blah blah blah blah blah blah blah blah blah blah blah
<br><p></b></font>
<p>
<a href="post.htm"><img src="back.gif" align=middle border="0">
<font size=+1> Back to Jobs Posting  </a></font> <br>
<a href="hrol.htm"> <img src="back.gif" align=middle border="0">
<font size=+1> Back to HR On-Line </a></font> <br>
<a href="hrol.htm"> <img src="home.gif" align=middle border="0">
<font size=+1> Home </a></font> <br>
<p>
<a name="106">
<img src="spectbar.gif" width="100%" ><br>
<font size=5.0><b>Job 106: Sales Representative  <br></font> </b>
<font size=3>The following job position is blah blah blah blah
blah blah blah blah blah blah blah blah blah blah blah blah blah
blah blah blah blah blah blah blah blah blah blah blah blah blah
blah blah blah blah blah blah blah blah blah blah blah blah blah
blah blah blah blah blah blah blah blah blah blah blah blah blah
blah blah blah blah blah blah blah blah blah blah blah blah blah
blah blah blah blah blah blah blah blah blah blah blah
<br><p></b></font>
<p>
<a href="post.htm"><img src="back.gif" align=middle border="0">
<font size=+1> Back to Jobs Posting  </a></font> <br>
<a href="hrol.htm"> <img src="back.gif" align=middle border="0">
<font size=+1> Back to HR On-Line </a></font> <br>
<a href="hrol.htm"> <img src="home.gif" align=middle border="0">
<font size=+1> Home </a></font> <br>
<p>
</body>
</html>
```

Figures 10-23 and 10-24 show what the user sees when he or she selects a listed job posting.

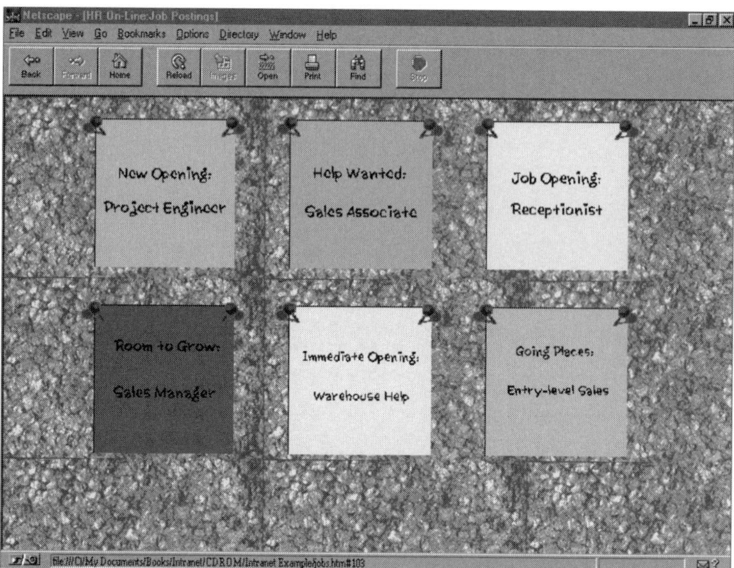

FIGURE *The Job Postings Page*
10-23

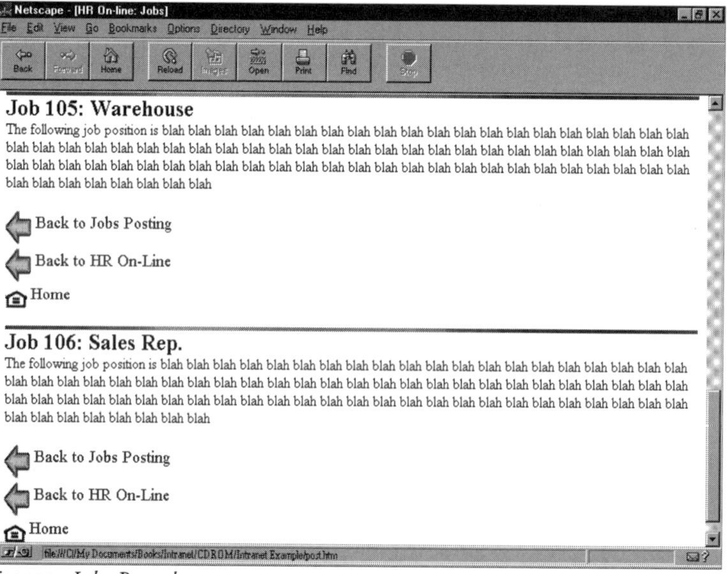

FIGURE *Jobs Posted*
10-24

Suggestion Box	The HR department also has a department-specific suggestion box it wants to duplicate on the intranet. Because the Human Resources department is one of the driving forces behind the company's intranet effort, it is especially interested in obtaining feedback on how well it is serving the users needs.

The suggestion box was written as a JavaScript application. Responses to the questions are sent via e-mail to the HR director's attention. Because confidentiality is a concern, an optional file was included for the sender to enter his or her name and telephone extension.

The following source code is the template used for the HR Online Suggestion Box application. The complete source code can be found on the companion CD-ROM.

```
<HTML>
<HEAD>
<TITLE>HR On-Line: Suggestion Box</TITLE>
<SCRIPT LANGUAGE="JavaScript">
function mailMe(form){
        Subject=document.suggestion.inputbox1.value
        Message= document. suggestion.inputbox2.value
        Name= document. suggestion.inputbox3.value
        Phone= document. suggestion.inputbox4.value
        location = "/cgi-
bin/mailto.cgi?director@hronline.com?subject="+Subject+"&mes-
sage="+ Message+"&name="+Name+"&phone="+Phone
        return true;
}
</SCRIPT>
</HEAD>
<BODY bgcolor="#FFFFFF"><center>
<h2> HR On-Line Suggestion Box</h2></center>
<b>From the Director of Human Resources:</b><br>
We are committed to improving the HR On-Line portion of this com-
pany's intranet. With that in mind, we are open to suggestions on
how we can make this site work for you.<p>
Tell us what you like, what you don't, and what you would like to
see us provide in the line of information and services. We are
here for you!<p>
<hr size=3>
<FORM NAME="suggestion" onSubmit="return mailMe(this.form)">
Pleas Let us know what you think of HR On-Line: <BR>
<INPUT TYPE="text" NAME="inputbox1" VALUE="What do you think of
our site?" SIZE=50><P>
What would you like to see us do differently? <BR>
<INPUT TYPE="text" NAME="inputbox2" VALUE="How can we improve
this site?" SIZE=50><P>
(Optional) Tell us who you are: <BR>
<INPUT TYPE="text" NAME="inputbox3" VALUE="Anonymous" SIZE=50><P>
```

```
(Optional) How may we contact you?: <BR>
<INPUT TYPE="text" NAME="inputbox4" VALUE="Phone Number"
SIZE=50><P>
<INPUT TYPE="submit"><BR>
</FORM>
</BODY>
</HTML>
```

When a user accesses the suggestion box page of the HR Online intranet site, he or she will see the screen shown in Figure 10-25.

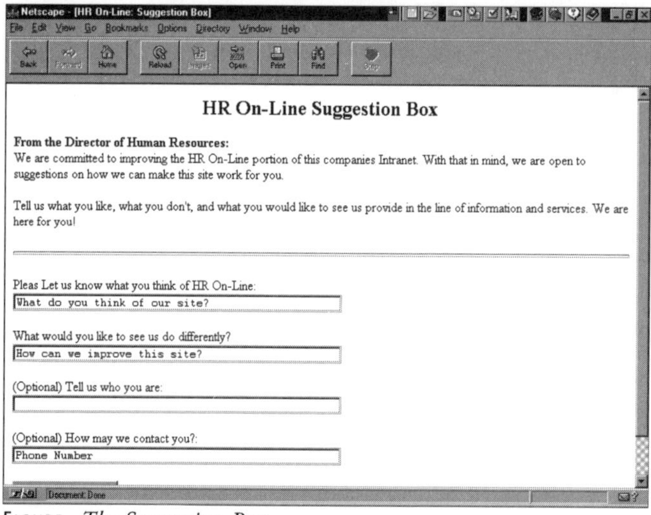

FIGURE *The Suggestion Box*

10-25

| **Corporate Events Calendar** | The Corporate Events Calendar is a monthly list of events within the organization. The goal is to provide employees with a central location to view all events, event updates, and scheduled meetings. Eventually, this application will provide such functions as conference room scheduling and vacation tracking. |

The calendar template needs to be created for each month of the year. The next version of this applet performs this function automatically.

Figure 10-26 shows the screen the user sees when he or she launches the calendar application.

The following source code is the HTML code for the Corporate Events Calendar screen. The source code can be found on the companion CD-ROM in the back of this book.

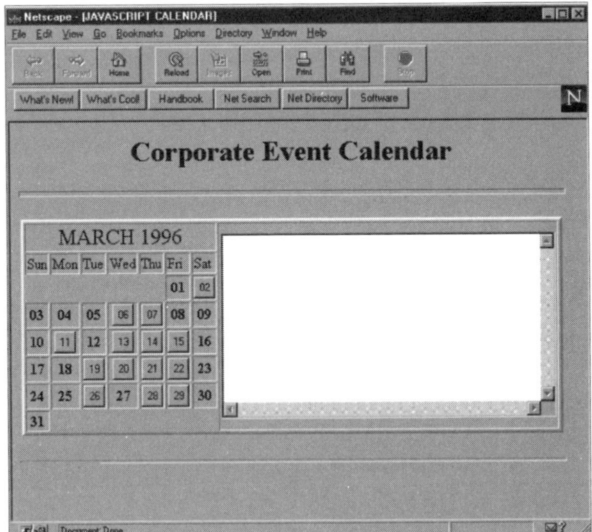

FIGURE *The Corporate Events Calendar Screen*
10-26

```
<HTML>
<HEAD>
<TITLE>JAVASCRIPT CALENDAR</TITLE>
<SCRIPT LANGUAGE="JavaScript">
<!- Begin to hide script contents from old browsers.
function compute(form, day) {
  form.content.value = form[day].value;
  }
// End the hiding here. ->
</SCRIPT>
</HEAD>
<BODY >
<center>
<h1>Corporate Event Calendar</h1>
</center>
<p><hr size=5><p>
<FORM METHOD="post">
<INPUT TYPE="hidden" NAME="0" VALUE="zero based arrays!">
<INPUT TYPE="hidden" NAME="1" VALUE="">
<INPUT TYPE="hidden" NAME="2" VALUE="March 2: Saturday
Advertising and Marketing Seminar
   -9:30 am - 5:00 pm
   -Conference Center ">
<INPUT TYPE="hidden" NAME="3" VALUE="">
<INPUT TYPE="hidden" NAME="4" VALUE="">
<INPUT TYPE="hidden" NAME="5" VALUE="">
<INPUT TYPE="hidden" NAME="6" VALUE="March 6: Wednesday
Networking Reception
   -5:00 - 8:00 pm
   -Conference Center">
```

```
<INPUT TYPE="hidden" NAME="7" VALUE="March 7: Thursday
Interviewing Techniques Workshop
     -12:45 pm
     - Room 104
Engineering Recognition Ceremony
     -12:45 - 2:30 pm
     -Room 120">
<INPUT TYPE="hidden" NAME="8" VALUE="">
<INPUT TYPE="hidden" NAME="9" VALUE="">
<INPUT TYPE="hidden" NAME="10" VALUE="">
<INPUT TYPE="hidden" NAME="11" VALUE="March 11: Monday
intranet Overview
     -4:00 pm
     -Room 73 ">
<INPUT TYPE="hidden" NAME="12" VALUE="">
<INPUT TYPE="hidden" NAME="13" VALUE="March 13: Wednesday
President's Reception for
Distinguished Employees
     -5:00 - 10:00 pm
     -The Supper Club ">
<INPUT TYPE="hidden" NAME="14" VALUE="March 14: Thursday
Lotus Notes User's Group Meeting
     -1:00 pm
     -Room 120">
<INPUT TYPE="hidden" NAME="15" VALUE="March 15: Friday
Apple Computer Presentation
     -9:30 am - 12:00 pm
     - Conference Room">
<INPUT TYPE="hidden" NAME="16" VALUE="">
<INPUT TYPE="hidden" NAME="17" VALUE="">
<INPUT TYPE="hidden" NAME="18" VALUE="">
<INPUT TYPE="hidden" NAME="19" VALUE="March 19: Tuesday
Technology Fair
     -12:30 - 1:30 pm
     -Room 50 ">
<INPUT TYPE="hidden" NAME="20" VALUE="March 20: Wednesday
intranet Prototype Session
     -1:00 - 4:30 pm
     - Conference Room">
<INPUT TYPE="hidden" NAME="21" VALUE="March 21: Thursday
Communications Skills Luncheon
     -12:30 - 2:30 pm
     -Conference Room
     -By invitation
">
<INPUT TYPE="hidden" NAME="22" VALUE="March 22: Friday
Marketing Meeting
     -8:30 am - 5:00 pm
     -Atrium">
<INPUT TYPE="hidden" NAME="23" VALUE="">
<INPUT TYPE="hidden" NAME="24" VALUE="">
<INPUT TYPE="hidden" NAME="25" VALUE="">
<INPUT TYPE="hidden" NAME="26" VALUE="March 26: Tuesday
Regional Sales Meeting
```

```
    - ALL DAY
     -Conference Room ">
<INPUT TYPE="hidden" NAME="27" VALUE="">
<INPUT TYPE="hidden" NAME="28" VALUE="March 28: Thursday
General Staff Meeting
     -12:40 pm
     -Conference Room
">
<INPUT TYPE="hidden" NAME="29" VALUE="March 29: Friday
Sales Presentation
     -9:00 am
     -Conference Room">
<INPUT TYPE="hidden" NAME="30" VALUE="">
<INPUT TYPE="hidden" NAME="31" VALUE="">
<center>
<TABLE BORDER=3 BGCOLOR=#ccffff>
<tr>
<td colspan=7><center><font size=+2>MARCH  1996</font></cen-
ter></td>
<TD rowspan=8 align=center><TEXTAREA NAME="content" ROWS=11
COLS=45></TEXTAREA><br></TD>
</tr>
<TR>
<TD>Sun</TD>
<TD>Mon</TD>
<TD>Tue</TD>
<TD>Wed</TD>
<TD>Thu</TD>
<TD>Fri</TD>
<TD>Sat</TD>
</TR>
<TR>
<TD align=center></TD>
<TD align=center></TD>
<TD align=center></TD>
<TD align=center></TD>
<TD align=center></TD>
<TD align=center><b>01</b></TD>
<TD align=center><INPUT TYPE="button" VALUE="02" onClick="com-
pute(this.form,2)"></TD>
</TR>
<TR>
<TD align=center><b>03</b></TD>
<TD align=center><b>04</b></TD>
<TD align=center><b>05</b></TD>
<TD align=center><INPUT TYPE="button" VALUE="06" onClick="com-
pute(this.form,6)"></TD>
<TD align=center><INPUT TYPE="button" VALUE="07" onClick="com-
pute(this.form,7)"></TD>
<TD align=center><b>08</b></TD>
<TD align=center><b>09</b></TD>
</TR>
<TR>
```

```html
<TD align=center><b>10</b></TD>
<TD align=center><INPUT TYPE="button" VALUE="11" onClick="com-
pute(this.form,11)"></TD>
<TD align=center><b>12</b></TD>
<TD align=center><INPUT TYPE="button" VALUE="13" onClick="com-
pute(this.form,13)"></TD>
<TD align=center><INPUT TYPE="button" VALUE="14" onClick="com-
pute(this.form,14)"></TD>
<TD align=center><INPUT TYPE="button" VALUE="15" onClick="com-
pute(this.form,15)"></TD>
<TD align=center><b>16</b></TD>
</TR>
<TR>
<TD align=center><b>17</b></TD>
<TD align=center><b>18</b></TD>
<TD align=center><INPUT TYPE="button" VALUE="19" onClick="com-
pute(this.form,19)"></TD>
<TD align=center><INPUT TYPE="button" VALUE="20" onClick="com-
pute(this.form,20)"></TD>
<TD align=center><INPUT TYPE="button" VALUE="21" onClick="com-
pute(this.form,21)"></TD>
<TD align=center><INPUT TYPE="button" VALUE="22" onClick="com-
pute(this.form,22)"></TD>
<TD align=center><b>23</b></TD>
</TR>
<TR>
<TD align=center><b>24</b></TD>
<TD align=center><b>25</b></TD>
<TD align=center><INPUT TYPE="button" VALUE="26" onClick="com-
pute(this.form,26)"></TD>
<TD align=center><b>27</b></TD>
<TD align=center><INPUT TYPE="button" VALUE="28" onClick="com-
pute(this.form,28)"></TD>
<TD align=center><INPUT TYPE="button" VALUE="29" onClick="com-
pute(this.form,29)"></TD>
<TD align=center><b>30</b></TD>
</TR>
</tr>
<TD align=center><b>31</b></TD>
<TD align=center></TD>
<TD align=center></TD>
<TD align=center></TD>
<TD align=center></TD>
<TD align=center></TD>
<TD align=center></TD>
</tr>
</TABLE>
</center>
</FORM>
<p><hr size=3><p>
</BODY>
</HTML>
```

About Our Department Pages

As with most organizations, there is always some confusion and misconception about the roles and responsibilities of other departments within the company. The intranet committee agreed that each department within the company should be allowed to put up a page on the intranet. Thus was born the "About Our Department" pages. This page could be virtually anything the department wants to allow each department to showcase itself to the rest of the organization.

Because the departments are new to HTML programming, the intranet committee decided for Phase 1 of the intranet to solicit a one-page description from each department, which describes its roles and responsibilities. The Webmasters or the intranet committee can then convert the one-page document into HTML.

Again, the goal for Phase 1 is simplicity. As each department begins to get comfortable with the corporate intranet, they begin to modify and add to their intranet page. In fact, if desired, they can expand their own section as the Human Resources department has.

The following source code is the HTML code written for the "About Our Department" pages. Each department uses this template for its associated pages. The source code can be found on the companion CD-ROM.

Note: As with all the examples in this book, the actual data has been omitted so you may more easily reuse or modify these templates for your own intranet applications.

```html
<html>
<title>About… Engineering</title>
<body bgcolor="#FFFFFF">
<h2>About … Engineering</h2>
<img src=" ">
The Engineering Department plays a vital role in the blah blah
blah blah blah blah blah blah blah blah blah blah blah blah
blah blah blah blah blah blah blah blah blah blah blah blah blah
blah blah blah blah blah blah blah blah blah blah blah blah blah
blah blah blah blah blah blah blah blah blah blah blah blah blah
blah blah blah blah blah blah blah blah blah blah blah blah blah
blah blah blah blah blah blah blah blah blah blah blah blah blah
blah blah blah blah blah blah blah blah blah blah blah blah blah
blah blah blah blah blah blah blah blah blah blah blah blah<p>
One of Engineering's primary responsibilities is to blah blah
blah blah blah blah blah blah blah blah blah blah blah blah blah
blah blah blah blah blah blah blah blah blah blah blah blah blah
```

```
blah blah blah blah blah blah blah blah blah blah blah blah blah
blah blah blah blah blah blah blah blah blah blah blah blah blah
blah blah blah blah blah blah blah blah blah blah blah blah<p>
The Engineering Department is comprised of the following opera-
tional area:<p>
<ul>
<li>Area 1
<li>Area 2
<li>Area 3
<li>Area 4
</ul>
<p>
Engineering's latest achievement is blah blah blah blah blah blah
blah blah blah blah blah blah blah blah blah blah blah blah blah
blah blah blah blah blah blah blah blah blah blah blah blah blah
blah blah blah blah blah blah blah blah blah blah blah blah blah
blah blah blah blah blah blah blah blah blah blah blah blah blah
blah blah blah blah blah blah blah blah blah blah blah blah blah
blah blah blah blah blah blah blah blah blah blah blah blah blah
blah blah blah<p>
</body>
</html>
```

Figure 10-27 shows what the About Our Department pages look like to the user.

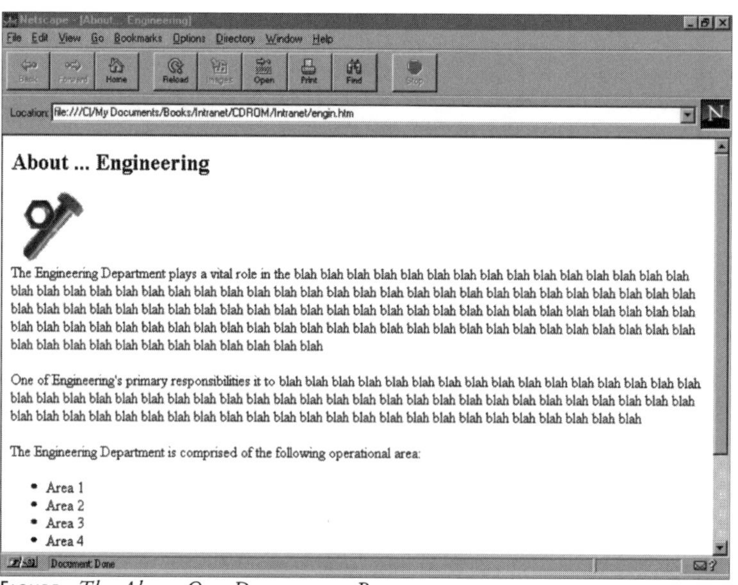

FIGURE
10-27

The About Our Department Page

UPDATE AND MODIFICATION OF PHASE 1 APPLICATIONS

The overall response to the initial corporate intranet was favorable. Some users would like to see more applications up and running, but the feedback the intranet committee received (both over the intranet and in person) is that of excitement and interest in seeing the corporate intranet grow. All the departments have been constructing "wish lists" of new applications they want added to the intranet. The trickle turned into a deluge.

With Phase 1 of the intranet up and running, the intranet committee needed to reconvene to discuss changes, modifications, and additions to the corporate intranet. One of the initial discussions was to clean up the overall "look" of the site. Standard headers and footers do not appear on each intranet HTML document. In addition, standard navigational tools and buttons are not used. On some pages, an HTML horizontal rule <hr> tag was used, yet on others, an image was used instead. Some pages have background images; others use simple color. The intranet Committee decided the pages should be reworked for consistency.

Where applicable, the intranet committee also agreed to increase the use of JavaScript and Java applets. These applications received the most positive feedback. Although these applications take longer to create, they do have the most user impact, which is what the intranet is for. The front end to the corporate intranet will also be redone as an imagemap using Macromedia's Applet Ace and Java. The revised applets and front end will be ready for the Phase 2 roll-out.

The intranet committee also prepared a status report for upper management. This report summarizes the total number of applications created for the intranet, the approximate number of hours it took to get the project up and running, and the user feedback received. The report also includes budgetary numbers for any new equipment or software required for Phase 2, as well as anticipated man hours needed to create the Phase 2 applications.

Virtual Company Store

Getting the company store up on the corporate intranet is one of the early ideas that came out of the intranet Committee's brainstorming sessions. The Company Store is a place employees can visit and buy products the company manufactures. However, the company store was only open during lunch hour, and many of the employees complained about this.

The concept of putting the Company Store on the intranet was simple: Place an online order form on the intranet. The employee can "shop" by selecting the items and quantity of each item that he or she wants. The order form totals the order and mails the form to the warehouse. The order is at the warehouse and the employee receives an e-mail indicating that their order is ready. Because the warehouse never closes, the employee can pick up his or her products any time.

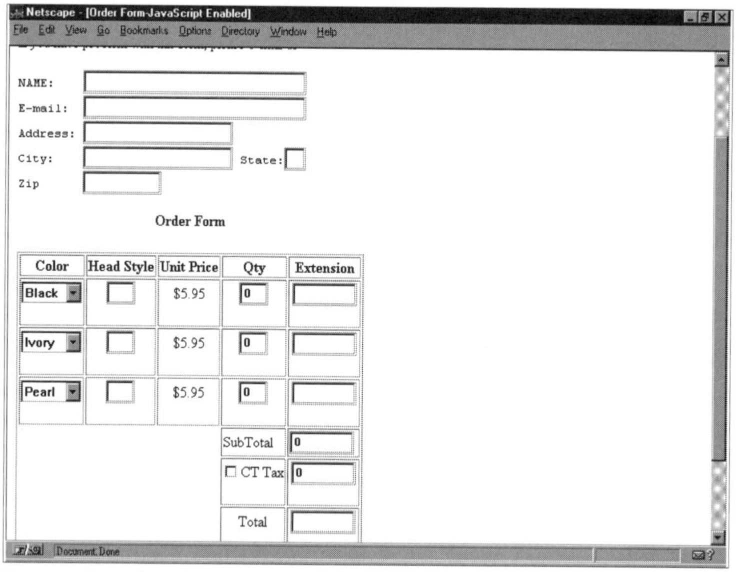

FIGURE
10-28 *Pure JavaScript Example*

The order form is a JavaScript application. As with any forms processing on the Web, the parsing of the form is accomplished through a CGI application running on the intranet Web server. The submitted form is e-mailed to the warehouse operator who fills the order and then e-mails a reply to the employee once the order has been completed.

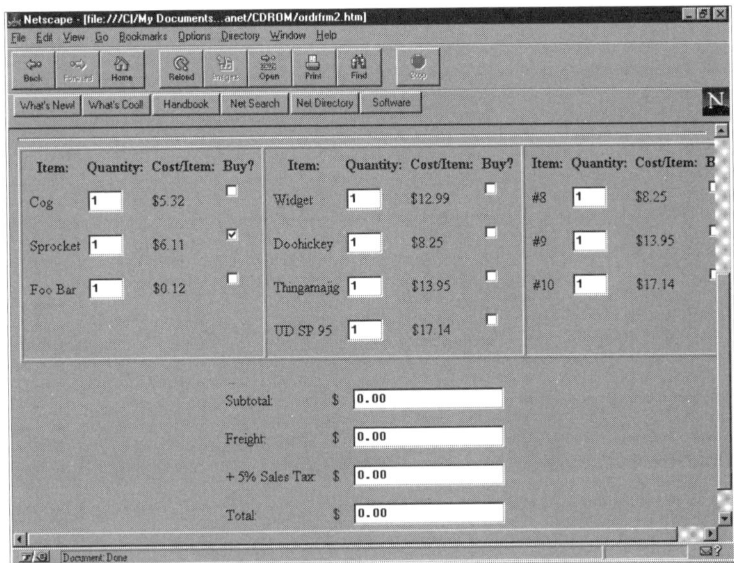

FIGURE *Virtual Company Store*
10-29

The following source code is the online order form for the Virtual Company Store.

```
<html>
<head>
<title>Sample intranet: JavaScript-enabled Order Form</title>
<script>
var subtotal=0
function update(form)
{
form.fldTotal.value    = parseFloat(form.fldExtens1.value) +
parseFloat(form.fldExtens2.value) +
parseFloat(form.fldExtens3.value)+ parseFloat(form.fldTax.value *
1)
}
function multiply(form)
{
form.fldExtens1.value = (form.fldQty1.value) *
(form.fldPrice1.value)
form.fldExtens2.value = (form.fldQty2.value) *
(form.fldPrice2.value)
form.fldExtens3.value = (form.fldQty3.value) *
(form.fldPrice3.value)
form.fldSub.value = parseFloat(form.fldExtens1.value) +
parseFloat(form.fldExtens2.value) +
parseFloat(form.fldExtens3.value)
```

```
checkTax(form)
}
function checkTax(form)
{
if (form.fldCT.checked)
form.fldTax.value = (form.fldSub.value*0.06)
else form.fldTax.value = 0;
update(form)
}
</script>
</head>
<body bgcolor="#FFFFFF" >
<H2> JavaScript enabled order form.</H2>
<p>
<form NAME="frmRegister" METHOD="POST" ACTION="/cgi-bin/mail-
form.pl" >
<pre>
NAME:    <input TYPE="text" NAME="fldName" size=30 value=""
maxlength=30>
E-mail:  <input TYPE="text" NAME="fldEmail" size=30 value=""
maxlength=30>
Address: <input NAME="fldAddress" Value="" maxlength="60">
City:    <input Name="fldCity" Value="" maxlength="35" size=20>
State:<input NAME="fldState" Value="" maxlength="2" size=2>
Zip      <input NAME="fldZip" Value="" maxlength=10 size=10>
</pre>
<table >
<caption ALIGN=top>
<center><p><b>Order Form</b></p></center>
</caption>
<tr>
<th>Item</th>
<th>Unit Cost</th>
<th>Qty</th>
<th>Extension</th>
</tr>
<tr>
<td align=middle>
<center><p> <input size=10 name="fldStyle1" value=""
maxlength=20> </p></center>
</td>
<td>
<center><p> <input size=5 name="fldPrice1" value="0" maxlength=5
onBlur="multiply(this.form)"> </p></center>
</td>
<td align=middle>
<center><p> <input size=3 name="fldQty1" value="0" maxlength=3
onBlur="multiply(this.form)"> </p></center>
</td>
<td align=right>
<center><p><input size=8 name="fldExtens1"></p></center>
```

```html
</td>
</tr>
<tr>
<td align=middle>
<center><p><input size=10 name="fldStyle2" value=""
maxlength=20></p></center>
</td>
<td>
<center><p> <input size=5 name="fldPrice2" value="0" maxlength=5
onBlur="multiply(this.form)"> </p></center>
</td>
<td align=middle>
<center><p><input size=3 name="fldQty2" value="0" maxlength=3
onBlur="multiply(this.form)"></p></center>
</td>
<td align=right>
<center><p><input size=8 name="fldExtens2"></p></center>
</td>
</tr>
<tr>
<td align=middle>
<center><p><input size=10 name="fldStyle3" value=""
maxlength=20></p></center>
</td>
<td>
<center><p> <input size=5 name="fldPrice3" value="0" maxlength=5
onBlur="multiply(this.form)"> </p></center>
</td>
<td align=middle>
<center><p><input size=3 name="fldQty3" value="0" maxlength=3
onBlur="multiply(this.form)"></p></center>
</td>
<td align=right>
<center><p><input size=8 name="fldExtens3"></p></center>
</td>
</tr>
<tr>
<td></td>
<td></td>
<td>SubTotal</td>
<td>
<input NAME="fldSub" size=8 value=0>
</td>
</tr>
<tr>
<td></td>
<td></td>
<td>
<center><p><input TYPE="checkbox" NAME="fldCT"
onClick="checkTax(this.form)">NJ
Tax</p></center>
```

```
</td>
<td align=right>
<center><p><input size=8 name="fldTax" value=0></p></center>
</td>
</tr>
<tr>
<td></td>
<td></td>
<td>
<center><p>Total</p></center>
</td>
<td align=right>
<center><p><input size=8 name="fldTotal"></p></center>
</td>
</tr>
</table>
<center><p>
<input TYPE=SUBMIT VALUE="Submit" Name="btnSubmit">
<input TYPE="reset" VALUE="Clear">
</form>
</p></center>
</body>
</html>
```

About Our Company Kiosk

Another project the intranet committee wanted to undertake was a Company Kiosk. The idea behind the Company Kiosk was to create an informative system company visitors can access in the front lobby. The kiosk highlights company milestones and achievements. It can also include an employee phone directory and a guest book for visitors to sign.

The corporate standard is to use the Netscape Navigator client, so the intranet committee wants to be able to use this software as the kiosk front-end. However, unlike Mosaic, the intranet committee cannot find any documentation about running Netscape Navigator in kiosk mode.

As it turns out, Netscape Navigator has command-line switches that let you run the Navigator client in a kiosk mode. In fact, there are several command-line options for the Windows and Windows 95 versions of Netscape Navigator. These command-line switches are explained in Table 10-2.

You can also use the kiosk-mode switches to specify a file that is stored on the client workstation's local hard disk drive.

```
netscape.exe -k -hc:\html\intranet\homepage.htm
```

The kiosk-mode switch will keep the casual user under control, but will not be effective for the experienced user or hacker. This is because kiosk mode does not enable the Netscape Navigator hot keys or keyboard control keys. Table 10-3 lists the Netscape Kiosk-Mode Commands and their functions.

Table 10-2. Netscape Navigator Kiosk-Mode Switches

Switch	Explanation
-h	This option allows the defined "homepage" to be launched when Netscape is started. netscape.exe -hhttp://www.test.com/test.htm
-i	Allows you to specify a different netscape.INI file. netscape.exe -imyfile.ini
-k	Netscape Navigator is launched with most of the menus disabled. Used in conjunction with the -h switch. netscape.exe -k -hhttp://www.test.com/test.htm
-news	Launches Navigator 2.0 news window. netscape.exe -news
-mail	Launches Navigator 2.0 mail window. netscape.exe -mail

Table 10-3. Netscape Kiosk-Mode Commands

Keystroke Combination	Function
Control + L	Open Location (for a new URL)
Control + S	Save as (used to save to a file)
Control + W	Close
Control + F	Find the next occurrence of a word
Control + R	Reload
Control + P	Print
Control + B	Bookmarks
Esc	Stop Loading
Alt + Arrow Key	Go forward or backward in history list

If you need to restrict access further, you will need programming skills and permission from Netscape to modify the Netscape Navigator client.

Company Newsletter	The Company Newsletter has been a popular method of communicating events and product announcements throughout the organization. Traditionally, the newsletter has been produced quarterly by the marketing department, which is responsible for printing the newsletter. With the introduction of the corporate intranet, marketing will produce the newsletter as an intranet application.

By placing the newsletter on the intranet, marketing will not have to worry about printing or distribution issues. In addition, it will be easier to generate updates more frequently. It is the marketing department's goal to eventually make this a weekly publication. The newsletter has also been produced as a black-and-white document. By using the intranet as a publishing and distribution media, color can be introduced into the newsletter.

The newsletter has been produced as a multicolumn document, similar to how a newspaper is laid out. With this in mind, when the marketing department created the intranet version, they used the HTML <TABLE> tag to create three distinct columns. In addition, each page is set to a definitive amount of text. For a reader to "turn" pages, navigational tools were built into the documents. Each newsletter "page" is created as a separate HTML document.

A table of contents is also created for the newsletter. When a reader "clicks" on a desired topic, he or she will be brought to that section via the HTML <NAME> tag.

The following source code was written for the Corporate Newsletter. The source code can be found on the companion CD-ROM.

Note: Only the first page of the newsletter has been supplied.

```html
<html>
<title>Sample intranet: Newsletter</title>
<body bgcolor="#FFFFFF">
```

```html
<Img src="bisbanr.gif" width="100%"><p><hr size=3>
<table cellpadding="15%" cellspacing="5" >
<tr><td valign="top" align="justify" >
<b>Bright Ideas Solutions</b><p>
<font size=-1>A Quarterly Newsletter</font><p><hr size=1>
To contribute to "Solutions", send your articles, ideas, case
studies and customer testimonials to: <a href="mailto:editor@com-
pany.com">Editor in Chief</a><br><hr size=1>
<p>
<b>IN THIS ISSUE:</b><br>
<font size=-1>
<ul>
<li><a href="#pselect">Learn about Pselect <I>Lite</I></a>
<li><a href="#intranet">Company intranet goes On-Line</a>
<li><a href="#supereq">Super-EQ  gets released</a>
<li>Book Review: CNE Guide to NetWare 4.1
</ul>
</font>
<p>
<hr size="4">
<a name="pselect">
<b>PSelect <I>Lite</I></b><p>
Bright Ideas Software today announced a comprehensive network
printer selection utility for Microsoft Windows. The software
assists network users in selecting a networked printer from
within any Windows application. The product is PSelect (pro-
nounced <I>"Select"</I>), and works with the Windows clients for
Novell, Banyan, and Microsoft Windows NT networks.<p>
Bright Ideas Software is currently shipping what they refer to as
the <I>"Lite"</I> version of  PSelect, which allows you to select
the print queue associated with a specific print driver. Bright
Ideas Software will release PSelect Professional in Q1 of 1996,
which will be a 32-bit Windows 95 application.<p></td><td
valign="top" align="justify" >
James D. Cimino, president and CEO said, "Networks are supposed
to allow us to share resources, yet printing over the network is
still considerably more difficult than it should be. Typically, a
network has more than one sharable printer, yet end-users are
configured to use only one or two available devices. This is done
more out of convenience for the network administrator than the
end user. What PSelect <I>Lite</I> does is it takes the cryptog-
raphy and confusion out of selecting a network printing
resource."<p>
PSelect <I>Lite</I> allows a network administrator to configure
up to four network print devices. You can list each network
printer resource by queue name, by a user-assignable alias name,
or in any combination of the two. PSelect <I>Lite</I> can be con-
figured as a Windows "Stay on Top" utility, and can be visible as
either an application bar or as an icon. Clicking on either will
give the user a "drop-down" listing of the available printers. A
```

```
user then selects the printer that they want to use, with a sim-
ple mouse "click."<p>
PSelect <I>Lite</I> also has a feature known as "flashback". What
"flashback" does is it allows you to define a default printer,
and PSelect <I>Lite</I> will automatically return to that default
device after each job. For example you might configure your
"flashback" device as a laser printer, and select a dot matrix
printer (your check printer) for a payroll run. When the check
printout has completed, PSelect <I>Lite</I> will "flashback" to
you laser printer for you. This way, if you started a different
Windows application, and forgot to reset your printer, your word
processing document will not be printed on your check
stock.<p></td><td valign="top" align="justify" >
<hr size="3">
<a name="intranet">
<b>Company intranet Goes On-Line</b><p>
Our company intranet is on-line!  This is phase one of this pro-
ject, and is only the beginning of what we hope will go into our
Corporate Information Network. The intranet is the combined work
of many employee's within this organization, and with the help of
some outside consultants. <p>
If you have any comments or suggestions to improve the intranet,
you can use the intranet Suggestion Box, which is a totally
anonymous method for getting your two cents in. <p>
If you would like to take an active role in the company intranet,
contact your department head, or write to the <a
href="mailto:webmaster@company.com">webmaster</a>.<p>
<hr size="3">
<a name="supereq">
<b>Super-EQ Released!</b><p>
Bright Ideas Software today announced a comprehensive network
server administration utility for Novell NetWare 3.12. The soft-
ware, which is a NetWare Loadable Module (NLM), assists network
administrators by allowing them to create a supervisor-equivalent
user from the file server console. The product is Super-EQ, and
currently only works with NetWare 3.12 server. A version for
NetWare 4.X is planned. <p> Super-EQ is serialized on a per-
server basis, and is tied directly to the NetWare serial number.
In so doing, Super-EQ can only be used on the server it was seri-
alized for. This prevents a copy of Super-EQ from being used on
any other file server.<br>(continued on next page)<p>
<a href="page2.htm"><img src="right.gif" border=0 align="center"
hspace="10">Next Page</a></td></tr></table>
<hr size=3>
</body>
</html>
```

Figure 10-30 shows how the front page of the intranet newsletter looks from the user's point of view.

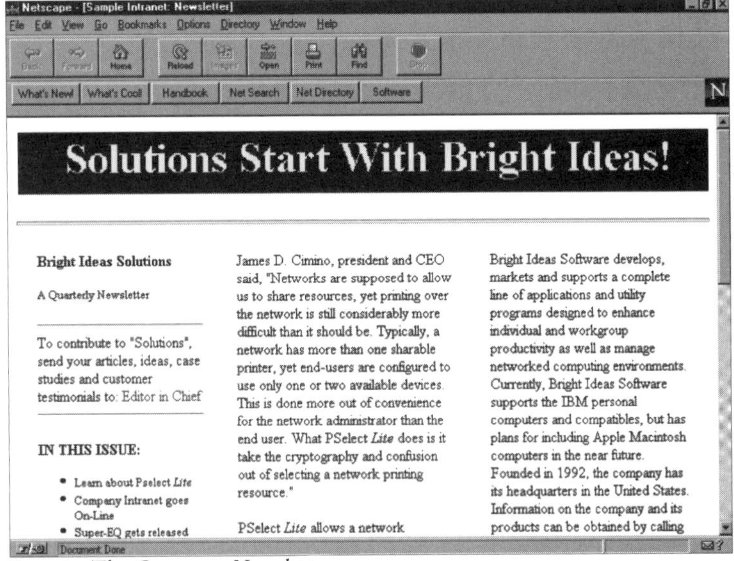

FIGURE **10-30** *The Company Newsletter*

As this application evolves, the marketing department wants to incorporate Java and JavaScript to add animation and interactive graphic elements. Another feature marketing wants to implement is an automatic subscription service that updates users with the latest information when it is available. A readership-tracking application is also in the works.

11

The Intranet Menu System

CONTENTS

The universal client can be used, in conjunction with your HTML documents, to create a common menu system for each user. This menu could be used to launch intranet applications (such as HTML documents and Java applets) as well as commercial applications (such as Microsoft Excel, Corel's WordPerfect, etc.).

Standard Internet applications, such as HTML documents and Java applications, can be opened by implementing standard URLs and hypertext links. Browsers such as Netscape Navigator and Microsoft Internet Explorer are designed to recognize these file types and launch these documents. However, applications such as Microsoft Word or Excel, or Corel's WordPerfect are not natively recognized by HTTP servers or clients. This is where MIME and a browser's capability to support external applications (Helper Applications in Netscape) come in.

To deliver documents of new and different types from your server, configure the correct content type for each type of document, and use the proper extension when naming the file on the server. If the document type is highly unusual, users will need to know what content type to configure their browsers for, and what application to launch for that content type.

If Netscape Navigator is your universal client, you will use the General Helpers Preferences panel to create or reconfigure how a file's format maps to an external helper application. Netscape has the built-in capability to interpret and display several formats, including the HTML format used by HTTP servers. Helper applications are used by Netscape to interpret files it has retrieved but can't read. You can designate MIME file types (a method of differentiating file formats using a suffix appended to a file name), helper applications and their associated actions.

When the Netscape Helpers General Preferences panel is displayed, you will see a scrolling text field that lists the file formats and helper applications available. You can add or modify the information for each application. Each line contains information about a specific application, such as:

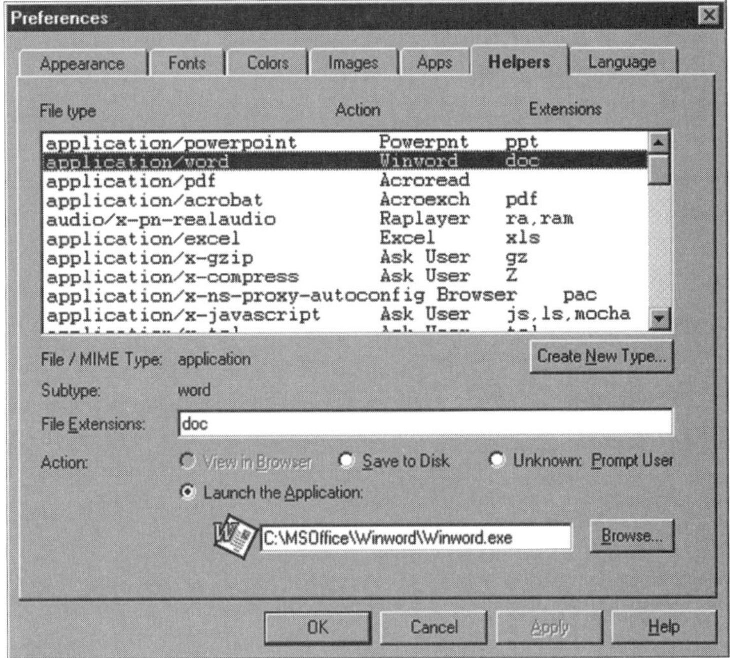

FIGURE **11-1** *Netscape Helpers General Preferences Panel.* Copyright 1996 Netscape Communications Corp. All Rights Reserved. This page may not be reprinted or copied without the express written permission of Netscape.

- the file type and application name;
- the action the helper application takes when it encounters the file; and
- the file extension(s) associated with the file format.

TO CREATE A HELPER APPLICATION IN NETSCAPE NAVIGATOR

1. Select the General Preferences menu selection from the Options menu.
2. Enter the Helpers Tab under the Preferences screen.

3. Click on the Create New Type button. The following dialog box will appear:

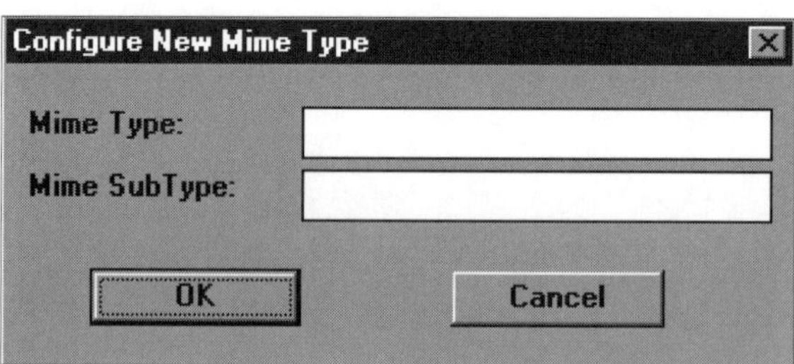

FIGURE *Configuring A New Mime Type.* Copyright 1996 Netscape Communications Corp. All Rights Reserved.
11-2 This page may not be reprinted or copied without the express written permission of Netscape.

4. Enter in the MIME Type and Subtype in the appropriate fields, and click on *OK* to continue. You will return to the Helper Configuration screen.

5. At File Extensions, enter the file extension(s) associated with the file format (for example, .txt for a text file). Separate multiple extensions with commas (for example, avi, txt, html). You don't need to include a period (.) before the extension.

6. Select the action the helper application executes when it encounters the file:

Select	Action
View in Browser	Opens the downloaded file in the content area (if Netscape supports it).
Save to Disk	Saves the file to disk.
Unknown: Prompt User	Notifies you to take further action.
Launch the Application	Opens the file with the specified application. Click on *Browse* to select a different application.

7. If you are launching a program, click on the Browse button and select an application from the scrolling field. You can also manually enter in the full pathname to the application you wish to add. Applications can be local to the workstation (stored on the local hard drive) or be located on a shared volume (a network drive).

8. When you have finished making your changes, click on *OK.*

TO MODIFY AN EXISTING HELPER APPLICATION IN NETSCAPE NAVIGATOR

1. Select the General Preferences menu selection from the Options menu.
2. Select the Helpers Tab under the Preferences screen.
3. Scroll down the list of applications until you locate the helper application you want to modify.
4. At File Extensions, enter the file extension(s) associated with the file format (for example, .txt for a text file). The most obvious application for this is when you have a new file extension you want an application to support. Separate multiple extensions with commas (for example, avi, txt, html). You don't need to include a period (.) before the extension.
5. When you have finished making your changes, click on *OK*.

MIME Document Types	To deliver documents of new and different types from your server, you need to configure the correct content type for each document type and use the proper extension when naming the file on the server. If the document type is unusual, users will need to know what content type to configure their browsers for, and what application to launch for that content type.

To deliver documents of new and different types from your server, you need to configure the correct content type for each document type and use the proper extension when naming the file on the server. If the document type is unusual, users will need to know what content type to configure their browsers for, and what application to launch for that content type.

Seven main classifications of MIME media content data types exist. They are:

- application
- image
- multipart
- video
- audio
- message
- text

Table 11-1 lists the better-known content types. The original list of content types was taken from the public domain NCSA Web page <URL:http://hoohoo.ncsa.uiuc.edu/>.

Note: New content types are coming into existence regularly.

Table 11-1. Media Content Types

Media Content Type	Comments
application/activemessage	
application/andrew-inset	
application/applefile	
application/atomicmail	
application/dca-rft	
application/dec-dx	
application/mac-binhex40	
application/macwriteii	MacWrite Document
application/msword	Microsoft Word Document
application/news-message-id	
application/news-transmission	
application/octet-stream	Use for binary file downloads
application/oda	
application/pdf	Adobe Acrobat Documents
application/postscript	PostScript
application/remote-printing	
application/rtf	Rich Text Format
application/slate	
application/wita	
application/wordperfect5.1	WordPerfect 5.1 Documents
application/wordperfect6.0	WordPerfect 6.0 Documents
application/x-bcpio	
application/x-cpio	cpio tape format (UNIX)
application/x-csh	Potentially dangerous [1]

Table 11-1. Media Content Types *(continued)*

Media Content Type	Comments
application/x-dvi	TeX/LaTeX Output (not TeX source)
application/x-gtar	gnu tar tape format (Unix)
application/x-hdf	
application/x-latex	LaTeX Source
application/x-mif	
application/x-netcdf	
application/x-sh	Potentially dangerous [1]
application/x-shar	Potentially dangerous [1]
application/x-sv4cpio	
application/x-sv4crc	
application/x-tcl	Potentially dangerous [1]
application/x-tex	TeX Source
application/x-texinfo	
application/x-troff	Troff Formatter Source
application/x-ustar	
application/x-troff-man	Troff Source, -man argument assumed
application/x-troff-me	Troff Source, -me argument assumed
application/x-troff-ms	Troff Source, -ms argument assumed
application/x-wais-source	
application/zip	Many users have ZIP helper apps
audio/basic	Sun-style .au format audio
audio/x-aiff	Amiga-format .aiff audio
audio/x-wav	Microsoft Windows-format .wav audio
image/gif	CompuServe GIF 8-bit lossless images
image/ief	
image/jpeg	JPEG lossy photographic images
image/png	w3 consortium PNG lossless images

[1] Browsers should almost never be configured to execute shell scripts. This is a dangerous practice, as the script in question could simply consist of `rm *` or another harmful command. Those interested in sending code to the browser should consider safe scripting languages such as Java, Safe-TCL, and PGP-SafePerl.

Table 11-1. Media Content Types *(continued)*

Media Content Type	Comments
image/tiff	TIFF format images
image/x-cmu-raster	
image/x-portable-anymap	netpbm/pbmplus images (any subtype)
image/x-portable-bitmap	netpbm/pbmplus black and white images
image/x-portable-graymap	netpbm/pbmplus grayscale images
image/x-portable-pixmap	netpbm/pbmplus truecolor images
image/x-rgb	
image/x-xbitmap	X Window System black and white images
image/x-xpixmap	X Window System color images
image/x-xwindowdump	X Window System screen dump format
message/external-body	
message/news	
message/partial	
message/rfc822	
multipart/alternative	
multipart/appledouble	
multipart/digest	
multipart/mixed	Server push
multipart/parallel	
text/html	HTML documents
text/plain	Plain ASCII text
text/richtext	This is not RTF (see above)
text/tab-separated-values	Useful for spreadsheet interchange
text/x-setext	
text/x-sgml	SGML documents, not limited to HTML
video/mpeg	MPEG video format; common on PCs, UNIX
video/quicktime	Apple video format
video/x-msvideo	Microsoft/Intel AVI video format
video/x-sgi-movie	

BUILDING THE MENU

Once you have added the support for your local applications, you are ready to create your HTML menu. Because your browser will now recognize these file types, you can launch these applications using the standard <A HREF=> tag. One trick is to create a generic "blank" file type for each application in the user menu. A blank document is simply a default document or file created when the application is launched, but no data has been entered.

For our sample menu, we'll use Microsoft Word, Excel, and PowerPoint as our applications. This does not mean you are limited to these applications.

Sample Menu Procedure

1. Create the appropriate helper applications for each menu application (Word, Excel, and PowerPoint).
2. Make sure all file extensions you want to support have been added to the program's helper application.
3. Create your MENU HTML document. You can get as elaborate as you want. Here is the code for a basic HTML menu:

```
<html>
<head>
<title>Applications Test Menu</title>
</head>
<body bgcolor="#FFFFFF">
<hr size=4>
<p> Welcome to the <b>Bright Ideas Software</b> Corporate
Applications Menu. <br><p>
<a href="blank.doc" ><img src="hbut1.gif" align=center
hspace="6" vspace="4">MS Word </a>
<a href="blank.xls" ><img src="hbut1.gif" align=center
hspace="6" vspace="4">MS Excel </a>
<a href="blank.ppt" ><img src="hbut1.gif" align=center
hspace="6" vspace="4">MS PowerPoint </a> <br>
<hr size=4>
</body>
</html>
```

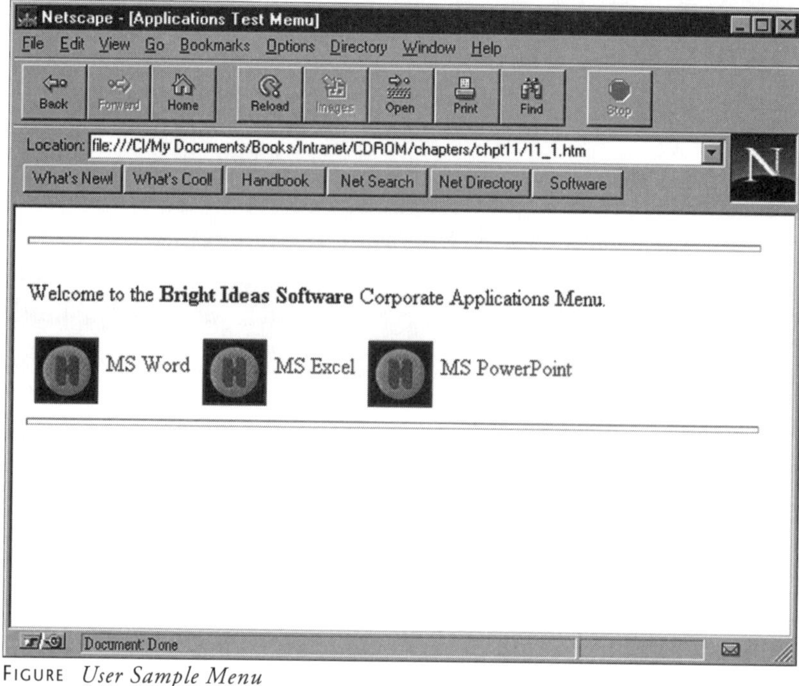

FIGURE *User Sample Menu*
11-3

When you launch this HTML document under Netscape, you get the display in Figure 11-3.

Provided you have set up your helper applications for all of your workstation client types (Macintosh, Windows, Windows 95, UNIX, etc.), this menu will look and function the same for all your client workstations.

In the previous example, when a user clicks on any of the buttons, the associated application is launched with a "blank" document. The user may then create new documents, edit existing documents, or do whatever he or she would normally do in that application. When the application is closed, the user will be returned to the Netscape menu.

In our menu example, we provided users with "blank" documents. We can also use this menu format to provide users with common documents or templates. For example, you can provide an Excel document for expense reports, a PowerPoint technical sales presentation, and a listing of employee resumes in MS Word. Remember, you are not limited to these applications: They are used here only for example purposes. You are limited only by your imagination!

Here is the same menu HTML document, modified as a front end for the Bright Ideas Software sales organization:

```
<html>
<head>
<title>Applications Test Menu</title>
</head>
<body bgcolor="#FFFFFF">
<center> The <b>Bright Ideas Software</b> Corporate Menu. <br><p>
<h3>Proposal Tools</h3>
<a href="sow.doc" ><img src="hbut1.gif" align=center hspace="30"
></a>
<a href="intro.doc" ><img src="hbut1.gif" align=center
hspace="30"></a>
<a href="refernc.doc" ><img src="hbut1.gif" align=center
hspace="30" ></a><br>
<a href="sow.doc" >| Statement of Work |</a>
<a href="intro.doc" >| Introduction Letter |</a>
<a href="refernc.doc" >| References | </a><br>

<hr size=4>
<h3>Reporting Tools</h3>
<a href="expense.xls" ><img src="hbut1.gif" align=center
hspace="20" > </a>
<a href="pipeline.xls" ><img src="hbut1.gif" align=center
hspace="20" > </a>
<a href="order.xls" ><img src="hbut1.gif" align=center
hspace="20" > </a> <br>
<a href="expense.xls" >| Expense Report |</a>
<a href="pipeline.xls" >| Sales Forecasts |</a>
<a href="order.xls" >| Order Form | </a> <br>
<hr size=4>
<h3>Presentation Tools</h3>
<a href="sales.ppt" ><img src="hbut1.gif" align=center
hspace="10" > </a>
<a href="about.ppt" ><img src="hbut1.gif" align=center
hspace="10" > </a>
<a href="product.ppt" ><img src="hbut1.gif" align=center
hspace="10" > </a> <br>
<a href="sales.ppt" >| Sales |</a>
<a href="about.ppt" >| Corporate |</a>
<a href="product.ppt" >| Product |</a>
<br></center>
<hr size=4>
</body>
</html>
```

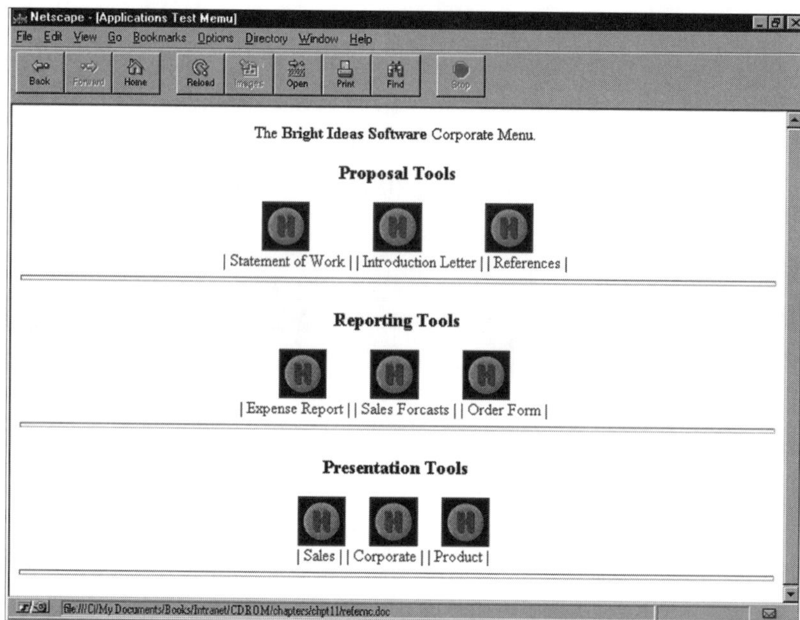

FIGURE *User Menu for Sales Organization*
11-4

When this HTML document is run under Netscape, you get the page shown in Figure 11-4.

For the previous example, we are accessing all the applications, documents, and files from a single HTML document or page. You are not limited to this configuration. You can create individual HTML documents for the various document types or for different divisions within your organization. Again, your options are limited only by your imagination. (By the way, if you are wondering why the Netscape screen changed in the above example it's because the Show Toolbar, Show Location, and Show Directory Button options were turned off from the Netscape menu to provide more screen area.)

Lotus Notes

CONTENTS

Lotus Notes allows you to communicate with colleagues, collaborate in teams, and coordinate strategic business processes. What's more, Notes acts as a central access point to find and share information, whether it's located in e-mail messages, relational databases, in documents created with desktop tools, or on the World Wide Web.

Lotus Notes is, in fact, a document database. The basic element in a Notes database is the individual document. A Notes document is defined by a form, which contains a number of fields. For example, a customer service document might include a date field; fields for customer name, ID number, and technician name; a field for a freeform text description of the customer problem; and a status field.

Users examine Notes documents using views. Notes lists field names as columns when it presents a view to the user. For example, Notes could present a view of the documents sorted by the values entered into the date field if the user wants to search through documents by date. Other field information is listed in columns to the right. Notes views are flexible and are based on an expand-and-collapse outline-like metaphor.

NOTES FEATURES

Notes can store and manage collections of data that do not readily lend themselves to relational or other database systems because the basic element of a Notes database is the document itself. In addition, Notes documents can contain both structured and unstructured content. Notes also provides the following features:

- Rich-text/multimedia — The Notes object store is a container that is optimized to distribute and manage business information efficiently. This information can be a variety of data types, such as tabular data (data from a database or a spreadsheet), formatted text, World Wide Web pages, graphics, or linked or embedded objects, as well as multimedia objects (scanned images, faxes, voice or sound, and video).

- Full-text search — Notes incorporates a full-text search engine to allow users to index and search Notes documents based on user queries. Documents matching the search criteria are displayed by Notes and sorted in user-specified order.

- Version control — Lotus Notes provides versioning capabilities to facilitate tracking of changes made to a single Notes document by multiple users. Automatic versioning can be implemented in a form whereby each edit is posted as a main document or as a response to the original. Thus, changes made to a Notes document by one user are not overwritten when another user saves changes to the document.

- Document links — Much like World Wide Web HTML documents, Notes is a hypertext-based system. A Notes document can contain a link to another document in any Notes database or to documents stored on the World Wide Web. Links from one page to another can be easily created by individual users using a single click of the mouse.

- Replication — Notes replication is unmatched in its functionality and granularity. A groupware platform uses replication technology to allow a remote site in, to make a copy of a database in another location and to store it on a local server. Replication allows workgroups to keep their information synchronized across geographically dispersed sites. Features of Notes replication include:

  1. Bidirectional — Notes' bidirectional replication synchronizes all changes made at sites, including propagation to remote servers. Thus, users in multiple sites to which the database is replicated can make changes to the database, add new documents, modify others, and delete others, without losing any of the changes made.

  2. Efficiency — When synchronizing databases, only those fields within documents that are new or have been changed on either side of the replication process need to be replicated. Field-level replication ensures the shortest synchronization cycles and optimum use of resources.

3. Client replication — Notes replication is not limited to server-to-server connectivity, but also includes client-to-server connectivity. Because connected workgroup members (such as mobile users) working at a remote site or home office need the same level of access to information as connected users, Notes replication updates local databases on the mobile workstation after reconnection to the Notes network.

4. Selective replication — A Notes user can replicate a subset of information contained in a Notes database with only a few mouse clicks. Notes allows users to define the profile of documents that need replication to client workstations.

5. Background replication — Conducting the replication process should not mean that other work on a laptop or home computer must cease, especially for mobile users. Notes replication can run in the background, allowing the user to continue to work on other tasks.

LOTUS NOTES AND THE INTERNET

The Internet and the World Wide Web provide intra-enterprise and inter-enterprise connectivity and application hosting on a scale unimaginable just a few years ago. Like the Web, Lotus Notes is based on a rich document-oriented database, fielded forms, and document linking. Lotus Notes is ideally suited as a development and deployment platform for Web applications.

Lotus Notes provides native support for Internet and Web protocols directly. Web application developers and users can use Notes' application development, client/server messaging, and distributed object store technology. This lets Web developers leverage the groupware functionality of Notes to reach non-Notes clients via Internet protocols and formats.

Security	The key to security in a distributed system is encryption. The *de facto* industry standard for access to X.500 directories is the X.509 certificate, which is based on RSA public key encryption technology, recognized as the only encryption system without an exposed point of compromise. Using cryptography and other security facilities, Lotus Notes provides four levels of security: authentication, access control, field-level privacy, and digital signatures.
Messaging	Notes messaging is used for interpersonal communication as well as for collaborative work among team members. It is a critical component of workflow applications, as well as a platform for group calendaring and scheduling.
E-mail	Notes messaging provides novice users with a simple-to-use mailbox while giving power users quick access to the message management tools they need to process and organize large volumes of mail. For users, the Notes user interface looks like cc:Mail. Notes includes a powerful editor for rich text, multiple fonts, colors, and a variety of formatting options. Notes R4 also includes agents that perform client tasks, such as looking through files attached to incoming messages for keywords and filing them in the appropriate folder. It also includes numerous server-based tasks, such as monitoring Web sites for new or specified information. In addition, Notes includes file viewers for the most popular desktop applications, so users do not need to have an application on their desktop to read or print data generated in that application.
Workgroup Collaboration	Notes' integrated messaging and groupware combines push-pull methods of information sharing to give users an intuitive and efficient means of collaborating. For example, when creating a document for review, a user

can send an e-mail message that contains a "doclink" to all reviewers. Each reviewer receives the message and simply clicks on the doclink to launch the document, thus giving each user access to the same, most recent version. Mail messages can contain links to any document in a Notes database, including discussions, customer profiles, documentation, Web pages, and news feeds.

Workflow

In most workflow applications, there is a need to notify a person or update a document based on the value of a field or the state of a process. Notes workflow applications also monitor this process, so if the process stalls, Notes sends another set of e-mail messages.

Directory Services

Notes contains a single directory, the Notes Name & Address Book. The Name & Address Book manages all resource directory information, from individual user addresses for mail to connection records defining how and when replication occurs throughout the network. Inheriting the benefits of Notes' document database architecture, the Name & Address Book allows Notes administrators to manage user information, database information, and server information, such as replication schedules through a single, integrated directory. There is no additional administrative overhead, directory maintenance, or synchronization infrastructure to manage separately.

The Notes Name & Address Book is simply another Notes database. This makes the directory extensible beyond its traditional role as the white pages and yellow pages of employee names and locations. The Notes directory is the hub of the enterprise network that binds all corporate assets — people, places, documents, and applications. In addition, the Notes directory inherits all the attributes of the Notes' shared object store, making it a richer source of name and address information than traditional messaging system directories.

Application Development Environment	The key to Notes' applications is its application development environment. These applications not only manage documents and data, but also manage the flow of work among team members who use and need those documents.

The Notes platform includes an integrated development environment, providing rich tools to developers of varying expertise. Users with no programming experience can build and deploy a Notes application and professional developers can build powerful applications using Notes' native programming tools.

Once an application has been developed and made available on a Notes server, it can be accessed by and replicated to any client or server that has appropriate access. From then on, any changes made to forms, fields, views, or programming are automatically inherited by all clients, regardless of the server and client platforms on which they were developed and deployed.

THE VALUE OF THE NOTES SERVER

By opening Notes to Internet and Web standards, Lotus extends the value of the Notes server to support Web browsers as alternative clients. Joining Web protocols with Notes technology is logical, because of the similar architectures of both Notes environments and the World Wide Web..

The level of functionality that can be shared between any set of clients and servers is determined by the protocol over which the two components interact. Notes clients continue to use the native Notes protocol to exploit the Notes compound document object, store and Web browsers leverage Notes' native HTTP protocol and native HTML document format.

THE VALUE OF THE NOTES CLIENT

Full support for native Internet and Web standards also extends the value proposition of the Notes client to include user and team-oriented Web information management. Just as Notes clients use the Notes server to provide a central access point for corporate data (such as mail, Notes workflow applications, access to relational data, and access to desktop applications), the Notes client extends its services to exploit information on Web servers. That is, the Notes client now applies its functionality — disconnected use, client/server messaging, rich text, security, workflow applications, discussion databases, and document libraries — to information published in HTML format on HTTP servers.

| **Alternative Clients** | There are a number of alternative clients that can be used as front ends to Notes: |

- cc:Mail 7.0 — The client-server edition of cc:Mail directly accesses the Notes server as a message store. cc:Mail clients use the standard cc:Mail user interface.
- Other Mail Application Program Interface (API) enabled clients — MAPI-based clients, such as the mail client that ships with Windows 95, can also exploit Notes as a back-end messaging server. The Notes server includes a MAPI service provider interface.
- Web browsers — Standard Web browsers are able to access Notes directly through Notes native support for HTTP and HTML. Web browsers can read Notes documents and views, complete and remit Notes forms, and have access to the Notes full-text search engine.

INTERNOTES WEB PUBLISHER

Lotus InterNotes Web Publisher is a Notes server program that lets users publish information entered in Notes to the World Wide Web. By converting Notes forms, documents, views, and databases into HTML (the format used by standard Web browsers such as NCSA Mosaic and

Netscape Navigator), InterNotes Web Publisher provides a simple, automated process for creating and managing intranet and public Web sites.

InterNotes Web Publisher lets you build interactive Web applications using Notes. Simply design a Notes form and use InterNotes Web Publisher to publish it in HTML format. Web users can then update the Notes databases in real time using standard Web browsers. When users submit data this way, any Notes workflow process can be triggered. Web users can also search published Notes databases from the Web.

With InterNotes Web Publisher, you can take advantage of Notes' collaborative authoring environment and workflow capabilities to automate creating, approving, and consolidating Web content from multiple departments and locations, ensuring a constant flow of current information to the Web site. InterNotes Web Publisher automatically converts items in Notes views and links Notes documents to HTML hypertext links, automating the process of managing and updating documents published on the Web. In this way, InterNotes Web Publisher lets you centralize and simplify management of your Web site.

When you publish a Notes database, InterNotes Web Publisher performs the following functions:

1. publishes the About Database document in the Notes database and makes it the home page for the database;
2. lists the database views as hypertext links on the home page;
3. converts each Notes document into an HTML file;
4. converts Notes forms into HTML forms;
5. converts Notes doclinks, view links, and database links into hypertext links;
6. converts Notes tables into HTML tables;
7. converts Navigators into imagemaps;
8. converts bitmaps in Notes documents into inline GIF files;
9. preserves the full-text index so users can search the database and view the search results from the Web; and,
10. preserves attachments to Notes documents so users can download them from the Web with a Web browser.

The InterNotes Publishing Process

When a user submits a publishing request:

- WebPUB, the publishing module, converts the database information into HTML files;
- WebPUB places the files in the Web server's output directory;
- a Web browser requests a Web page;
- the Web server serves the page to the Web browser; and
- the Web browser displays the page.

When a Web user submits a form via a Web browser:

- the Web server passes the form information to the Internotes CGI program;
- the Internotes CGI program passes the information to INOTES, the interactivity module;
- INOTES passes the information to InterNotes Web Publisher; and
- InterNotes Web Publisher creates a new document in the Notes database, which contains the form information.

You can publish the Notes documents that contain the form information to the Web again by submitting another publishing request.

NETWORK REQUIREMENTS

InterNotes Web Publisher converts Notes databases to HTML files. To connect your Notes server to the Web, you need the following network connections:

1. an Internet connection through a leased line or dial-up line to an ISP, or a connection to a company LAN or intranet; and
2. TCP/IP on the Notes server on which the InterNotes Web Publisher software resides.

InterNotes Web Publisher supports the following TCP/IP implementations:

1. OS/2 Notes Server — IBM TCP/IP 2.0
2. Windows NT Server — TCP/IP bundled with the Windows NT software
3. Windows 95 Server — TCP/IP bundled with the Windows 95 software
4. NetWare Loadable Module (NLM) Server — Novell TCP/IP module
5. Sun Solaris 2.4 UNIX server — TCP/IP bundled with Sun Solaris software
6. IBM AIX 4.1.3 UNIX server — TCP/IP bundled with IBM AIX software

HARDWARE REQUIREMENTS

We recommend the following hardware:

- a one gigabyte (GB) disk drive; and
- 32MB of RAM (64MB for UNIX).

WEB SERVER AND CLIENT SOFTWARE REQUIREMENTS

InterNotes Web Publisher works with standard World Wide Web servers and browsers. You will need to install the following:

- a Web server to make the translated HTML documents available to Web clients; and
- a Web browser to browse the HTML documents.

InterNotes Web Publisher has been tested with several Web browsers, including InterNotes Web Navigator, NCSA MOSAIC, and Netscape Navigator.

SUPPORTED INTERNOTES WEB PUBLISHER CLIENTS

The InterNotes Web Publisher software supports all Notes clients release 3.1 or later.

Design Guidelines for Publications

When you design or customize a database for publication, keep the following tips in mind:

- Keep the database design simple. Hide information users don't need to see on the Web (for example, fields that contain internal information).

- The InterNotes Web Publisher uses certain conventions when naming the HTML files it creates when you publish a database. If you want to override the default naming scheme, you can add a field named HTMLFile to any Notes form. Select Text as the data type for this field. When you compose a document using this form, the text you enter in the HTMLFile field will be used as the filename of the resulting HTML file.

- If you want items to appear side by side in the published version and your Web browser supports the display of tables, enter the items in adjacent cells of a Notes table. For example, you can paste a graphic in one cell and some identifying text in the cell next to it. HTML preserves alignments in tables, but not in other text, so you can always enter items in Notes tables if you need to preserve their alignment settings.

- If you refer to the same image in more than one document, store the image in the Using Database document, and refer to it from the individual Notes documents. This will reduce the database size.

- You can add links in a Notes database to other Notes documents or views in the database, to Notes documents or views in other Notes databases, or to other pages on the Web. You can create links using regular Notes doclinks, or indicate links by enclosing a Uniform Resource Locator (URL) in square brackets. If you enter links in square brackets, you can enter the links in one of two ways: in a Notes pop-up using the Edit-Insert-Popup command, or following underlined text. For compatibility reasons, you should use Notes doclinks whenever possible; entering a URL can sometimes have unexpected results if the source database changes (for example, through replication).

- If you use pop-ups to create the links, make sure the Borders Visible box is checked in the Insert PopUp dialog box. This makes it easy to locate the pop-ups in the Notes document.

- Set up an internal Web site so you can view published databases internally before you make them publicly available on the Web.

- If you have scheduled databases for frequent publication, disable publishing before you edit the Database Publishing Record. Otherwise, you may have a conflict with the server when you attempt to save the Database Publishing Record. If the Notes server attempts to read the Database Publishing Record while you are saving it, an error occurs.

- InterNotes Web Publisher can publish a database on any server to which it has access — a user simply submits a Database Publishing Record. For security reasons, you may want to restrict the server on which you install the InterNotes Web Publisher so it cannot access confidential databases.

- To restrict the server on which you install the InterNotes Web Publisher, modify the Access Control List (ACL) for any database that contains confidential information. For example, if you install InterNotes Web Publisher on a server named MyPublisher and you do not want the Web Publisher to access a database named Internal Memos, add MyPublisher to the Internal Memos ACL and specify No Access.

- Because it is the central control for the InterNotes Web Publisher, you should restrict user access to the Configuration database. InterNotes Web Publisher runs as an add-in on a Notes for Windows NT Server. Therefore, users who are authorized to edit Database Publishing Records in the Configuration database will be able to submit a publishing request or edit a publishing record created by another user for any database to which the Notes server has read access.

History of Lotus InterNotes Product Offerings	InterNotes Web Publisher shipped in May 1995 for Windows NT and IBM OS/2. InterNotes Web Publisher Release 1.0 allowed users to statically publish information stored in Notes databases and documents to the Web, thereby making Notes data accessible to any Web client. To run InterNotes Web Publisher, you needed the Web Publisher code, a Notes server, and any Web server configured on the same machine because Notes didn't support HTTP natively.

InterNotes Web Publisher Release 2.0 added the capability to interact with Notes applications via forms submittal. With release 2.0, Lotus provided a way for users to leverage the Notes full-text search engine.

In InterNotes Web Publisher Release 4.0, Lotus added functionality to leverage Notes Release 4.0 (such as support for Navigators as imagemaps, subforms, bulleted and numbered text paragraph styles, folders, and hide-paragraph formulas). In addition, Lotus added support for more platforms — Solaris, AIX, and Windows 95 (running on Windows NT or OS/2).

Note: Lotus also released InterNotes Web Publisher Release 2.1 for Notes Release 3.x servers on Windows NT and OS/2 platforms.

DOMINO: THE LOTUS NOTES WEB SERVER

Domino represents the first integrated Notes/HTTP server from Lotus Development. Domino makes Notes applications securely accessible to any Web browser. With Domino, users have dynamic access to and interaction with Notes data and applications (HTML on-the-fly, and the ability to open, edit, create, and delete documents from the Web browser).

Domino is the next product offering from the InterNotes Web server team. Currently slated for delivery in Notes release 4.5 (January, 1997), Domino will allow anyone with a Web browser to participate in Notes applications securely.

Using Domino, users can securely extend the reach of Notes applications to anyone with a Web browser. Domino enhances the marriage of Notes and the Internet; thus, users will experience a more meaningful representation of and interaction with Notes applications.

Domino extends Notes security concepts applied to Web browser access though Access Control List (ACL) reader fields. Domino also provides dynamic access to any Notes data based on who you are. More importantly, Domino provides usable Notes applications without the need for a Notes client: just use your Web browser. In addition, using Domino simplifies the creation and management of good-looking, effective Web sites. Domino is the solution of choice for existing Notes installed base and represents unique advantages to non-Notes users as well.

Key Features

Domino's features are:

- Real-time Notes to HTML translation;
- full database transaction support — Insert, Update, and Delete;
- real-time view updates;
- real-time full-text search updates;
- real-time database macro support;
- expand or collapse views;
- frames support;
- Extended Notes security model — user registration and authentication via name and password (leverage ACL lists, groups, and rights);
- Notes API URL syntax;
- Lotus script integration; and
- triggered agents.

B Out-Sourcing Case Study
Forman Interactive

CONTENTS

An alternative to building and hosting your own Web server is having a Presence Provider do it for you. One provider, Forman Interactive, in addition to being an "Internet Presence Provider," also manufactures the Internet Creator, a software package for creating Web sites quickly and easily. The Internet Creator, for Windows and Windows 95, is included on the companion CD-ROM in the back of this book.

The Forman Interactive Story

Forman Interactive started when Richard Forman (CEO of Forman Interactive), Peter Forman (president of Forman Interactive), and their partner Dan Levine experienced frustrations involved in getting up and running on the Internet.

Like many others, Forman Interactive's founders experienced first-hand the lack of standards, exorbitant costs, and the staggering amount of research required to establish a Web site. So, they did something about it.

Forman Interactive now develops and hosts Internet Web sites for small and medium-size organizations. Forman Interactive's products and services include state-of-the-art hosting capabilities as well as in-house proprietary client and server software. Forman offers a number of services including:

- HTML authoring;
- custom graphic design;
- Perl and CGI scripting; and
- Java scripting.

Forman Interactive is one of the nation's leading full-service Internet hosting firms. They make it easy and affordable for you to get up and running on the Internet.

- Step 1: Using Forman Internet Creator software, you can build your own Web site in less than one hour.
- Step 2: Once your site is built (whether you build it yourself or they do it for you), Forman will provide you with the Forman Internet Connector Software, which will connect you to the 'Net via a selected Service Provider.
- Step 3: Forman will host your Web site on its low-cost, state-of-the-art servers and you will be able to conduct full electronic commerce over the Internet — worldwide — for as little as $59 per month.

Technical Support	Forman Interactive's in-house design and programming staff has experience in:

- programming — in C, Perl, FoxPro (.dbf applications) and Visual BASIC; porting CD-ROM applications to the Internet;
- operating systems — UNIX, Xenix, DOS, and Windows;
- hardware — Sun Sparcstation 2, RS-6000, Silicon Graphics (SGI) Indy, and Intel co-processors; and
- server-based applications — Web forms, CGI-bin, daemons, mailing lists, procmail, and major domo.

When Forman started, its primary focus was to provide low-cost Web site creation software for companies that required an Internet presence. The company's vision was to develop a proprietary software product that allowed businesses to create and maintain an Internet Web site without the need for external (and typically high-priced) consultants.

Forman Interactive wanted its software to permit a business to design, build, and publish a complete Web site in under an hour — without the need to learn or use HTML. This simple, easy-to-use software was called Internet Creator.

And, as Forman's customers created their Web sites, they turned to an array of IPPs (Internet Presence Providers) to host their sites. Often, they came back, frustrated that they weren't able to find a low-cost, quality service provider.

Forman Interactive set up its own Web hosting service that included top-of-the-line Silicon Graphics (SGI) Challenge S servers and high-speed T-1 communication lines.

COMMON QUESTIONS AND ANSWERS FOR SELECTING A WEB SERVICE PROVIDER

Why shouldn't a company set up its own Web server?

For no reason whatsoever. However, for most small to medium-size organizations, it's just not economically practical.

First, you need to specify and purchase the hardware. Then, you need to get it installed by experienced consultants. Next, you need Web server software and communication lines. You then need to write your own HTML and CGI code. Finally, once you've spent anywhere from $10,000 to $80,000 setting up the server, you still need a system administrator to maintain the server and make sure it's operational 24 hours a day, seven days a week (another $40,000 to $60,000 per year).

The alternative to this is to use a hosting service that allows you to build and maintain your own Web site. Forman Interactive has set up a powerful server with high-speed communication lines for its customers.

What is a server?

It is a computer or software package that provides a specific kind of service to client software (such as a browser) running on other computers. The term can refer to a particular piece of software, such as a WWW server, or to the machine on which the software is running.

What is a domain?

A domain identifies a part of the Internet space managed by the Domain Name Service (DNS). Usually, a person or company will register a domain with the global registration authority and will give its computers names in their own domain.

What is the difference between domain- and sub-domain-level service?

A domain name is your unique address on the Internet. It's the clearest, simplest way for customers to find you. Domain names are made up of two or more parts, separated by a period (called a dot).

For example: Let's say you're a widget importer and are able to get "WidgetsDirect" as your domain name. On the World Wide Web, your address would be:

```
www.widgetsdirect.com
```

The address is short and easy to remember. In time, it will become as critical a component of your business identity as a logo, brand name, or toll-free phone number. A domain name is like having your own stand-alone electronic building.

What is a sub-domain?

A sub-domain is like renting space in an office park or retail space in an established shopping mall. Forman Interactive has created its own electronic mall just for this purpose called, "register.com."

A sub-domain is perfect for the small-business person who wants to congregate with other businesses so "traffic" will stop on the information superhighway. Using the widget business again as an example, the sub-domain Internet address would be:

```
www.register.com/widgetsdirect
```

As you can see, sub-domain names have more words, dots, and slashes because there need to be more "directions" to find you.

What is a domain name?

A domain name is a unique address on the Internet. Domain names are made up of two or more parts separated by a period. Let's say you're a widget importer and are able to get "WidgetsDirect" as your domain name. On the World Wide Web, your name/address would be:

```
www.widgetsdirect.com
```

Names are regulated and assigned by a quasi-public agency formerly called InterNIC, now Network Solutions.

How do I get a domain name?

You have to register for one. Names are assigned on a first-come, first-served basis. Once a domain name has been registered, it's unavailable to any other company or individual in the world. This means when "widgetsdirect.com" is gone, it's gone, even if 16 other widget importers want it. In 1994, there were about 200 domain name requests a month. In 1995, requests jumped to about 20,000 a month. If you're considering getting an address on the Internet, you should act fast.

One of the services Forman Interactive provides is helping select, research and register your domain name with the organization in charge of all name registration, the InterNIC, Network Solutions. Your domain name will be valid for two years from the date of activation, and thereafter can be renewed annually at a modest price ($50/year payable to InterNic [Network Solutions]).

What is a sub-domain name?

This account name is linked from an existing domain such as register.com. If you were to sign up with Forman Interactive's server your Internet address would be:

```
www.register.com/yourname
```

How long can my account name be? Sub-domain? Domain?

A sub-domain name is limited to 22 characters in the form `www.register.com/acme`. A domain name can be 22 characters (before the .com) drawn from the alphabet (a-z), digits (0-9), and minus sign (-). No blank or space characters are permitted.

How can people find or search for my Web site?

The best way for someone to find you is to give them your address. You can mention it on the phone, put it on your business card, or highlight it in your correspondence or newsletters.

Telling people you already know is only the first step. There are more than 35 million people who have access to the Internet. They are typically higher-than-average wage-earners and consumers of both goods and information.

What is an Internet Service Provider?

A service provider is a company that provides you with your connection to the Internet. Just as you have many choices of long-distance companies that can connect you to the telephone network, you have many choices as to who can connect you to the Internet.

Forman Interactive is not an Internet Service Provider (ISP). It is an Internet Presence Provider. Forman Internet Connector, which allows you to immediately connect to the Internet via a Service Provider, is included free with its services.

Do I still need my service provider to gain access?

Yes, you still need your service provider to provide you with basic Internet access. Internet Presence Providers, such as Forman Interactive, take responsibility for your organization's hosting needs. An Internet Presence Provider can provide you with other services such as domain name registration services and e-mail POP3 (Post Office Protocol #3) services that allow you to have an e-mail address in the form of john@acme.com.

What is a Web site host server?

It is a network of computers that have special software that let you access your Web site on the World Wide Web. This operation would be accessible 24 hours a day, seven days a week.

What is a host (or hosting service)?

It is a powerful server linked directly to the Internet that serves as a "host" or repository for one or more Web sites. Most businesses use a hosting service's server as the home (or base location) for their Web sites.

What should I look for in a quality Web site hosting service?

- T1 lines for high-speed communication
- Powerful servers
- Secure transactions using Secure Sockets Layer (SSL)
- Shopping basket ordering modules
- Daily and monthly statistical reporting logs and graphs
- Daily backups

- Business services — such as e-mail, domain name registration, and seeding so your Web site is listed on the major directories
- Marketing support — the Internet is a new medium requiring both traditional marketing skills and a firm footing on the information superhighway to help you generate traffic to your Web site.
- Customized services — you should be able to simply tell the hosting service what you need and let them have their talent and technological expertise work for you.

QUESTIONS AND ANSWERS ABOUT FORMAN INTERACTIVE

If Forman Interactive registers my domain name, am I required to use its hosting services?

No, you are not required to use Forman's hosting service if you register your domain name. You are free to choose. In the event you want to move your site or domain name to another service, send Forman a signed letter spelling out the details of where you want your service transferred and Forman will do it for you immediately. At no charge.

What is the register.com mall?

It is an electronic hosting service that runs 24 hours a day, seven days a week. It delivers information globally and sells your products or services with no additional effort on your part. It is state-of-the-art in electronic marketing and provides customers with:

- online searching;
- electronic commerce;
- market basket ordering;
- secure transactions; and
- seeding of key worldwide databases.

Forman Interactive makes sure that register.com is an attractive and exciting place for customers to visit. Forman is constantly making improvements to make sure your customers come, stay, and have a good time.

What happens if I want to change information on my site?

All you need to do is make the changes you want locally (which is as simple as it was to create it originally if you built it using Internet Creator) and upload the information to Forman's server. It's that simple.

How often can I change the information on my Web site?

As often as you like — no matter how often you update your site, there are no additional charges.

Can I have a downloadable file on my site that my customers can FTP?

Yes. That's very simple to set up and is a good service to provide to your customers.

How much does hosting cost?

Forman Interactive's rates are:

> $59.00 a month for sub-domain level; or
> $99.00 a month for domain level.

What do I get for this price?

- 20MB of disk space
- 300MB of transfers a month
- SGI Challenge S server (IRIX 5.3)
- Full T-1 line-order processing
- Secure online order processing
- POP3 e-mail
- Complete FTP server
- Daily and monthly statistical reporting
- Logs and graphs
- Daily backups
- Complete consulting services

Glossary

ADDRESS

The address is a unique name or number that identifies a computer. Each packet of data communicated across the network is addressed much like a letter.

ADDRESS RESOLUTION

Address resolution performs the translation of the IP address to the workstation's physical address.

ANONYMOUS FTP

Anonymous FTP is a service that allows file availability. It lets a user connect to a remote computer to transfer public files to their computer.

ARCHIE

Archie catalogs programs on a set of computers and allows users to find files that are available by anonymous FTP.

COMMON GATEWAY INTERFACE (CGI)

CGI allows HTTP programs to execute and interface with World Wide Web pages.

DOMAIN

A domain is a category used to identify groups of computers on a network. A domain name is separated by dots (.). Domains are identified by domain names.

DOMAIN NAME

A name with multiple parts for a computer or group of computers, which uniquely identifies them to the Internet. Domain names are converted by the domain name system to IP addresses for communication across the Internet via the Internet protocol (IP). Domain names are organized from the least specific to the most specific characteristics, for example, company.organization.department. A domain name starts with the type of protocol it accepts. For example, Bright Ideas Software is a World Wide Web address and is characterized by the name www.bright-ideas.com.

DOMAIN NAME SYSTEM (DNS)

The domain name system converts Internet names to Internet numbers. DNS lets you use the Internet without remembering a list of numbers.

FTP

The File Transfer Protocol is the protocol users use to download files from FTP servers. When a user connects to an FTP server, he or she enters "anonymous" as the logon ID and his or her e-mail address as the password. The user can then browse through and download any files the FTP server designates as public.

GOPHER

Gopher is a program users use to find programs and resources.

HOME PAGE

The home page is the entry point to a company's or individual's documents on the Web.

HYPERTEXT MARKUP LANGUAGE (HTML)

HTML is a simple script-like programming language that is used to imbed graphics, text, audio, and hypertext within a screen that is decoded and displayed by a user's Web browser.

HYPERTEXT TRANSPORT PROTOCOL (HTTP)

HTTP is the protocol that makes hypertext browsing possible and allows users to transfer binary and ASCII files. It makes hypertextual browsing through the World Wide Web possible. HTTP allows ASCII and binary file transfers. Via

HTTP, users click on links in a hypertext document, and are moved automatically to that document irrespective of where the document or computer that stores it is located.

HYPERTEXT

Hypertext is non-linear data. In a hypertext document, the user moves throughout the document by clicking on links to different parts of the document.

IP ADDRESS

The IP address identifies a computer to the Internet and allows the computer to communicate with the Internet. IP addresses consist of 4 octets of data.

LISTSERV

A listserv manages mailing lists programs by responding to requests and providing responses to requests.

MAILING LIST

A possibly moderated discussion group, distributed via e-mail from a central computer maintaining the list of people involved in the discussion.

MOSAIC

Internet navigation software that allows Internauts to access information through a graphical, point-and-click interface rather than text-only screens or menus. Mosaic is known as a web browser because it accesses World Wide Web information formatted into special pages using hypertext.

MULTIMEDIA

The integration of at least two of the five types of electronic information (text, voice, video, graphics and data) for presentation on a personal computer or other device. Multimedia computers are here; networks capable of delivering multimedia are coming.

NAMESERVER

A computer in a network responsible for keeping the name and address mapping tables, and for providing information on request (usually from other machines, not people directly).

NEWSGROUP

A Usenet discussion group about a particular topic. Over 14,000 newsgroups now exist.

NFS (NETWORK FILE SYSTEM)

A set of protocols that allows you to use files on other network machines as if they were local. So, instead of using FTP to transfer a file to your local computer, you can read, write, or edit it on the remote computer.

NNTP (NETWORK NEWS TRANSFER PROTOCOL)

The standard for Internet exchange of Usenet messages.

POP

Point Of Presence, which refers to an internet connection that allows individuals to connect to the 'Net.

POP

Post Office Protocol is an electronic mail server used to store E-Mail messages until retrieved by a user.

PPP (POINT TO POINT PROTOCOL)

A protocol that allows a computer to use the TCP/IP (Internet) protocols (and become a full-fledged Internet member) with a standard telephone line and a high-speed modem. (Replaces SLIP)

PROTOCOLS

A formal description of message formats and the rules two computers must follow to exchange messages. Standard protocols allow computers from different manufacturers to communicate, providing programs running on both ends agree on what the data means.

ROUTER

A dedicated computer (or other device) that sends packets from one place to another, sort of like a crossing guard.

SERVICE PROVIDER:

Business that provides an Internet connection.

SIMPLE MAIL TRANSFER PROTOCOL

The Internet standard protocol for transferring electronic mail messages from one computer to another. SMTP specifies how two mail systems interact and the format of control messages they exchange to transfer mail.

SLIP (SERIAL LINE INTERNET PROTOCOL)

Allows computer to connect to the Internet using a modem and a telephone line. Users then explore using Internet navigation software on their own computer. This type of connection simulates a network connection to the Internet.

SMTP

Simple Mail Transfer Protocol is used to send E-Mail through an Internet host from a TCP/IP, LAN, or SLIP connection.

TCP/IP

The set of protocols that determine how data is transmitted on the Internet. Transmission Control Protocol controls the transport of data, ensuring that it is delivered. Internet Protocol determines the packet structure of data and the addressing used to deliver data to its destination.

TCP/IP STACK

Software used to manage Internet data packets on your computer.

TELNET

The Internet standard protocol for providing connection to a remote computer (remote login). Telnet allows a user at one site to interact with a remote system at another site as if the user's terminal were connected directly to the remote computer.

TERMINAL SERVER

A small, specialized, networked computer that connects many terminals to a LAN through one network connection. Any user on the network can then connect to various network hosts.

UUCP (Unix to Unix Copy Program)

A store-and-forward system primarily for Unix systems but currently supported on other platforms.

URL

Uniform Resource Locator is a standard way to refer to resources that specify the type of service as well as the exact location of the directory or file in.

Usenet

A worldwide Unix-based network that supports the distribution of messages.

Usenet Newsgroups

Areas for Internet conversations covering thousands of subjects where users share information.

Veronica

A Gopher service that provides keyword searching of Gopher menu items.

WAIS (Wide Area Information Servers)

Client software providing searching and retrieval of various databases.

World Wide Web (WWW)

The fastest growing part of the Internet. The Web links servers around the world with a common protocol, allowing users to surf among a huge variety of multi-media offerings and commercial services. Software such as Netscape provides an easy-to-use graphical interface for the Web.

D Intranet and Web Software Vendors

A

Abacus Accounting Systems Inc.
P.O. Box 1471
Minot, ND 58702-1471
Web Order Taker

ACI US Inc.
20883 Stevens Creek Blvd.
Cupertino, CA 95014
4D Web SmartServer

Actuate Software Corp.
999 Baker Way, Ste. 330
San Mateo, CA 94404
Web Agent

Adobe Systems Inc.
1585 Charleston Rd., P.O. Box 7900
Mountain View, CA 94039-7900
Adobe SiteMill (v1.02)
Adobe Acrobat Search
Adobe Acrobat Exchange (v2.1)
Adobe PageMill (v2.0)
Adobe Acrobat Reader (v2.1)
Frame & Adobe Internet Publishing Solution
HTML Add-on for Word for Windows

ADVANCED BusinessLink Corp.
155 108th Ave., NE, Ste. 210
Bellevue, WA 98004
BusinessLink/WEB

Alias/Wavefront (subsidiary of Silicon Graphics Inc.)
110 Richmond St., E
Toronto, ON, CD M5C 1P1
Web/Animator

Allaire Corp.
8400 Normandale Lake Blvd., Ste. 410
Minneapolis, MN 55437
Cold Fusion Professional (v1.5)

Allen Systems Group Inc.
750 11th St., S
Naples, FL 34102
WebGalaxy (v1.0)

ANDATACO
10140 Mesa Rim Rd.
San Diego, CA 92121
Web Storage Manager (v1.0)

ANS CO+RE Systems Inc.
1875 Campus Commons Dr., Ste. 220
Reston, VA 22091
ANS InterLock Service

Apertus Technologies Inc.
7275 Flying Cloud Dr.
Eden Prairie, MN 55344
Enterprise/Access: Web Edition

Arbor Software Corp.
1325 Chesapeake Terrace
Sunnyvale, CA 94089
Essbase Web Gateway

Astea International Inc.
100 Highpoint Dr.
Chalfont, PA 18914
Astea Web Server

Asymetrix Corp.
110 110th Ave., NE, Ste. 700
Bellevue, WA 98004-5840
WebPublisher
Web 3D

Attachmate Corp. (Intranet Products Group)
1129 San Antonio Rd., P.O. Box 51860
Palo Alto, CA 94303-4310
Emissary Host Publishing System
Emissary Host Publishing Server
Emissary Workgroup
Emissary TCP Server

B

BBN Planet Corp. (subsidiary of Bolt Beranek and Newman Inc.)
150 Cambridge Park Dr.
Cambridge, MA 02140

BBN Internet Server
Internet Site Patrol
Web Advantage Gold
Web Advantage Bronze
Web Advantage Silver

Berkeley Systems Inc.
2095 Rose St.
Berkeley, CA 94709-4303
Web.Max
Web.Pet

Best Enterprises
118 Leroy St., Apt. D4
Potsdam, NY 13676
World Wide Web Weaver (v1.1)

Beyond Software Inc.
5201 Great American Pkwy., Ste. 351
Santa Clara, CA 95054
EnterpriseWeb/VM
EnterpriseWeb/MVS
Webshare

Blue Sky Software Corp.
7777 Fay Ave., Ste. 201
La Jolla, CA 92037
Help-to-HTML Converter
RoboHELP 95 HTML Edition
WEB Office
WinHelp Office 95 HTML Edition

Blueridge Technologies (subsidiary of Metters)
664 H. Zachary Taylor Hwy.
Flint Hill, VA 22627-0430
Optix-WEB

Bluestone Consulting Inc.
1000 Briggs Rd.
Mt. Laurel, NJ 08054
Sapphire/Web (v2.0)

Brock International Inc.
2859 Paces Ferry Rd., Ste. 1000
Atlanta, GA 30339-9851
TakeControl Web

C

Caldera Inc.
931 W. Center St.
Orem, UT 84057
Internet Office Suite (v1.0)

Campbell Services Inc. (subsidiary of FTP Software Inc.)
21700 Northwestern Hwy., Ste. 1070, 10th Fl.
Southfield, MI 48075
OnTime Web Server (v1.0)

CASPR Inc.
100 Park Center Plaza, Ste. 550
San Jose, CA 95113
LibraryNet WEB Server

CERFnet
P.O. Box 919014
San Diego, CA 92191-9014
CERF n' Web

Citrix Systems Inc.
210 University Dr., Ste. 700
Coral Springs, FL 33071

TCP/IP for WinView
WinFrame/Enterprise (v1.6)
WinFrame/Access
WinView for Networks (v2.3)

Clarity Software Inc.
2700 Garcia Ave.
Mountain View, CA 94043
Compatibility Server (v1.4)

CNet Technology Inc.
2199 Zanker Rd.
San Jose, CA 95131

Common Ground Software Inc.
    (division of Hummingbird Communications Ltd.)
303 Twin Dolphin Dr., Ste. 420
Redwood City, CA 94065-1409
CD-ROM Publishing System
Web Publishing System (v1.0)

CompassWare Development Inc.
18 West 27th St.
New York, NY 10001
CompasSearch Web Server

CompuServe Inc. (SPRY/Internet Division)
3535 128th Ave., SE
Bellevue, WA 98006
AIR Navigator (v3.0)
AIR Mail
AIR Series (v3.0)
AIR Connect (v3.0)
AIR tn3270
AIR Gopher
AIR Telnet
AIR NFS (v3.0)
AIR Mosaic (v1.1)
AIR X
AIR News
Internet in a Box (v2.0)
Internet Office Web Server
MOSAIC In A Box (v2.0)
Network File Manager
Spry Internet Office (v4.1)
Spry Web Server
Spry Badger
Spry SafetyWEB Server (v1.1)
SPRYNET

Cuadra Associates Inc.
11835 W. Olympic Blvd., Ste. 855
Los Angeles, CA 90064
STAR/Web

D

DataViz Inc.
55 Corporate Dr.
Trumbull, CT 06611
Web Buddy

Desktop Data Inc.
1601 Trapelo Rd.
Waltham, MA 02154
NewsEDGE/Web

Digital Equipment Corp. (DEC)
146 Main St.
Maynard, MA 01754-2571
Internet AlphaServer 400 4/166
Internet AlphaServer Software Kit (v2.0)
Internet AlphaServer 1000 4/266
Internet Portal (v1.1)
Internet AlphaServer 400 4/233
Pathworks Browser (v2.0)
Web AlphaServer 1000 4/266
Web AlphaServer 400 4/233
Workgroup Web Forum (v1.0)

Distinct Corp.
12901 Saratoga Ave., Ste. 4
Saratoga, CA 95070
Distinct NFS
Distinct Visual Internet Toolkit-32 (v1.1)
Distinct NetRover

E

Eastgate Systems Inc.
134 Main St.
Watertown, MA 02172
Web Squirrel

E.E.S. Companies Inc.
2 Vernon St., Ste. 404
Framingham, MA 01701
WEB Order Processing

Electronic Book Technologies Inc.
One Richmond Sq.
Providence, RI 02906
DynaWeb (v3.0)
WebTap (v1.0)
eSoft Inc.
15200 E. Girard Ave., Ste. 3000
Aurora, CO 80014
IPAD (Internet Protocol Adapter) (v1.1)

Excite Inc.
1091 N. Shoreline Blvd., 2nd Fl.
Mountain View, CA 94043
Excite for Web Servers (v1.1)

EXSYS Inc.
1720 Louisiana Blvd., NE, Ste. 312
Albuquerque, NM 87110
Web Runtime Engine
Professional (v5.0)
Linkable Object Modules
RuleBook/RuleBook Plus (v1.1)

F

Farallon Communications
2470 Mariner Square Loop
Alameda, CA 94501-1010

FileTek Inc.
9400 Key West Ave.
Rockville, MD 20850
Web-AMMO

5 Star Pioneer Group Inc.
1151 Clear Creek Canyon Dr.
Diamond Bar, CA 91765
Internet Publisher's Toolbox
Web Fever

Firefox Inc. (subsidiary of FTP Software Inc.)
2099 Gateway Plaza, 7th Fl.
San Jose, CA 95110-1017
Internet Document Server
NOV*IX for NetWare (v3.0)
NOV*IX Mail for NetWare (v3.0)
NOV*IX for Internet (v3.0)
Plus*Pack for NOV*IX

Folio Corp. (subsidiary of Reed Elsevier, PLC)
5072 North 300 West
Provo, UT 84604
Infobase Web Server
Web Retriever (v2.0)

FORMTEK Inc. (subsidiary of Lockheed Martin Corp.)
1801 Page Mill Rd., Bldg. 254
Palo Alto, CA 94304
FORMTEK: Web Gateway

Frontier Technologies Corp.
10201 N. Port Washington Rd.
Mequon, WI 53092
CyberJunction
CyberSearch (v2.0)
Intranet Genie
SuperTCP Suite 96
SuperWeb Server
SuperHighway Access 2

FTP Software Inc.
100 Brickstone Sq., 5th Fl.
Andover, MA 01810
CyberAgent Software Development Kit (SDK)
Esplanade (v1.2)
FTP Secure WebServer (v1.1)
FTP WebServer (v1.1)

Fulcrum Technologies Inc.
785 Carling Ave.
Ottawa, ON, CD K1S 5H4
SearchBuilder EXPRESS
SearchBuilder (v2.0)
Surfboard (v2.0)
FIND!
SearchServer (v3.0)

G

General Magic Inc.
420 N. Mary Ave.
Sunnyvale, CA 94086
Telescript Active Web Tools
Telescript

Globalink Inc.
9302 Lee Hwy., 12th Fl.
Fairfax, VA 22031-1208
Web Translator

Gradient Technologies Inc.
2 Mt. Royal Ave.
Marlborough, MA 01752
WebCrusader Connect Server
WebCrusader Connect Client

H

Hertz Computer Corp.
325 Fifth Ave.
New York, NY 10016-5012
NT Web Server P-Pro P-200
NT Web Server Dual P-133
NT Web Server P-166
Web Basic Server P-133

Hewlett-Packard Co.
3000 Hanover St.
Palo Alto, CA 94304
HP Internet Advisor for WAN (v9.0)
HP Internet Reporter
HP Internet Advisor for LAN (v8.0)

Hummingbird Communications, Ltd.
1 Sparks Ave.
North York, ON, CD M2H 2W1
Columbus for Windows (v1.0)
eXceed X Development Toolkits
NFS Maestro for DOS and Windows (v5.1)

NFS Maestro for Microsoft TCP/IP (v5.1)
NFS Maestro for Windows 95 (v5.1)
NFS Maestro for Windows NT (v5.1)
TCP/IP Maestro (v5.1)

I

I/NET Inc.
643 W. Crosstown Pkwy.
Kalamazoo, MI 49008
Web Server/400

Ibex Technologies Inc.
4921 R.J. Mathews Pkwy.
El Dorado Hills, CA 95762
FactsLine for the Web

IBM (International Business Machines)
Old Orchard Rd.
Armonk, NY 10504
Internet Connection (v4.0)
Internet Connection Secured Network Gateway
Internet Connection Secure Web Explorer for OS/2
Internet Connection Servers
Internet Connection Secure Server (v1.1)

ICL Inc.
11490 Commerce Park Dr.
Reston, VA 22091
i500 Web Connector

Iconovex Corp. (subsidiary of Innovex Inc.)
7900 Xerxes Ave. S, Ste. 550
Bloomington, MN 55431
SWAPI (Syntactica Web API)
WebAnchor

Illustra Information Technologies Inc.
        (division of Informix Software Inc.)
1111 Broadway, Ste. 2000
Oakland, CA 94607
Web DataBlade (v2.2)

Individual Inc.
8 New England Executive Park, W, 4th Fl.
Burlington, MA 01803
First! Intranet
First! for Exchange

Intergraph Corp.
One Madison Industrial Park
Huntsville, AL 35894-0014
TD-10 Web Server
InterServe Web 30

Isys Odyssey Development Inc. (division of Odyssey Development Pty Ltd.)
8775 E. Orchard Rd., Ste. 811
Englewood, CO 80111
ISYS Web
ISYS/Netspace

J

JSB Corp.
108 Whispering Pines Dr., Ste. 115
Scotts Valley, CA 95066-4785
INTRAnet Jazz

JYACC Inc.
116 John St., 20th Fl.
New York, NY 10038
JAM/WEB (v1.0)

L

Little Men Studio
177 Highland Ave.
Redding, CT 06896
World's largest collection of custom-designed Web-ready art

Livingston Enterprises Inc.
6920 Koll Center Pkwy., Ste. 220
Pleasanton, CA 94566
FireWall IRX

Lotus Development Corp. (subsidiary of IBM)
55 Cambridge Pkwy.
Cambridge, MA 02142-1295
InterNotes Web Publisher

Luckman Interactive Inc.
1055 West 7th St., Ste. 2580
Los Angeles, CA 90017
Web Commander

Lundeen & Associates
909 Marina Village Pkwy., Ste.595
Alameda, CA 94501
Web Crossing (v1.2)

M

Marketing Masters
926 Willard Dr., Ste. 223
Green Bay, WI 54304
Survey Said for the WEB (v5.3)

McAfee Associates Inc.
2710 Walsh Ave., Ste. 200
Santa Clara, CA 95051-0963
WebScan (v1.0.1)
WebStor (v1.0)
WebShield

MCI Communications Corp. (Business Markets Division)
3 Ravinia Dr.
Atlanta, GA 30346
InternetMCI

MDG Computer Services
231 Faircroft Rd.
Bartlett, IL 60103-1363
Web Server 4D Developer Edition
Web Server 4D Runtime Version

MEGASOFT Online LLC
819 Hwy. 33, E
Freehold, NJ 07728-8431
Web Transporter

Microrim Inc. (subsidiary of Abacus Software Group)
15395 Southeast 30th Place, Ste. 200
Bellevue, WA 98007-9918
R: Web (v1.0)

Microsoft Corp.
One Microsoft Way
Redmond, WA 98052-6399
Internet Assistant for Microsoft Excel
Internet Assistant for Microsoft PowerPoint
Internet Assistant for Microsoft Word 95 (v2.0)
Internet Business Development Kit
Internet Assistant for Microsoft Office
Internet Software Development Kit
Internet Assistant for Microsoft Word 6.0 (v2.0)
Internet Explorer Administration Kit (IEAK)
Internet Information Server
Internet Assistant for Schedule+
Internet Starter Kit
Internet Assistant for Access
SGML Author for Word

MicroStrategy Inc.
8000 Towers Crescent Dr.
Vienna, VA 22182
DSS Web

Microsystems Software Inc.
600 Worcester Rd.
Framingham, MA 01701-5342
Cyber Patrol (v2.10.04)
Cyber Sentry

N

NaviSoft Inc. (subsidiary of America Online Inc.)
75 Second Ave., Ste. 710
Needham, MA 02194
GNNserver
NaviPress (v1.1)
World Wide Web (WWW)

NEC Technologies Inc. (Internet Business Unit)
110 Rio Robles Dr.
San Jose, CA 95134
PrivateNet

NetManage Inc.
10725 N. De Anza Blvd.
Cupertino, CA 95014
Chameleon Internet SDK
Chameleon Desktop (v4.6)
ChameleonNFS/X (v4.5)
Chameleon/X (v4.03)
ChameleonNFS Spanish (v4.5)
ChameleonNFS (v4.5)
Chameleon/D (v4.5)
Chameleon for Windows 95 (v6.0)

NetPhonic Communications Inc.
1580 W. El Camino Rd., Ste. 8
Mountain View, CA 94040
Web-On-Call Voice Browser

NeTpower Inc.
545 Oakmead Pkwy.
Sunnyvale, CA 94086-4023
Calisto Web Server Pentium Pro/200

Netscape Communications Corp.
501 E. Middlefield Rd.
Mountain View, CA 94043
Live3D
Navigator Gold 2.0
LiveWire
Directory Server
Proxy Server 2.0
SuiteSpot

NetScheme Solutions Inc.
201 Boston Post Rd., Ste. 400
Marlborough, MA 01752
InterMart Toolkit (v1.0)

The Network Connection Inc.
1324 Union Hill Rd.
Alpharetta, GA 30201
Cheetah Video-Web 2000

Network Engineering Technologies
1714 Ringwood Ave.
San Jose, CA 95131
Web Server

Neuron Data Inc.
1310 Villa St.
Mountain View, CA 94041
Web Element
Web Element Pro

Nomad Development Corp.
81 Vine St., Ste. 203
Seattle, WA 98121
WebDBC (v2.5)

Novadigm Inc.
1 International Blvd., Ste. 200
Mahwah, NJ 07495
EDM: Client for the intranet

Now Software Inc.
921 S.W. Washington St., Ste. 500
Portland, OR 97205-2822
Up-to-Date Web Publisher (v1.5)

O

Open Software Associates Inc.
20 Trafalgar Sq., 5th Fl.
Nashua, NH 03063
Web C/S Solutions

Open Text Corp.
180 Columbia St., W
Waterloo, ON, CD N2L 3L3
Livelink Intranet
Livelink Search 64
Web Search Server

Oracle Corp.
500 Oracle Pkwy.
Redwood Shores, CA 94065
Designer/2000 WebServer Generator
InterOffice

P

Paradigm Software Development Inc.
2510 Western Ave., Ste. 500
Seattle, WA 98121-1360
WorkWise-Employee File, Web Edition (v3.0)

PC DOCS Inc. (subsidiary of PC DOCS Group International Inc.)
25 Burlington Mall Rd.
Burlington, MA 01803
DOCS Interchange for the World Wide Web

PointCast Inc.
10101 N. De Anza Blvd., Ste. 400, 4th Fl.
Cupertino, CA 95014
I-Server

Portable Graphics Inc.
    (subsidiary of Evans & Sutherland Computer Corp.)
3006 Longhorn Blvd., Ste. 105
Austin, TX 78758
VRealm 3D Web Browser

Presence Corp.
5 Hillandale Ave.
Stamford, CT 06902
QM Web

Process Software Corp.
959 Concord St.
Framingham, MA 01701-9572
Purveyor IntraServer for Windows NT
Purveyor WebServer for NetWare
Purveyor Encrypt WebServer (v1.2)
Purveyor WebServer for OpenVMS (v1.1A)
Purveyor WebServer for Windows NT (v1.2)
Purveyor WebServer for Windows 95 (v1.2)

Prodea Software Corp. (subsidiary of PLATINUM Technology Inc.)
11095 Viking Dr., Ste. 225
Eden Prairie, MN 55344
InfoBeacon Web

Progress Software Corp. (Crescent Division)
11 Bailey Ave.
Ridgefield, CT 06877-4505
Web Jump Start Kit

Progressive Networks Inc.
616 First Ave., Ste. 701
Seattle, WA 98104
RealAudio Server (v2.0)

Pure Atria
1309 S. Mary Ave.
Sunnyvale, CA 94087
PureDDTS WebTracker (v3.2)
PurePerformix/Web

R

RAD Data Communications Inc.
900 Corporate Dr.
Mahwah, NJ 07430-2013
Web RANger

Raima Corp.
1605 N.W. Sammamish Rd., Ste. 200
Issaquah, WA 98027
Velocis Web Server Gateway

ResNova Software Inc.
5011 Argosy Dr., Ste. 13
Huntington Beach, CA 92649
NovaServer Web Starter Package

Rhode Island Soft Systems Inc.
P.O. Box 748
Woonsocket, RI 02895-0784
Web Whiz

S

Sax Software Corp.
950 Patterson St.
Eugene, OR 97401
Webster Control (v2.0)

Scitex Digital Printing (division of Scitex Corp. Ltd.)
3100 Research Blvd.
Dayton, OH 45420
Begin: Web Layout/Page Composition

Seagate Enterprise Management Software
        (division of Seagate Technology Inc.)
19925 Stevens Creek Blvd., Bldg. 150
Cupertino, CA 95014
Seasurf Internet/Web Server

Searchlight Software
6516 Detroit Ave.
Cleveland, OH 44102
BBS (v4.5)
Spinnaker Web Server

Secure Computing Corp.
2675 Long Lake Rd.
Roseville, MN 55113
Sidewinder (v3.0)

Shiva Corp.
28 Crosby Dr.
Bedford, MA 01730
WebRover for Internet

Silicon Graphics Inc.
2011 N. Shoreline Blvd.
Mountain View, CA 94043-1389
WebFORCE Indigo2 Extreme
WebFORCE Internet Gateway
WebFORCE Challenge S
WebFORCE Indy
WebMagic Digital Media Tools
WebMagic Pro
WebMagic Author (v1.0)
WebSpace Author (v1.0)
WebSpace Navigator (v1.1)

Silknet Software Inc.
1001 Elm St.
Manchester, NH 03101
Web Page Manager

Simware Inc.
2 Gurdwara Rd.
Ottawa, ON, CD K2E 1A2
Salvo Server Edition (v1.0)
Salvo Personal Edition

Software Artistry Inc.
9449 Priority Way West Dr., Ste. 100
Indianapolis, IN 46240
SA-Expert Web

Software Research Inc.
625 Third St.
San Francisco, CA 94107-1997
STW/Web

SourceCraft Inc.
20 Mall Rd.
Burlington, MA 01803
ObjectCraft
NetCraft

Specular International Ltd.
7 Pomeroy Lane
Amherst, MA 01002
3D Web Workshop

StarBase Corp.
18872 MacArthur Blvd., Ste. 300
Irvine, CA 92715
StarTeam Web Connect (v2.0)

Sun Microsystems Inc. (JavaSoft Division)
2550 Garcia Ave.
Mountain View, CA 94043-1100
HotJava
Java Workshop (v1.0)
Java Developer's Kit (JDK) (v1.1)
JavaOS
Java (v1.1)

SurfWatch Software Inc. (division of Spyglass Inc.)
105 Fremont Ave., Ste. F
Los Altos, CA 94022
Surfwatch (v1.0)

Sybase Inc.
6475 Christie Ave.
Emeryville, CA 94608
web.sql

Syntellect Inc.
15810 North 28th Ave.
Phoenix, AZ 85023
Web Access

T

Teubner & Associates Inc.
P.O. Box 1994
Stillwater, OK 74076-1994
Corridor: The Web to Host Passageway

TGV Systems Inc. (Internet Business Unit)
101 Cooper St.
Santa Cruz, CA 95060
Cheetah Web Server
MultiNet Information Server (v1.1)

Thuridion
269 Mt. Hermon Rd., Ste. 200
Scotts Valley, CA 95066-4029
CREW

Tivoli Systems Inc. (subsidiary of IBM)
9442 Capital of Texas Hwy., N, Arboretum Plaza One
Austin, TX 78759
net.Commander Internet/Web Server

Tomorrow's Horizons Inc.
950 Greentree Rd.
Pittsburgh, PA 15220
Visual Web

Traveling Software Inc.
18702 N. Creek Pkwy.
Bothell, WA 98011
WebEx

Trimco America Inc. (an Alpharel Co.)
15950 Bay Vista Dr., Ste. 140
Clearwater, FL 34620
Web Information Server and Distributed Object Maitre'd (WISDOM)

Trusted Information Systems Inc.
3060 Washington Rd., Rt. 97
Glenwood, MD 21738
Gauntlet Intranet Firewall (v3.2)

V

Ventana Communications Group
P.O. Box 13964
Research Triangle Park, NC 27709
HTML Publishing With Internet Assistant
Internet Publishing Kit
Internet Publishing Kit for Windows
World Wide Web Kit, Netscape Edition for Windows
World Wide Web Kit, Netscape Edition for Macintosh
World Wide Web Kit, Ventana MOSAIC Edition for Windows

Verity Inc.
1550 Plymouth St.
Mountain View, CA 94043-1230
Topic WebAgents Publisher's Toolkit
TopicCD-WEB PUBLISHER (v1.2)

Visix Software Inc.
11440 Commerce Park Dr.
Reston, VA 22091
Galaxy Application Environment (Rel.2.6)

VMARK Software Inc.
50 Washington St.
Westboro, MA 01581-1021
Web Developer's Kit

Voxware Inc.
305 College Rd., E
Princeton, NJ 08540
ToolVox for the Web

Vream Inc.
2568 N. Clark St., Ste. 250
Chicago, IL 60614
Web Interactive Reality Layer (WIRL)

VTLS Inc.
1800 Kraft Dr.
Blacksburg, VA 24060-6351
Virtua-Web Gateway

W

W3.COM
459 Hamilton Ave., Ste. 202
Palo Alto, CA 94301
W3 Personal Web Site Toolkit (PWS)

WebFlow Corp.
3160 De la Cruz Blvd., Ste. 206
Santa Clara, CA 95054
SamePage Intranet Work Processor

Westing Software
134 Redwood Ave.
Corte Madera, CA 94925
Bookends Web

Wholly Mac Software
P.O. Box 34046
Las Vegas, NV 89133-4046
Web ShortCuts

X

Xedia Corp.
301 Ballardvale St.
Wilmington, MA 01887
IP/Assist (v1.0)

XSoft (division of Xerox Corp.)
3400 Hillview Ave., P.O. Box 10034
Palo Alto, CA 94304
Astoria

Index